ADVANCED
Strategic
Planning

A New Model for Church and Ministry Leaders

Aubrey Malphurs

Baker Books

A Division of Baker Book House Co
Grand Rapids, Michigan 49516

Published by Baker Books
a division of Baker Book House Company
P.O. Box 6287, Grand Rapids, MI 49516-6287

Fifth printing, November 2002

Printed in the United States of America

Library of Congress Cataloging-in-Publication Data

Malphurs, Aubrey
    Advanced strategic planning : a new model for church and ministry leaders /
Aubrey Malphurs.
        p.   cm.
    Includes bibliographical references and index.
    ISBN 0-8010-9068-7 (pbk.)
    1. Church management. 2. Strategic planning. I. Title.
BV652.M3563   1999
254—dc21   98-55370

For current information about all releases from Baker Book House, visit our web site:
http://www.bakerbooks.com

Contents

Introduction

I spotted the creature sitting off in the distance almost by itself. With long arms that looked like a tangle of dark blue steel tentacles, it reminded me of a large octopus that had crawled out of the ocean nearby. It was nothing of the sort. It was one of several rides operated by a small, traveling carnival that happened to pass through our town close to where my family and I lived. I was alone with my daughter, Jennifer, who at the time was around the impressionable age of four or five. I decided to live a little and have a good time that would make a lasting impression on my little girl. She would discover that Dad wasn't afraid to try something new.

We boarded the monster and soon it was spinning around at breakneck speed while the tentacles frantically lashed up and down. It was frightening. I began to worry that one of the tentacles—the one that held us—could possibly tear loose with all the contortions it was going through. We would not survive if it did. I silently prayed and made a vow to God as I held Jennifer tightly against my chest. It went something like this: "God, if you get us off this ride alive and in one piece, I promise never to get on another ride for the rest of my life!" God answered my prayer, the octopus let go, and I have kept that vow.

More than any other time in history, North America, along with much of the world, is exploding with change—fast, frightening change. I refer to it as megachange. It has affected every institution—

business, government, the schools, and the church—and it is occur-
ring at a number of levels: national, corporate, and individual. The
result is a revolution taking place all around us that is likely to be as
profound as any in the past. Some wrongly advise us just to be patient,
that in time it will all pass. The reality is, however, that there is no end
in sight. We have climbed on board the octopus only to discover that
it will not let go.

What is the explanation for all this megachange? What is happening?
Peter Drucker sums it up best:

> Every few hundred years throughout Western history, a sharp trans-
> formation has occurred. In a matter of decades, society altogether re-
> arranges itself—its world view, its basic values, its social and political
> structures, its arts, its key institutions. Fifty years later a new world exists.
> And the people born into that world cannot even imagine the world in
> which grandparents lived and into which their own parents were born.[1]

Drucker's point is that we are living at one of those rare points in time
when an old worldview (modernism) and many of its trappings are dying
and another (postmodernism) is struggling to be born. The consequence
is a massive shift in our culture, science, society, and institutions. This
change is enormously greater than the world has ever experienced, and
we are caught in the middle of it. We are living at a frightening point of
absolute, chaotic discontinuity, watching the old die off and the new rush
in to fill the vacuum.

Where is the church in all this? How is it doing? The answer is, not
well. In one of my early books, I noted that in 1988 between 80 to 85
percent of churches in North America had either plateaued or were in
decline (dying).[2] As we enter the twenty-first century, that figure has not
changed appreciably despite a valiant surge in church planting. The number of unchurched people across America continues to be high, possibly
as high as 70 to 80 percent. Penny Marler comments that if the Gallup
surveys over the past thirty years that estimate the unchurched to be only
57 percent of the population were accurate, then people would be flock-
ing to our churches. But this is not happening.[3]

Based on my research and consulting ministry with churches, I am
convinced that the typical church does not understand the full implications of megachange. Even when a church has some understanding of
the implications, it doesn't know how to respond in effective ministry to
those immersed in the postmodern paradigm. I believe that the majority of seminaries that prepare people for ministry sit in the same boat

with the churches. They are still preparing future pastors for ministry to a modern, not a postmodern, world. Most training equips pastors for one hour on Sunday morning but ignores the other forty-plus hours of the week that demand leadership gifts and abilities and people skills. My studies and current pastoral experience indicate that pastoring a church is a leadership-intensive enterprise. It is imperative that a pastor be able, not only to preach to a congregation, but to lead and relate well to that congregation.[4]

Strategic Planning and the Church

The typical church in North America is like a sailboat without a rudder, drifting aimlessly in the ocean. As if that is not bad enough, the winds of change and the currents of postmodernism are relentlessly blowing and pulling the church even farther off course. I believe that the rudder that the church is missing is a good strategic planning process. Without it, the typical sailor—today's pastor—will find it difficult to navigate in any situation.

I came to this conclusion as a result of my own pastoral and consulting experience and after writing books on the concepts of vision, mission, core values, and strategy.[5] Early in the process of writing these books, I began to ask myself how each concept related to the other concepts and, if I put them all together, what the resulting product would be. The answer quickly became evident. I would have a strategic process that would help church leaders think through the core issues of ministry and then implement their conclusions.

Not enough church leaders understand and practice strategic planning. According to an article in *American Demographics*, Gary McIntosh of the American Society for Church Growth estimates that only 20 percent of America's 367,000 congregations actively pursue strategic planning. In the same article, George Hunter, professor of evangelism and church growth at Asbury Theological Seminary, warns that churches without plans for growth invariably stagnate.[6]

At the same time, the idea of strategic planning is often no longer held in high regard. A number of business writers and consultants play down the importance of and even the need for strategic planning.[7] Karl Albrecht, for example, writes, "In the Western business world most *conventional* thinking about 'strategic planning,' that is, setting goals and making plans to achieve them, is misguided and obsolete."[8]

In his book *Thriving on Chaos* Tom Peters presents a more balanced position that touches the heart of the problem.

> Sound strategic direction has never been more important—which is why the strategic planning process must be truly decentralized. Yet strategic planning, as we conventionally conceive of it, has become irrelevant, or worse, damaging.
>
> What is a good strategic *plan?* There is none. But there is a good strategic planning process.[9]

The conventional or traditional concept of strategic planning, as practiced up to the present, has become somewhat obsolete and irrelevant. The problem is not with "strategy," but with the particular concept of strategy that predominates in most companies and churches that attempt it. What a growing number of critics are rejecting is strategy that is a pedantic, incremental planning ritual that assumes tomorrow is just an extension of today. Ritualistic planning fails to provoke the deeper fundamental questions and debates about why the organization is, what drives it, where it is going, and how it will get there. Answering these questions is vital to an organization's health. Most often an organization's strategy begins with discussing what is and never gets around to asking what could be. For too many, a strategic plan means going through the motions of an annual planning event or slavishly following a long-range plan, while ignoring the profound, cataclysmic transformation of the world outside.

The purpose of this book is to provide the church and its leadership a good strategic planning process, such as Peters mentioned above. This is the necessary rudder that will biblically and thoughtfully guide the church through these and future times of unprecedented, convoluted change.

A good strategic planning process, as captured by a good strategic planning model, is important for numerous reasons. Here are eight:

1. The church decides on and envisions its God-determined future and how best, through specific strategies, to accomplish that future. This, in turn, affects the second.
2. The process prompts the church to be proactive not reactive—to be aggressive not passive—"salt and light" in this present world. That way churches can prepare for a future that honors Christ and they can make things happen, rather than waiting for things to happen and becoming victims of the times.

3. It forces churches to think about and focus on such deep biblical-theological issues as core purpose, mission, values, vision, and strategy.[10]
4. A good strategic model helps the ministry discover its strengths as well as its weaknesses, its opportunities as well as its threats.
5. Strategic thinking helps churches face the reality of chaotic change and make the tough decisions.
6. A good strategic planning model will help the church be positive, not negative, in its approach to ministry—to envision what it can do.
7. It invites the church to discover the trends driving both the secular world and the evangelical church and their positive or negative effect on the ministry.
8. The planning model gets everyone on the same page so that the entire church team has a common context for decision making and problem solving.

A Definition

What is strategic planning? I define it simply as the process of thinking and acting. It involves thinking through and then doing the church's ministry. It is a process, not something you do one time and then abandon. That means that it has to be a constant in the life of the church and the ministry of its leaders. We live in tough times. The constant and fast pace of change in our world means that no leader can afford to withdraw to the status quo. Leaders and their churches must constantly think strategically about the church and its ministry.

The process involves thinking. Perhaps that is its greatest value. It forces pastors and leaders to return to the basics, to dig deeply into the Scriptures. It compels them to think theologically and to ask the important, fundamental questions such as, What does the Bible say about why we are here? What drives us? What are we supposed to be doing? What does that look like? How will we accomplish what we are supposed to be doing?

But the process does not end with thinking through and discovering or rediscovering the core fundamentals. We must follow the thinking with action. One of the weaknesses of conventional strategic models is their failure to encourage implementation of the results. The findings are filed away in some ministry's filing cabinet under "plan." When that happens, the entire process is undermined. Eager participants feel as if they have been through nine months of pregnancy only to experience a still-birth. The church must become what Christ intended it to be. That calls for implementation.

Strategic thinking and acting is no stranger to the Bible. References to and examples of it are generously sprinkled throughout the Old and New Testaments. Numerous leaders in the Old Testament thought and acted strategically. Moses in response to God's mission to lead Israel out of Egypt led them strategically through the wilderness as recorded in the Pentateuch. In Exodus 18, Moses' father-in-law, Jethro, challenges him to think and act strategically in his counseling of individual Israelites. The leadership of Moses' successor, Joshua, was most strategic (Josh. 6:1–6; 8:3–23; 10:6–9). The writer of 1 Chronicles notes that the men of Issachar "understood the times and knew what Israel should do" (1 Chron. 12:32). Nehemiah thought and acted strategically as he led God's revitalization project in Jerusalem (Nehemiah 3–6). Proverbs presents God's wisdom and role in planning (Prov. 14:15, 22; 15:22; 16:3–4, 9; 19:21; 20:18; 21:30).

In the Gospels, Christ informs the church of its mission—the Great Commission (Matt. 28:19–20; Mark 16:15). The Book of Acts records how the Holy Spirit used the church strategically to implement this mission, especially through the missionary journeys (Acts 13:1–21:26). Paul did not wander aimlessly but appears to have carefully and strategically selected the cities he visited for ministry while on his missionary journeys. For example, he located in Ephesus because it was the gateway to Asia Minor (compare Acts 19:1 with 19:10). Even the Godhead thinks and acts strategically according to Luke (Acts 2:23; 4:28). In Ephesians 5:15–16, Paul encourages the Ephesian church to live strategically.

It becomes obvious, then, that God has sovereignly chosen to work through strategic thinking and acting to accomplish his divine will on earth. Accordingly, churches must be careful of those who advise them to ignore any planning and simply "let go and let God." This does not mean that we should trust our strategies and ignore the role of the Holy Spirit in the process. Proverbs 19:21 is clear that God's purpose will prevail regardless of our plans. John 15:5 warns that without Christ we can accomplish absolutely nothing. In Zechariah 4:6, the prophet reminds us as well as Zerubbabel, "Not by might nor by power, but by my Spirit, says the LORD Almighty." Letting go and letting God must work in conjunction with strategic thinking and acting. I tell my seminary students and my readers to hold their plans before the sovereign God of the universe in an open hand.[11]

I have observed a troubling trend among numerous well-meaning pastors who desire to minister effectively for God. They have a tendency to mimic the ministries of other effective, evangelical churches. Many of the latter are great churches that are led by unusually gifted leaders who minister to people in their own unique communities. More often than not, to ape their plans and strategies results in failure and disappointment.

The problem is that these leaders who are trying to duplicate someone else's ministry are attempting to implement a product without having gone through the process. I have discovered that the leaders of the truly great churches have consciously—and some unconsciously—thought and worked through a process that has led to their particular ministry or product. All leaders need to take their church through the process so that their ministry product is endemic to them, their people, and their unique ministry community.

The Process

This book is all about such a ministry process. It is the process of strategic planning. I have divided it into two parts. Part 1 consists of two chapters that seek to prepare leaders and their churches for strategic thinking and acting. Chapter 1 provides pastors with a seven-item preplanning checklist. It asks leaders to consider seven areas prior to taking a ministry through strategic planning: readiness, personnel, time, cost, place, tools, and decision making. Chapter 2 introduces churches to the important concept of the S-curve in helping them understand organizational (church) growth and development and then apply this knowledge to their church. It also provides a brief theology of change.

Part 2 consists of nine chapters that help leaders take their churches through the actual process of strategic planning (see figure 1).

The chapters guide ministers in thinking through and answering each of the nine most fundamental questions of their ministry.

I would ask church planters not to skip chapter 3 on conducting a ministry analysis. Though initially they have no ministry to analyze, analysis is still an ongoing process. Once they launch the ministry, they will need to know how to analyze what they are doing. I would compare it to the wise, seasoned doctor who regularly checks his patient's vital signs. Established and planted churches should think through and answer all nine questions presented in chapters 3–11. I must warn leaders that this is a soul-searching and potentially painful process. I know because I have taken the church I pastor through this process. Many who dare to pursue and answer these questions will find that somewhere the ministry has gotten off track. Also some will struggle even more as they attempt to implement the changes necessary to align their churches with God's directives in the Scriptures.

Finally, I have included analysis, discussion, and application questions at the end of each chapter. They will not only help you think through the material in each section, but aid you in the strategic thinking and acting process. To get the most out of this book, I suggest that first you quickly scan the book, catching its drift and general message. Then read back through it carefully, answering the questions and doing what each chapter asks of you and your ministry as you go through the strategic planning process.

Strategic Planning Model

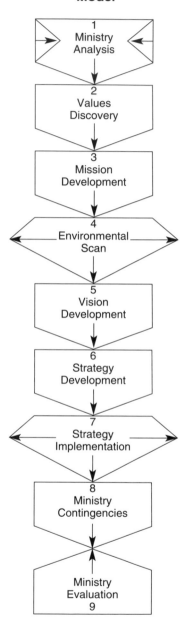

Figure 1

PART 1

The Preparation for Strategic Planning

1

Preparing to Think
and Act

Runners to Your Marks!

To alleviate our fear of flying, the various airlines assure us that traveling in one of their aircraft is safer than driving to the airport in your car. As a ministry consultant and trainer, I find that information comforting since I spend much time on airplanes flying to different places in North America and abroad. One of the reasons for the safety record of airlines is that pilots and mechanics carefully work through a preflight checklist. I have watched the captain walk around the plane, examining the engines and the flaps. On occasion I have even seen the captain kick the tires. When the flight personnel leave the cabin door open, you can watch them as they busily flip and check switches, examine various digital and modular instruments, and review their charts and flight plans. I have also observed mechanics running test programs to make sure that the plane's electronics are working properly. To do otherwise could prove disastrous.

Leaders, like airline pilots and mechanics, must also do some prework before attempting the strategic planning process. This chapter will serve as the leader's preflight checklist. The preplanning list consists of seven items.

The Church's Readiness for Thinking and Acting

The first item in the preplanning list is a ministry's readiness for strategic planning. My wife and I married at a young age and had all but one child while in our twenties. The result is that we are young grandparents. Our grandchild, Maria, is, of course, the most intelligent child on the face of the earth! My wife taught her how to read at the age of three and one half. She was ready; otherwise, any attempts at teaching her to read would have been futile. The point is that each child is unique in his or her intellectual development, and not every child—no matter how intelligent—is ready or able to read this early in life.

The readiness of churches to begin strategic thinking and acting varies, just as it does with children and their learning to read. To attempt to force the process on an unwilling subject is not wise. So the question becomes, Is this church ready to pursue strategic planning? How can you know if your ministry is ready to proceed with the process? Several keys can help you decide.

The Church's Openness to Change

One key is the church's openness to change. Good strategic planning will result in change. For many older, established churches this may mean deep change. If a ministry is not willing or able to undergo significant changes, then it should not attempt any in-depth strategizing.

How can you know if your church is open to change, and, if so, how much? I have provided a Readiness for Change Inventory in appendix A of this book to help you answer this vital question. You, as a church leader, could begin by taking the Inventory yourself. You should also ask other key leaders to take the Inventory, especially if you have been there a relatively short time. You may also select some of the questions and use them to quiz various congregants individually.

The Pastor's Attitude toward Change

A second key to knowing if your church is ready to pursue strategic planning is the attitude of the pastor, or the senior pastor in a multistaff situation. If the pastor sees the need for and understands the importance of strategic planning, then the process has a chance, depending on his abilities to persuade the board and other leaders. If he does not see the need, then the process simply will not happen. He will not push for it, and it will die for lack of a second.

Why might a pastor oppose strategic thinking and acting? One answer is lack of awareness. He may not be aware of or understand the process. Another is he may be resistant to change. Some temperaments fear or are suspicious of change. For those familiar with the temperament tools, they tend to be the S and C temperaments on the *Personal Profile* (DiSC System),[1] and the SJs on the *Myers-Briggs Type Indicator*.[2]

A third reason a pastor may resist strategic thinking and acting is that he is an old-paradigm thinker who lives and ministers in the past. Much of the change that has affected ministry has passed him by. Thus he sees no need to plan strategically. He is convinced that if something seems to no longer work, the staff needs to simply redouble its efforts and work harder.

A pastor may also fear failure. Making the kinds of deep changes that turn a ministry in a new direction requires the leader to take some big risks and step outside his and others' comfort zones. He has no guarantee that the church will follow him. Thus he is vulnerable as he walks into the land of uncertainty and the real possibility of failure. For many this is a terrifying choice that involves a dark night of the soul.

I have discovered that some strong, gifted, high-energy leaders—especially those with leadership gifts but no administrative abilities—find it difficult to take the time for any strategic thinking and acting. They neglect it at their own peril. Avoiding or rushing through strategic development is characteristic of a "quick fix" mentality. The result is a symptomatic solution that is temporary in nature because it fails to address the key issues of ministry at a fundamental level. Leaders who resist strategic planning would be wise to recruit and work closely with those who have gifts and abilities in this area.

Resistant Attitudes toward Change

1. A lack of awareness of change and the change process
2. A fear or suspicion of change
3. An old-paradigm perspective that clings to the past
4. A fear of failure
5. Not wanting to take the time

The Board's Attitude toward Change

A third readiness key is the church board's attitude toward change. Most churches have a board that functions in some way. Most often the board runs the smaller church. In larger churches, especially those over five hundred people, the staff runs the church and the board's role is diminished. In the smaller board-run churches, if the board does not support strategic thinking and acting, it will not happen. If the pastor pushes it, they may drag their feet, argue with him, vote it down, or fail to act. The potential pastor of a small church who is change-oriented should use the Readiness for Change Inventory or selected questions from it to assess where that board stands on change before taking the church. The pastor who finds himself in a church with a change-resistant board needs to be patient with them. I would recommend that he take at least three to five years—preferably five—to bring them along with him in his thinking, through education (reading books together on strategy and change), through visiting change-friendly churches that plan strategically, and through personal, individual counsel.

Three Readiness Keys for Change

- The church's openness to change
- The pastor's attitude toward change
- The board's attitude toward change

The Church's Personnel for Thinking and Acting

Critical to any church's ministry is the people who make up its leadership. A ministry is only as good as the people who lead it. Therefore the question is, Who will be involved in the strategic planning process? The answer is, as many people as possible. The more people you involve in the process, the greater the ownership of the results. However, ultimate responsibility for thinking and acting rests with the leadership. This includes the following people.

The Pastor

I am convinced that the point or senior pastor should be the primary leader and responsible person for the planning process. That is why he must see the need for and agree with the importance of strategic planning for the church. It helps if he has skills and abilities in strategic thinking and acting and he should also be knowledgeable about the process. One of the reasons I have written this book is to help leaders become more knowledgeable. The senior pastor of a large church or the sole pastor of a small church should take the responsibility for the initial development of the strategic plan.

Significant Others

The strategic plan, however, is not to be the product of the pastor alone. While he initiates and guides the process and shapes the initial plan, he needs significant others to get their fingerprints all over the product as well. Significant others include church staff, board members, other church members either involved in leadership or being considered for leadership, small-group leaders, and those who exert influence over the congregation but do not have an official position of leadership.

A Woman

Often a viewpoint that is missing in strategic thinking and acting is that of the women in the church. If the church has few or no women in leadership positions, it would be wise to solicit a female perspective. Otherwise the process will not have important female insight, especially in the area of women's ministries. The church that I pastor, Northwood Community Church in Dallas, Texas, believes that women should not be elders. However, we have a women's advisor to the board who sits in on our meetings and regularly provides us wisdom from a woman's perspective.

An Outside Consultant

I believe that, if possible, a church is wise to employ the services of an outside consultant. A consultant can make a significant difference in several ways. First, one who is knowledgeable in the area of strategic planning can guide and instruct the pastor and other leaders. Since the consultant has been through the process and knows where the "sticking points" lie, he can save the church much time. Second, since he is an outsider, he brings necessary objectivity. Third, he can serve as a confidential sounding board for the pastor who may become extremely frustrated with the process and those involved in it. Fourth, he lends his credibility to the process. This is an interesting phenomenon. No matter how well trained or competent the pastor is, members of North American churches grant more credibility to specialists who come in from the outside than they do to their own pastor. People tend to respect, trust, and listen to a consultant when they would not give the same attention to a pastor. I have labeled this phenomenon "the prophet is without honor syndrome."[3]

The Benefits of a Consultant

1. They guide the church through the process.
2. They provide necessary objectivity.
3. They serve as a confidential sounding board.
4. They bring credibility to the process.

A Planning Team

Some churches prefer to use a special ad hoc planning team or a strategic planning committee made up of a representative cross section of the church. If you should decide to use this approach, or if it is a part of your church's tradition, then consider the following advice. Select seven to nine people who really want to be on the committee and for the right reasons. (A bad reason is to function as a watchdog to protect the church's cherished traditions. A good reason is to advance the cause of Christ in the church's ministry community.) Select people who are easy to work with but are willing to express their viewpoint. This will serve to enrich the process and limit any hidden surprises from surfacing at the last minute and undermining the final product. The pastor will need to work closely with the committee and make sure they are properly trained for the work they have to accomplish.

The Number of People Involved

The number of people taking part in the planning process is an important issue. Research indicates that the number of people primarily involved in crafting the product should range between five and twelve, with the ideal being from seven to nine.[4] Fewer than five people limits representation of various viewpoints. More than twelve is problematic because it makes scheduling meetings difficult, larger groups can become unwieldy, each member of the group has less time to talk and make contributions, and "reading" groups larger than twelve is difficult in terms of group process.

The Size of Planning Groups

Good size: 5–12 people
Ideal size: 7–9 people

③ The Church's Time for Thinking and Acting

The two most frequently asked questions regarding the strategic process concern time commitment and cost. A characteristic of most people in the twenty-first century, especially in urban North America and urban centers abroad, is busyness and limited discretionary time. Consequently people's time is a major factor that leaders and pastors must consider in attempting the strategic planning process.

How Long Will It Take?

The question on many people's minds is, How long will it take? Initially it will take ten to twenty full days, depending on such factors as prior preparation, knowledge of the process, and the use of a consultant. Since few—including staff—can set aside ten to twenty days without interruption, the time will consist of some full-day meetings, some half-day meetings, and a few hours here and there. Wisdom says that it will take longer than you think. Thus pastors should make no promises concerning time, which would risk their loss of credibility.

The time-consuming phase of strategic thinking and acting is the initial ten- to twenty-day period. However, you are not finished when you have completed the initial thinking and you are implementing the results. The process will continue for the life of the church. When the leadership of a ministry ceases to think and act strategically, the ministry will not survive times of chaotic and overwhelming cultural change.

Other Factors

Some other factors that affect planning time are initial agreement on core issues such as values and mission, the availability of data, and the use of creative, timesaving techniques such as storyboarding. I will say more about the latter at the end of this chapter.

Already have Core Values + mission statement

The Cost of Thinking and Acting

Another concern for most ministries as they consider strategic planning is cost. Can we afford to do strategic thinking and acting? It is a legitimate concern because several cost commitments may be involved.

There may be an expense for the personnel who are responsible for doing the primary crafting of the process, unless the staff are already on the payroll. Should the church decide that it is best for the strategists to get away periodically for their planning sessions, they should include such expenses as meals and lodging.

If a church follows my advice and uses a consultant, this will be an additional expense. But the difference a good, qualified consultant makes to the process may be the difference between success and failure. A few denominations have consultants on staff and provide their services at little cost to the church. Most consultants charge from five hundred to several thousand dollars a day. Usually, the better consultants have a higher fee.

There may also be a cost for good research. Those who do strategic planning must do some research—especially in the environmental analysis. This research looks at trends in both the secular world and evangelical churches by using demographic and psychographic materials. However, those who provide these research materials charge nominal fees for the information. I will say more about this in a later chapter.

Strategizing Cost Factors

- Cost of ministry personnel
- Cost of any travel, meals, and lodging
- Cost of a qualified consultant
- Cost of research (demographics and psychographics)

 ## The Place for Thinking and Acting

The strategic thinking team will need a place where it does its work. It must ask, Where will we do our thinking and acting?

A Church Facility

Since so much must be done in brief snatches of time (an hour here and one-half hour there), the church facility will be the best place for much of the work.

The Team Center

Taking a cue from the people at Disney World, innovative companies are developing team centers where their people gather to do some of their most creative work. Team centers are resource-rich rooms where people gather to work together, using creative thinking and planning techniques.

A church could create a team center within its own facility. The ideal is a room with the most current technologies, such as Internet access and video equipment, and ample wall space for visualization techniques—whiteboards, slide and overhead projection. However, most churches do not have the money to provide such a center. Thus the pastor's office or a classroom will suffice. What a team needs is sufficient room for a group of five to twelve people to meet comfortably around a table. I do some of my most creative church work in a classroom with an overhead projector, markers, and spacious whiteboards. My creative assistant at Dallas Seminary, David Ward, does much strategizing with students in his office, using only a three-by-two-foot whiteboard and a variety of color markers.

Other Facilities

Though the team will accomplish much of its work at the church, it would be wise to get away periodically and use other facilities for longer planning sessions. Often these meetings prove to be highly creative with fewer interruptions. Teams have used such places as a large private house, a conference center, a private club, a lake house or mountain cabin, a hotel or motel meeting room, and the boardroom of a bank or other professional organization. Some teams accomplish more by spending the night at a conference center or motel. However, I prefer not to travel too far because sleeping in one's own bed and seeing one's family makes for more productive work the next day.

Creative Tools for Thinking and Acting

In my consulting and training ministry and at my church, I use several helpful creative tools that save time and enhance the planning process as well as other leadership activities. I teach these methods to seminarians for use in their future ministries.

I discovered some of these tools in Mike Vance and Diane Deacon's book *Think Out of the Box*.[5] They have created them or collected them from others, and Vance popularized them at the Disney Company. However, I have personalized and altered the tools so that they match my style and best facilitate the particular activity I happen to be conducting. I will cover five tools here: the powwow, brainstorming, workouts, mindquakes, and storyboarding. I will cover a final tool, scenarios, in the last section under decision making.

Powwows

Use

The powwow is an excellent icebreaker. I use it primarily with new, small groups of people who plan to minister together and need to get to know one another quickly—it initiates vital community. I use this tool in the early formative stages of ministry or creative planning (most often the first meeting).

Participants

The participants in a powwow are people who will work together on some kind of team. It works best with smaller groups of people (no more than fifteen).

Setting

A relaxed environment such as a private home, mountain cabin, lake home, or a retreat facility is best.

Purposes

The powwow accomplishes several purposes. People get to know one another quickly and informally. It lays the foundation for a positive working relationship. It provides the important element of socializing. Powwows establish a pattern of open, authentic communication. They often set in motion the creative processes, and you get an early read on the composition and makeup of the team.

Characteristics

Powwows are intentionally open, authentic, friendly, nonthreatening, casual, not highly directive or structured, open-ended, and relaxed.

Process

The way I conduct a powwow is to gather the new group of people together at their earliest convenience for a casual meeting. I announce that I want to use this opportunity for all of us to get acquainted and I suggest that each person answer some or all of the following. What is your background? Comment on where you are from, your parents and siblings, and your early years. What are your gifts, passion, and interests? Where do you see yourself going in life and ministry? What are your honest feelings about this process, project, or class?

I have written the questions on a whiteboard or a large writing tablet mounted on an easel. I start the process by answering some or all of the questions myself. This allows me to model the process for them. Then I ask the same questions of the others in turn. If someone is too brief or unclear, I gently probe that person with questions for more information. Since this tool serves as an icebreaker, there is no need to take notes.

Brainstorming

Use

I use brainstorming when a group needs to generate as many ideas as possible over a short period of time. It works well anytime during a session except at the end, for it does not bring closure.

Participants

The participants are usually teams such as a board, planning group, or church-planting core group.

Setting

Brainstorming takes place best in a semiformal environment where no interruptions will occur.

Purposes

Brainstorming accomplishes several purposes. First, it stimulates a quick, free flow of numerous ideas. Next, it generates and often captures important preliminary concepts. Finally, it gives ownership of these concepts to the participants.

Characteristics

Brainstorming is fast paced, positive, smooth running, and nonconfrontational. The leader will need to establish and enforce the following ground rules: No confrontation or criticism of ideas, defer any negative thoughts or feelings, no speeches, and quantity is more important than quality.

For later thought and use, the various concepts should be recorded. They can be written on a whiteboard, three-by-five-inch cards, or Post-it notes.

Process

I conduct brainstorming sessions by gathering the group together, explaining the purpose for the session, and announcing the topic, often in the form of a question. Examples of topics are: How can we find more space for our crowded children's ministry? What could we do to reach out to some of the ethnic groups in our community?

Then I announce the ground rules given above. As people voice their ideas, I ask one member of the group to write them. When people run out of ideas, it is time to stop the exercise.

Workouts

Use

I use workouts to address any proposals or issues with which a group or an individual is wrestling. Often these are issues that surface during a brainstorming or mindquake session. Workouts provide closure. Consequently they fit best at the end of a strategic planning session or project.

Participants

The participants are usually teams, boards, planning groups, project development groups, and others.

Setting

Like brainstorming, workouts need to take place in a semiformal setting where there will be few interruptions.

Purposes

Workouts lead to solutions and bring closure to the work that has been done. They help to work through disagreements and differences of opinion.

Characteristics

Workouts are slow paced, reflective, confrontational (potentially the most confrontational of any of the tools), and dialogical, with few restraints.

Process

Workouts are somewhat the opposite of brainstorming and may be conducted in many different ways. Participants are urged to refine their thinking by prioritizing ideas that have already been gathered and discarding the ones that will not lead to the achievement of the group's goal. I provide an example of how I conduct a workout in the storyboarding process described below.

Mindquakes

Use

Mindquakes are excellent for helping groups see beyond or break out of their paradigms and solve difficult problems. Like brainstorming, mindquakes may be used at any time except at the end of a process or project. They are not meant for closure.

Participants

Any board or staff working toward a common goal can use mindquakes.

Setting

Mindquakes should be used when there will be no interruptions. Any disturbance will disrupt the creative processes of individuals and interactions taking place within the group.

Purposes

Mindquakes have several purposes: They catalyze thinking "outside the box," they give participants permission to "color outside the lines," they stimulate breakthroughs in new-paradigm thinking, and they generate and capture fringe and way-out ideas.

Characteristics

A mindquake is usually fast paced, chaotic, free-flowing, fun, sometimes confrontational, and may engender arguments. Nothing is out of bounds.

Process

After bringing together the group, the leader may conduct a mindquake by announcing that their help is needed in solving a difficult problem. The leader gives the group permission to pursue any direction they want, including apparent "rabbit trails," in their effort to think of a solution. Have someone record the ideas on a whiteboard or large tablet. When the group runs out of ideas, then it is time to stop. But do not assume that long pauses mean that they are out of ideas.

Storyboarding

I have used storyboarding more than any other tool in my leadership tool kit. Some refer to it as compression planning because it condenses planning processes into a short period of time. Also, more leaders have asked me to teach them the storyboard process than any other tool.

Use

Storyboarding helps teams accomplish a number of different tasks but is especially helpful in planning. Unlike the preceding tools that are used as part of a bigger process, storyboarding is a complete process in itself.

Participants

As few as five people or as many as fifteen to twenty people may be involved in storyboarding. Figure 2 shows you how to arrange the tables where the participants sit in relation to the storyboard and the facilitator. The facilitator is responsible for guiding the process, encouraging participation and idea development, and keeping the group on track. I suggest that a group have at least two recorders who will write down words and ideas on the three-by-five-inch cards as the participants call them out.

Setting

Storyboarding, like mindquakes, should take place in a location where there will be no interruptions.

Purposes

Storyboarding helps teams do planning in a shorter period of time. It also accomplishes problem solving. A third purpose is to help a ministry discover its core values.

Characteristics

Storyboarding involves creative thinking (brainstorming) and critical thinking (a workout).

Process

First, you will need to purchase the proper supplies—the storyboard itself, which is a 3-by-4-foot sheet of cork or bulletin board covered with cloth, pushpins, several felt-tip markers, color-coding labels (1/2" red dots), and a liberal supply of index cards in several sizes (mostly 3-by-5-inch yellow and some 5-by-8-inch red or blue). These supplies are not expensive and are easy to find, but you may wish to purchase them from the McNellis Company, which offers materials specifically made for the storyboarding process. I would suggest that you at least order a catalog from them at P.O. Box 582, New Brighton, PA 15066 (1-800-569-6015). If you do not wish to use the cork storyboard to which you pin cards, you can use a wall or whiteboard and stick Post-it notes to it. The problem is that when you move the Post-its around, they will curl up. Another option is to stick removable poster tape on the back of cards, but this is a more time-consuming process.

I begin storyboarding by explaining the four rules that I have written on a large card and pinned to the upper left side of the board. The four rules that apply to only the brainstorming part of storyboarding are the following:

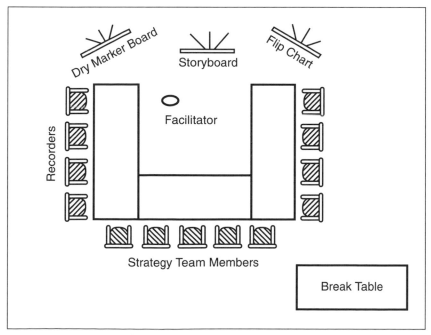

Storyboarding Room Arrangement

Figure 2

1. Suspend all judgment
2. Quantity, not quality
3. Please, no speeches
4. No killer phrases

Examples of killer phrases are: We have never done it that way before, That's not in the budget, and It cannot be done. I give each participant three small foam balls. They are to throw them at people who violate the rules. This serves to break tension and facilitate fun.

I explain what we hope to accomplish in the storyboarding session. I have written this on a card that is placed below the four rules. One example could be "to discover our core values." Another is "to develop a mission or a vision statement."

The first part of the exercise is a brainstorming, or creative thinking, session. If the group is discovering the church's core values, for example, the participants call out what they believe are the church's values—strong leadership, the lordship of Christ, celebrative worship, and others. The recorders write the responses on cards, and the pinner pins them to the board. This may go on for fifteen to twenty minutes.

When the facilitator senses that the group has exhausted its ideas, then it is time to shift to part two. This is the workout, or critical thinking, process. During this time the group will prioritize ideas, look for trends and recurring themes, remove any duplicates or false concepts, refine and collate concepts, and tie up any loose ends. If the group is discovering core values, they will eliminate values that are not true of the ministry, toss duplicate values, and identify items that are not actually values.

I have found it helpful in prioritizing ideas to give each participant a limited number of color-coding labels. Then I ask them to come up during the break and stick the labels on the cards with the most important ideas. If we are discovering core values, they would place the labels on the cards they believe are the actual values of the organization. Then we can quickly eliminate any ideas without labels.

A wonderful feature of the storyboarding process is that no one has to take notes. When you are finished, you merely collect the cards and give them to a secretary who will compile and record them for future use.

Do not allow all the detail to discourage you from using this tool. Once I learned how to do it, I began to use it all the time. And the only way to learn how is to practice it until you become proficient. It is a very visual and creative process that will save you much time in strategic thinking and acting and any other work you may attempt for the Savior.

Scenarios

Use

A sixth tool that I have recently begun to use in my church for strategic planning is the scenario. It is a tool that unlocks fresh perspectives about the future. Though it has been largely overlooked by most planners, some leaders are beginning to discover and use scenarios as the basis for an imaginative launch into the future. Scenarios are used primarily for investigating and making important decisions in the present that affect the future.

Participants

Scenarios are best used in a team context. Through a team, research can be done efficiently, and the different perceptions and insights of the team members help develop probable scenarios.

Setting

Once the team has done all its research and meets together, scenarios should take place in a semiformal setting where there will be few, if any, interruptions. Any disturbance may hamper the creative flow of ideas.

Purpose

We do not know the future yet we have to make decisions that affect our ministry in the future. When faced with such decisions, leaders use research to develop several stories that represent potential futures for their organization or elements within them. The result is that the leader is able to make strategic decisions about several different possible futures. Consequently no matter what the real future is, the leader has anticipated it and is better prepared to deal with it.

Characteristics

Scenario planning will take time because of the need to do research and to interact together as a team with the material gathered.

Process

First, the team must articulate the decisions to be made. Then, they must do research, looking for trends that will influence the future. Finally, based on the trends they observe, they are ready to develop possible scenarios for the future of the church. See appendix B for more information on developing scenarios.

Decision Making for Thinking and Acting

All organizations, whether Christian or non-Christian, have to make numerous decisions on a daily basis. Most are minor, but some are critical. How can a church or Christian ministry make good decisions? The best answer is to study and know the Scriptures. The following are some tools that will facilitate the application of that knowledge to strategic thinking and acting.

Scale of 1 to 10

The first is the scale of 1 to 10. A quick way to discover where people are on a particular decision or issue is to use the scale of 1 to 10 (see the

Creative Strategic Planning Tools

Tool	Use	Timing	Characteristics	Setting
Powwow	icebreaker, creates community	first meeting	open, non-threatening, casual	informal
Brainstorming	generates new ideas, problem solving	anytime except at end of meeting	fast paced, positive, non-confrontational	semiformal
Workout	arrive at solutions, make final decisions	end of meeting (closure)	slow paced, reflective, confrontational	semiformal
Mindquake	breaks through old paradigms, solves difficult problems	anytime except at end of meeting	fast paced, free-flowing, sometimes confrontational	semiformal
Storyboarding	planning, values discovery, mission development	an event in itself	all of the above at various times during the process	semiformal
Scenario	decision making for the future, explore organization's potential future	an event in itself	all of the above	semiformal

scales in the preplanning checklist at the end of this chapter). If the leader of a group such as a board wants to know where people stand on an issue, he or she can ask each one for a number between 1 and 10. A 1 says the person is strongly against the issue, and a 10 indicates that he or she is adamantly for it. A 5 or 6 means not sure.

If all those in a group give a 10 to a particular issue, such as a change of worship style from traditional to contemporary or hiring a new staff person, then the leader can move forward without unnecessary discussion. The leader knows that the group is convinced of or behind the proposal or decision. If most of them give a 1, this signals that they do not support the issue. Since it is obvious that the group is decidedly opposed, the leader will not want to spend time discussing the issue any further. When most of the group give a 5 or 6, it shows that they are undecided and need to spend some time in discussion.

Consensus

Some argue that church boards and committees should not take action unless they are unanimous in their decision. However, a unanimous decision is a rare occurrence in the real world of church boards and committees. Often church people do not see issues the same way. This is one of the reasons for working in teams—to get other people's viewpoints. But to come to a decision, two options are available: compromise and consensus.

Some leaders pursue compromise when a unanimous decision is needed. They encourage everyone to give a little or a lot for the sake of the entire church. This prevents gridlock and supposedly promotes unity. However, my experience is that when people have to compromise their views, no one is happy regardless of the decision.

A second and much better option is consensus. To best understand consensus decision making, we will first probe what it is and then what it is not.

What Consensus Is

Team or board members approach a decision with the attitude that they will attempt to support the decision of the team—even if they disagree with it—because their view has received a fair hearing. If they feel that for conscience sake they cannot agree with the majority decision, then they agree to disagree and to not cause a disturbance.

What Consensus Is Not

Consensus decision making as I am using it here must not be confused with majority rule as practiced by the typical church. Many churches practice majority rule by asking the congregation to vote on various matters, from the color of the new carpet to a new pastor. Sometimes you want the majority to rule, for example, when you want to know if people will financially support a new building proposal. If you begin a building program and your people are against it, the church will incur an insurmountable debt from which it might never recover. The problem with majority rule is that most churches have more immature believers than mature believers. Thus the spiritually immature could control the direction or lack thereof in the church. This happened with the majority and minority reports from the twelve spies that Moses sent in to spy out the Promised Land (Numbers 13). Contrary to God's direction, the majority (ten leaders) voted not to enter the land (Deut. 1:26).

The difference between consensus as I am using it and majority vote is the people. A group of spiritually mature people are able to make decisions by consensus. They are the people who make up the ministry teams, leadership boards, and staffs of many congregations. Much effective ministry in the New Testament was accomplished by such teams. The history of the church in Acts is replete with the names of various Pauline teams consisting of godly people. How might a group of mature leaders come to a decision where disagreement exists? The answer is consensus.

Scenarios

A third helpful tool in making decisions is the scenario. As I listen to people speak, I note that they often use the term *scenario*. However, if I

Helpful Tools for Decision Making

Tool	Primary Purpose
Scale of 1 to 10	Determines if group is ready to make a decision (saves time and eliminates unnecessary discussion)
Consensus	Prevents gridlock so group can come to a decision (promotes unity among the group)
Scenarios	Help ministry make decisions about the organization's future (anticipates and prepares for the future)

asked them to define or explain what a scenario is, I doubt they would be able to do so. To develop this concept as in-depth as is necessary, I have placed an extensive explanation in appendix B. Since this concept is so important to strategic thinking and acting in the future, and it will surface again in the next chapter, please turn now to appendix B and read about scenarios before going on to the next chapter.

Preplanning Checklist

Using the scale of 1 to 10, rate how well you believe your ministry is prepared to think and act strategically. Circle the appropriate number under questions one through five (1 indicates strongly against, 10 strongly for, and 5 or 6 not sure).

1. Is your church ready for strategic planning?

Comments:

2. Do you have the right personnel (pastor, board, staff) for change?

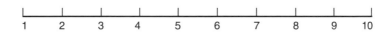

Comments:

3. Is this ministry willing to take the necessary time to do strategic planning?

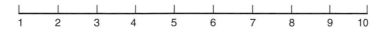

Comments:

4. Is the church willing to spend the necessary funds to think and act strategically?

Comments:

5. Is this organization willing to meet in the best possible place to accomplish its planning?

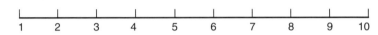

Comments:

6. Which strategic-thinking tools would help you in your ministry? Which ones will you try? Which will you not attempt? Why?

7. Which decision-making tools would help you in making decisions? Which ones will you use? Which will you not attempt? Why?

2

Understanding Organizational Development

The Sigmoid Curve

That people are born, grow, age, and, in time, die does not catch anyone by surprise. That is the human life cycle and it is old news. However, new news is that since the 1900s, the average life span for a North American has increased from forty-seven years to seventy-six years in the 1990s. The fastest-growing segment of the American population is the elderly. The number of people eighty-five and older grew 242 percent during the thirty years between 1960 and 1990.[1]

Like people, churches have a life cycle (figure 3). In general, a church is born and over time it grows. Eventually it reaches a plateau, and, if nothing is done to move it off that plateau, it begins to decline. If nothing interrupts the decline, it will die.

Unlike the elderly American population, the number of older American churches is not growing. Gary McIntosh writes that churches tend to reach their peak in health around their twentieth year after which many plateau and begin to decline. The majority of churches (70 percent) do not reach age one hundred.[2]

The Life Cycle of a Church

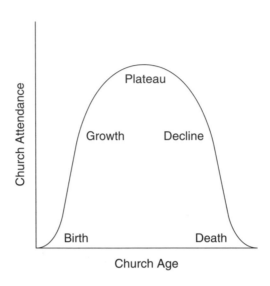

Figure 3

In this chapter I will address three areas. First, I will answer the question, Where is the North American church in terms of the church life cycle? Is it growing, plateaued, or declining? The answer is that the church is not doing well, so I will present this fact in the form of a problem to be solved. Second, I will provide an explanation for what is happening to the church in terms of the sigmoid curve. Understanding the concept of the sigmoid curve is imperative to dealing with North America's current church dilemma. Finally, in light of the explanation, I will venture a solution to the problem.

The Problem

The problem is that churches all across North America are not doing well. If the typical, traditional church checked into the hospital, chances are good that the doctors would put it on life support. However, before we examine what is taking place in North America, we need to look at the condition of the church in western Europe.

The Church in Western Europe

Often what takes place in western Europe reflects what eventually will be true of North America. The philosophical and theological ideas that have aged and cured over time in the intellectual wine cellars of Europe are still imported and served in the intellectual cafes of America. Consequently, if we examine what has taken place in the churches of western Europe, we might anticipate what will happen in our churches in North America.

The following table indicates that if the typical American church checks into the hospital, the typical church in western Europe will have to move over to make room for it.[3] Far too many western European churches are ornate tombstones scattered around the cemetery of European Christianity. The table compares the average church attendance (of at least one time a month) with the percentage of people affiliated with a church in many countries in western Europe. Only the church attendance in Catholic Ireland is impressive (82 percent). However, I would suspect that the political climate of Ireland has more to do with this than religion alone. The church attendance in the Netherlands (27 percent) is not reflective of attendance in the key urban centers. For example, I have ministered in Amsterdam where some estimate that approximately 2.5 percent of the people are churched.

	Church Attendance (at least once a month)	Church Affiliation (percentage of population)
Belgium	30%	74%
Denmark	4%	93%
France	13%	73%
Germany	21%	89%
Ireland	82%	98%
Italy	36%	93%
Netherlands	27%	58%
Spain	14%	90%
United Kingdom	11%	85%

The Church in North America

What has taken place in Europe has migrated to the United States. Religious bodies, in general, have hit a snag. Jackson W. Carroll, Douglas W. Johnson, and Martin E. Marty report that a study of Protestant, Catholic, and Jewish membership trends in America from 1947 to 1973 shows a flattening out followed by a slight decline in growth compared to the American population.[4]

Statistics of Decline

Several observers of the American church scene have observed the same. In 1988 Win Arn wrote, "Today, of the approximately 350,000 churches in America, four out of five are either plateaued or declining." Then he adds, "80–85% of the churches in America are on the downside of this growth cycle."[5] In 1995 Lyle Schaller wrote, ". . . two-thirds to three-fourths of all congregations founded before 1960 are either on a plateau in size or shrinking in numbers."[6] Charles Truehart wrote in 1997, "Little congregations of fewer than a hundred at worship, in rural communities and inner cities, are shutting their doors at the rate of fifty a week, by one estimate."[7]

Mainline Churches Are Declining

A large number of the churches that are declining are mainline (see table below). For example, the *Yearbook of American and Canadian Churches* reports that in 1965 the United Methodist Church had approximately 11 million members. However, by 1996 they reported 8.5 million. In 1965 the Presbyterian Church, U.S.A., reported 4 million members, but by 1996 the figure had dropped to 3 million. The Disciples of Christ had 2 million members in 1965 but dropped to 1 million in 1996. The Episcopal Church dropped from 3.4 million members in 1965 to 2.5 million in 1996.[8]

Church	1965	1996
United Methodist Church	11 million	8.5 million
Presbyterian Church, U.S.A.	4 million	3 million
Disciples of Christ	2 million	1 million
Episcopal Church	3.4 million	2.5 million

Evangelical Churches Are Declining

Some studies report that while most mainline churches are declining, the more conservative churches are growing. This may be true of a few such as the Assemblies of God and the Christian and Missionary Alliance churches.[9] My experience in working with a number of smaller evangelical denominations is that this is not true of the majority. One study citing conservative church growth points out that it came as a result of what the authors termed "a kind of circulation process, by which evangelicals move from one conservative church to another." (Church growth people refer to this as the "recirculation of the saints.") The study adds the following: "Bibby and Brinkerhoff conclude that conservative churches do a better job of retaining those already familiar with evangelical culture—both transfers and children of members—than moderate and liberal churches do in retaining their members."[10]

How are some of the larger evangelical denominations doing? Some people proudly cite the growth of the Southern Baptist Convention (SBC)—the largest evangelical denomination in America. However, the denomination reports that 70 percent of its churches are either plateaued or in decline (the 1994 Annual Church Profile reports that 49.5 percent of SBC churches are plateaued; while 20.2 percent are in decline).[11]

In several places in this section, I have intentionally referred to the church in North America. I include Canada as well as the States. The question is, Are the churches in Canada growing, plateaued, or in decline? My studies indicate that the situation is much worse in Canada than in the United States. In *Reclaiming a Nation,* Arnell Motz writes the following:

> The decline of religion in Canada has first been marked by the attendance drop-off in Protestant and Catholic churches alike. This was the beginning point of Bibby's analysis as he showed how in 1946 two-thirds of Canadians claimed (on a Gallup poll) to attend church weekly but by 1986 that number had dropped to one-third. . . . To those who circulate among various denominations, the number seemed to be high. In fact, I personally would be encouraged if I could find one-third of a community in church on a Sunday morning. So we checked attendance in several major urban centers across Canada and found attendance between 5 and 10 percent of the population; in the smaller towns it was 10 and 46 percent.[12]

Evangelical Churches and the Great Commission

Perhaps we could debate whether conservative churches are growing. However, the more important question is, Are conservative North American churches implementing the Great Commission (Matt. 28:19–20)? How well are they accomplishing the evangelism of the lost and the edification of the saints?

The answer is that both are casualties of decline. For example, Bill Hull writes that according to a 1980 Gallup survey of 22 million evangelicals who attend church, only 7 percent have taken any training in evangelism and only 2 percent claim to have led someone to faith in Christ.[13] In 1994 Bob Gilliam developed the "Spiritual Journey Evaluation" as an attempt to determine if today's church is making disciples. The survey included almost four thousand attenders in thirty-five churches in several denominations scattered from Florida to Washington. After analyzing the results, Gilliam observed that, "Most people in these churches are not growing spiritually. Of those taking this survey, 24 percent indicated that their behavior was sliding backward and 41 percent said they were 'static' in their spiritual growth."[14] Therefore, 65 percent of those responding indicated that they were either plateaued or declining in their spiritual growth.

The Explanation

The information above indicates that the North American church is not on a plateau but in decline. It is over the life cycle hump and moving downward. Before venturing to offer a solution to the problem, I want to look at an explanation for the problem. I believe that an understanding of why the problem exists is a major step toward solving the problem.

Experts have put forth numerous explanations for why the North American church is struggling. Many lay blame. Based on the information above, you could blame the church for not doing a better job of evangelism and edification. If 65 percent of the people in the churches are either plateaued or declining in their spiritual growth, then it is no wonder that so many churches are struggling.

You might also blame the seminaries and colleges that train the church's leaders. A scan of the typical seminary curriculum would reveal that far too many are not aware of what is taking place in North American culture and its impact on the typical church. Though many seminaries and Christian colleges have begun to use the new technology, they are typically business as usual when it comes to the curriculum.

My view is that the problem is not what evangelical seminaries teach but what they do not teach. Many evangelical seminaries teach the Bible and theology, and it is imperative that they do so. However, they often do not provide strong training in leadership, people skills, and strategic-thinking skills and this is poor preparation for ministry in today's shrinking world, which is undergoing intense, convoluted change.

The Sigmoid Curve

It is easy to lay blame, and many need to wake up or pull their heads out of the sand. However, a bigger, more fundamental explanation is represented by the sigmoid curve. We can better understand much of what is taking place in North American Christianity in general and churches in particular if we understand the concept of the sigmoid curve.

What Is It?

The term *sigmoid* simply means S-shaped (see figure 4). The S-shaped curve represents the natural development of one's personal life and relationships. It also represents the natural development of biological systems, institutions, worldviews, civilizations, and organizations including the church.

The S-shaped curve is essentially the life cycle pattern, covered in the first section of this chapter as it relates to the church. The curve depicts how virtually everything in life begins, grows, plateaus, and then ultimately dies. This pattern is represented by a curve in the shape of an S. I noted at the beginning

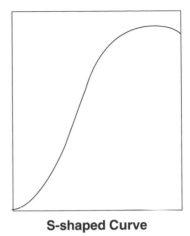

S-shaped Curve

Figure 4

of the chapter that this pattern is true of human beings. It also may be true of relationships such as marriage. It is true of civilizations as proved by the Greek and Roman empires in the past and the Russian empire today. The Fortune 500 companies demonstrate that it is true of businesses as a number of companies who made the list one, two, or more years ago are not on that list today. In physics, it is the second law of thermodynamics. In biology, it is extinction. In terms of worldview, it is the shift from theism to deism and then to naturalism or modernism. And today it is the shift from modernism to postmodernism. As demonstrated above, not even the church is an exception to the pattern. In short, the world and everything in it are all somewhere on the S-shaped curve.

The Message

The message or lesson of the sigmoid curve is that all good things (and even some bad things) end. In a world of constant, turbulent change, many relationships and most organizations do not last. The pattern is that they wax and eventually wane. Even brand-new institutions and organizations such as a church will, in time, plateau and then die. One of the fastest-growing and largest churches in North America is Willow Creek Community Church in northwest Chicago. However, a staff person recently told me that it has plateaued. No matter what institution it is, organizational "dry rot" sets in. The institution becomes brittle, ceases to function, and expires.

This concept has been true since the fall of mankind as recorded in Genesis 3. The bad news for the twenty-first century is that today decline is happening faster than ever before. In the first three quarters of the twentieth century, for example, decline was a relatively slow process. It took time for things to change and eventually die. You had some advance warning and time to address it. However, writing in 1994, Charles Handy warns, "Those units of time are also getting depressingly small. They used to be decades, perhaps even generations. Now they are years, sometimes months. The accelerating pace of change shrinks every sigmoid curve."[15] I would add that it has shrunk not only to years and months but in some cases to days.

While it does prove helpful to examine specific reasons why churches are declining, the lesson is that it will happen anyway. We can learn from this information and research what to do as well as what not to do. Regardless, in time the end is inevitable. This was true of the spiritually strong and not so strong churches of the first century. Those ministries live on today in the churches of the twenty-first century. However, the original churches are no longer. If you travel to the Middle East, you will not find any of them.

A Solution

The concept of the sigmoid curve raises a critical question for the North American church: Is there anything a church can do to circumvent or at least put off eventual decline and death? The answer is yes, and it is threefold. First, churches and denominations must start new S-curves. They need to launch out in new directions. Second, they need a strategic planning process that helps them start new sigmoid curves. They need to know how to think and act in the twenty-first century. Third, they need a theology of change that will guide them in starting new S-curves and implementing the change process.

Starting New S-Curves

The answer to the problem of church decline is to start new S-curves. This should occur in several contexts: church planting, church growth, and church revitalization.

Church Planting

The first context in which to start new S-curves is new church starts. Birthing new churches was the early church's response to Christ's Great

Commission. The church's three missionary journeys found in Acts 13:1–21:26 involved church planting.

A number of organizations and denominations have caught a vision to parent Great Commission churches all across North America. They refuse to bury their heads in the sand and ignore all that is taking place around them. The Assemblies of God and the Southern Baptists launched bold church-planting programs at the end of the twentieth century. A number of smaller denominations such as the Missionary Church, Lutheran Church-Missouri Synod, the Evangelical Covenant Church, the Church of the Nazarene, and others have followed suit.

Church planting involves starting a new or first S-curve (see figure 5). The new church has no prior history. It is at the very beginning of the church life cycle. While this can be a very disorganized time in the church's history, it is also a time of great excitement and anticipation. The core group is asking, What is God going to do? To what extent will God use us to make a difference in our world in the twenty-first century? Typically, churches at this early stage are very evangelistic and reach out to people in the community and beyond.

The concept of the S-curve teaches us that for the universal church to survive, it must plant churches. Since every church in time will wane and die, it is imperative that we start new churches, or the church as a whole will cease to exist.

Church Growth

The second context for new S-curves is the growing church. The key to continued growth and renewal is not only to start new first-curve churches (church planting) but to start a new second curve in the existing church before it plateaus.

Like church planting, this is a proactive response. The church starts the second curve while it is still virile and growing. It is at this stage that the ministry has the time, resources (people and finances), energy, spirit, and the drive to launch the new curve. Many in the church, however, will view this as foolish if not insane (they have not learned from companies like IBM that made the exact same mistake and as a result don't have the market share they once had).[16]

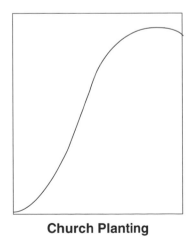

Church Planting

Figure 5

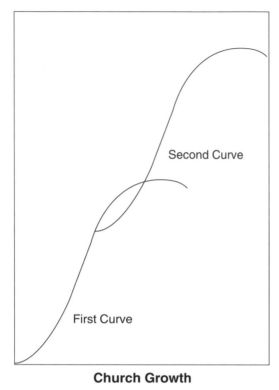

Church Growth

Figure 6

Why start a new course when the present course is so successful? Someone will quip, "If it ain't broke, don't fix it!" This calls for a strong leap of faith, as the need for and evidence in support of a new direction will not be obvious. This is a paradox. Leaders must push ahead in spite of the seeming evidence that the current ministry is doing well. It is tantamount to letting go of the trapeze with no net in sight. It takes leaders of strong faith and vision to pull it off.

Most leaders wait until the church has plateaued or is in decline before they seek renewal. This is the crisis or reactive mode. But people do not lead and respond well in a crisis context for several reasons. One is that the leaders are discredited. They are the very ones who led the organization into its state of decline, so they are not considered competent as leaders or worthy of trust.

People will also respond poorly because of lack of resources. Declining ministries are like sinking ships. People are quick to abandon them and take their money with them. There will also be poor esprit de corps. People are down emotionally, which drains them of the energy needed to be involved in renewal.

At this point, an important question for growing churches is, How can we know where our church is on the first curve and when it is time to start the second curve? The answer to both questions is that you cannot know for sure. However, the following hints may prove helpful. First, it is always safe to assume that you are close to a plateau. If you are not close, you can be sure that one is lurking somewhere off in the distance. Handy candidly points out that an organization needs a new direction every two to three years.[17] This is because not only is there more change today, but it happens in a shorter amount of time.

It may be helpful to ask an outsider (another pastor or consultant) for his evaluation. He will be more objective in discerning where the ministry is. Finally, younger people in the church and younger leaders will often be more aware of where the church is than older members. The older and established leaders, however, may hold different assumptions, views, or paradigms that blind them to the real situation. This is why I and others advise older leaders and retiring pastors not to stay in the church. It is imperative that those who cannot embrace the new curve step aside, and, usually, leave the church. This may seem harsh, but the church as a whole is more important than a handful of former leaders. These older leaders could move to other churches where they would be able to serve with less influence as lay leaders or as ministers in small-group communities.

Not only is it difficult to convince people in a growing church of the need to start a second curve, but it is difficult to accomplish the same. For a time, various currents will be pulling in different directions. The old and new curves will coexist causing much confusion. Conflict will surface between leaders and their followers invested in the first curve and those invested in the second curve. In addition, as the second curve starts up, it may wane before it takes over. The result will be even more criticism of the leaders of change. This makes it easy for them to lose heart, give up on the new curve, and return to the old or resign. The answer for leaders of change is to exercise great patience with the process. Do not be too quick to decide it's not working.

Some second-curve events. How do growing churches launch new S-curves? What are some second-curve events? One is a church relocation. Lakepointe Baptist Church is a growing Southern Baptist church located in Rowlett, Texas (a suburb of Dallas), with an average of two to three thousand attenders. They relocated to a larger facility that is located four or five miles away, facing a four-lane interstate highway, and attendance has jumped to over three thousand.

Another way to initiate a second curve is to implement some or, better, all of the concepts in chapters 3–11 of this book: discovering your core values; developing a mission, a vision, and a strategy; and so forth. For those who have already discovered and developed these concepts, begin a second curve by revisiting and updating or rethinking them.

Other events are the addition of a more contemporary worship service, transitioning the traditional church service to a contemporary service, adding a service to attract and win seekers, redesigning the traditional Christian education program, launching a vibrant small-groups ministry, and challenging all the people to go through a process of discovering their divine designs and then investing their lives in some aspect of church ministry.[18]

Warning. Every church is unique. Consequently, what works for one church may not work for another. Relocation worked well for Lakepointe—a healthy church. It could prove disastrous for you. The same is true for transitioning from a traditional to a more contemporary format, adding a service, and so on.

Some events result in deeper changes than others. A relocation or transition in style may bring changes only at the church's edges. This depends on the church and its particular culture, needs, and problems. Usually the kind of events that launch new S-curves result in substantial changes at the organization's heart and not just around its edges. Often, they involve a change in paradigm. While a church relocation or transition from one style to another is optional, discovering core values, developing a mission, vision, and strategy are not. When an entire church concurs and decides to pursue these, the result, most likely, will be a new S-curve.

Church Revitalization

The third context for starting a new sigmoid curve is the revitalization of plateaued or dying churches. The hope is that it is not too late. A plateaued church can move in a new direction. It starts the new S-curve while on the plateau (figure 7). However, when enough new people are coming into the ministry to offset those exiting, the leaders may find themselves dealing with some of the same problems as that of growing churches.

When a church waits until it is dying to make changes, it finds itself in a reactive, not a proactive, mode. It may be too late to start a new sigmoid curve. The church may have used up much of its resources in trying to keep the sinking ship afloat. Few people are willing to invest in a ship that is listing badly, and many head for the lifeboats. Those who decide to stay with the ship find themselves constantly wrestling with discouragement. As difficult as church planting and starting a new curve in a growing work are, revitalization of a declining ministry is the most difficult and the least likely to succeed.[19] However, if it is to survive at all, it must start a new S-curve as soon as possible (figure 8).

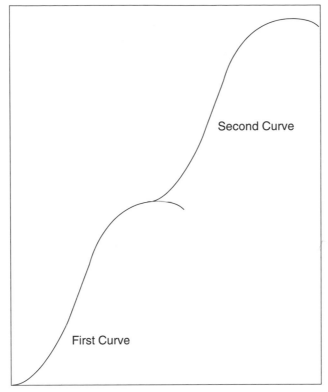

The Plateaued Church

Figure 7

The Strategic Planning Process

Before and after an organization starts a first or second sigmoid curve, certain specifics should be in place. They are all aspects of the strategic thinking and acting process and vital to successful new curves. This process is what the rest of this book is about. It consists of nine steps that ask leaders to answer nine basic questions relating to their ministry. These steps are vital to the life and future of every church. I will briefly overview them here.

The Ministry Analysis

The first step in strategic thinking and acting is the ministry analysis. It asks, What kind of church are we? Before leaders kick up their heels

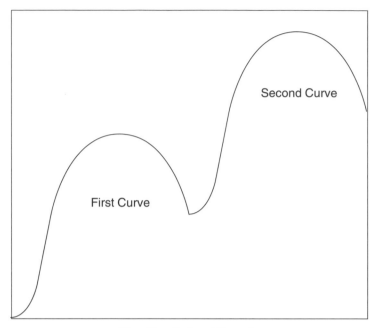

The Declining Church

Figure 8

and dream about what could be, they need to be in touch with reality or what is. If done authentically, this knowledge will help them spot the flaws and weak places in the organization's underside. It consists of a number of ministry audits that assess the church in such areas as its resources, place on the life cycle, culture, spirituality, esprit de corps, and performance. When performed properly, the analysis should help old-paradigm thinkers see the need for a new paradigm or direction.

2   Values Discovery and Development

The second step is values discovery and development. It asks, Why do we do what we do? The answer will reveal the church's core values. They are what drive the church. The values are the hidden motivators that dictate every decision and determine ministry priorities. They are timeless and do not vary no matter how much change may swamp the organization. This is why it is essential that every church discover, develop, and articulate its core values. Of all the steps in the thinking and acting process, this may be the most important because a ministry's values determine the answers to the other vital ministry questions in the strategic planning process. So this step must be taken early on.

3 Mission Development

The third step is mission development. The church's mission statement answers the functional questions, What are we supposed to be doing? What is our mission in life? In the marketplace this would correspond to the question, What business are we in? Christ has already predetermined the church's mission—it is the Great Commission (Matt. 28:19–20). Consequently, like the core values, the mission statement will not change appreciably. However, each church must personalize the Great Commission so that its people understand it and implement it in their unique ministry context.

4 Environmental Scan

Next is the environmental scan. It answers the question, What is going on out there? The purpose of the scan is to keep the church in touch with what is taking place in the world in general and in the world of the church. It helps churches anticipate trends and coming changes in the general environment that affect society, technology, economics, politics, history, philosophy, and theology. It also aids them in discovering what other churches are doing in response to these trends that might prove helpful. Most important, it fosters creative, proactive thinking that anticipates the future so that the organization is not overwhelmed or left behind in its ministry.

5 Vision Development

The fifth step is vision development. The articulation of a clear, succinct vision answers the question, What kind of church would we like to be? Whereas the ministry analysis focuses on what is, the vision focuses on what could be. It has much in common with the core mission, for it too is directional. The mission provides a statement of where the church is going, while the vision paints a picture of what that will look like. The importance of the vision is that people need to be able to see the church's future for it to happen.

6 Strategy Development

The next step is strategy development. The strategy answers the question, How will we get to where we want to be? Once the ministry knows (mission) and sees (vision) where it is going, it must decide how it will get there. A well thought-through strategy consists of a target group (the people we will reach), a specific, working strategy (how we will reach them), personnel (who will reach them), finances (how much it will cost to reach them), and facilities (where we will reach them). Unlike the core values and mission, the strategy is not timeless but timely. It should not only be open for change, it must never stop changing.

7   Strategy Implementation

Next comes strategy implementation. It answers the questions, Where do we begin, when, and with whom? Some writers on planning identify implementation as the greatest problem in any planning process. They argue that leaders design good plans but too often fail in their efforts to implement them. In some cases they do not know how to implement them. The result is that the entire plan dies for lack of implementation. This step involves determining specific action steps, deciding which are priorities, setting deadlines for them, deciding who will implement them, communicating those steps, and reviewing the entire process at a monthly implementation review (MIR) meeting.

8   Ministry Contingencies

The eighth step is preparing for ministry contingencies. This part of the process answers the question, How will we handle pleasant and not so pleasant surprises that could affect the strategy? Churches need to prepare for contingencies—both harmful and helpful. Potentially harmful contingencies are heart attacks during the service, an accusation of sexual harassment or molestation, an AIDS baby in the nursery, and others. Not all contingencies are harmful. Some are potentially helpful, such as a large financial donation, the visit of a celebrity, a revival, and others. This step is important because even the smallest contingency, helpful or harmful, if handled poorly, could ultimately cause the demise of the ministry.

9   Ministry Evaluation

The final step is ministry evaluation. It asks, How are we doing? Churches that do not evaluate what they are doing and the people who are doing it will struggle to improve. What gets evaluated gets done, and usually gets done well.

A Theology of Change

This chapter and this book emphasize the important role of change in North America and its impact on the church. Not only are there many changes, but they are taking place over a shorter time. The waves of change are pounding the typical church boat and they refuse to let up long enough for it to bail out the water. The purpose of this book and the strategic thinking and acting process is to place the church in a position where it can function at its best in preparation for and during the pounding.

Every institution—whether for profit or not for profit—must wrestle with the vexing question of what in the organization should change and what should never change. Opinions in both contexts range from one extreme (nothing should change) to the other (everything should change). Thus it is imperative that the church and its leaders have a biblical theology of change that guides them, especially during the pounding when it is so difficult to think clearly. A good theology of change addresses two areas: function and form.

Functions

The functions of the church are those timeless truths that must never change. They are the same for the church of the twenty-first century as they were for the church of the first century and all the centuries in between. Some examples of functions are evangelism, worship, prayer, and fellowship.

For the purposes of strategic planning, you must decide, through the nine-step process described above, what is timeless and should not change. I believe that the church's values, mission, and purpose are timeless core ingredients of the ministry.[20] They make up the congregation's heart and soul. Once the ministry has discovered and articulated its values, mission, and purpose, it must not change them except to reword or rephrase them for purposes of communication

Strategic Thinking and Acting Model

1   ⟶ Ministry Analysis ⟵

2   Values Discovery

3   Mission Development

4   ⟵ Environmental Scan ⟶

5   Vision Development

6   Strategy Development

7   ⟵ Strategy Implementation ⟶

8   Ministry Contingencies

9   Ministry Evaluation

Figure 9

and remaining culturally current. They are core ministry ingredients that will define and direct the organization's future.

Forms

The forms of the church are timely vehicles that are tied in some way to the church's culture. They implement the functions. The problem is that most churches tend to equate the church's functions with the cultural forms that express them whether local, national, or international. For example, the cultural forms of the European churches have exerted a strong influence on many traditional North American churches. Far too many people in these churches believe, for example, that the New Testament prescribed the great hymns of the faith for worship. However, men such as the Wesleys and Martin Luther wrote these in the context of the western European mindset and culture. Regardless, these forms must change if the church is to speak to its culture.

Theology of Change

Functions (never change)	Forms (must change)
worship	hymns/praise songs
evangelism	altar call/acts of kindness
community	potluck/small groups

Again, for strategic planning purposes, you must decide what is open for change. My view is that only the core values, mission, vision, and purpose of the church are timeless. Thus everything else—the church's strategy, structures, systems, policies, and procedures—are subject to change and should regularly change. The vision expresses the church's direction in a cultural context. While the direction (to make disciples) will not change, the cultural context (who, where, when, and how) will change over time.

Strategic Thinking and Acting

Timeless	Subject to Change
values	structures
mission	strategy
purpose	systems
vision	policies

Questions for Analysis and Discussion

1. Where is your church on the church life cycle—growing, plateaued, or declining? Has the church equipped its people for evangelism? Are the people growing and developing spiritually? Why or why not?

2. Based on your church's position on the church life cycle, where would you start a new sigmoid curve? What are some of the difficulties that you anticipate if you start a new S-curve? Have you considered church planting?

3. Did the information on a theology of change prove helpful? Do you agree with the function-form concept? If not, why? This chapter holds that, while their wording will vary as times change, a ministry's core—values, mission, vision, and purpose—should never change; everything else in the process is subject to change. What do you believe should and should not change in the strategic planning process?

PART 2

The Process
of Strategic
Planning

3

Analyzing the Ministry
What Kind of Church Are We?

I am a visionary, and my wife, Susan, is a realist. I spend much time dreaming about what could be. She spends her time thinking about what is—reality. We have been involved in several difficult church revitalization projects. In each situation, she asks, "Do you know what you are getting yourself into? Are you sure you want to do this?" I need to hear those questions. I usually follow them with one of my own, "But don't you see what could be?" She needs to hear that. Though this difference in our way of thinking can lead to strong disagreements, it helps us balance each other and see both sides of an issue or decision. I help her think about and envision what could be; she helps me think about and examine reality. Both are vital to any ministry situation.

The first step in strategic thinking and acting is to conduct a ministry analysis. It invites churches to ask the basic questions, How are we doing? and What kind of church are we? This forces people like me to face and deal with reality. It grabs the proverbial ostrich around the neck and pulls its head out of the sand. Since no organization is perfect, it helps each leader see the need for strategizing and provides both information

Ministry Analysis
Values Discovery
Mission Development
Environmental Scan
Vision Development
Strategy Development
Strategy Implementation
Ministry Contingencies
Ministry Evaluation

for the process and a realistic picture of the work that needs to be accomplished. In Nehemiah 2:11–17, Nehemiah conducted a ministry analysis when he and his leaders rode through Jerusalem, examining the walls (vv. 13, 15). He did this before communicating the mission for the Jerusalem Reclamation Project (v. 16b). Then he used the results of his findings to establish the need for his mission (v. 17a) and to challenge the Jewish remnant living in Jerusalem to attempt that mission.

I must stress the need for objectivity as you and your team move through this first step. At times, you and others will face the temptation to distort or minimize the information you uncover, especially that which surfaces your personal failures or those of the ministry. This analysis contains some gut-wrenching questions. It pokes and prods the ministry's tender underside. Nevertheless, operate with candor, openness, and accuracy as you work through the process. Otherwise, the results will be skewed and misleading.

This chapter and those to follow will not say much about prayer and trusting God for this entire strategic process. That is because I assume the importance of both. If you and your team do not bathe the entire process in prayer and trust God each step of the way, then you are doomed to failure (Prov. 14:2; 16:3).

The ministry analysis has two parts. The first is the internal analysis. It consists of a number of audits taken on the ministry as a whole. The second is the external analysis. It considers both any threats to the church's ministry and any opportunities for ministry.

The Internal Analysis

The internal analysis consists of several audits that are designed to give everyone a read on how the church is doing in such areas as performance, direction, energy, finances, and other key areas. I have not placed these in any particular order.

The Life Cycle Audit

The life cycle audit assesses where the ministry is on the church life cycle, covered in chapter 2 (see figure 10 on p. 63). This information determines if and where the church will start a second S-curve.

Every church can find itself at some point on this life cycle. The job of the assessors is to identify and come to an agreement as to where that is. To begin, ask each person involved in the analysis to circle the

The Life Cycle of a Church

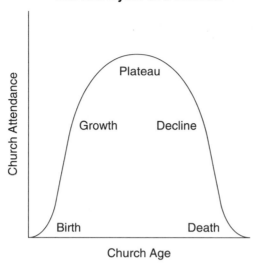

Figure 10

number that corresponds to where he or she would place the church (see figure 11).

Next, add all the numbers together and divide by the number of assessors. The result will be the group's estimation of whether the church is growing, plateaued, or dying. Announce the finding and then allow for discussion.

Here are some questions that you should discuss:

- If the ministry is growing, do we know why? How close is it to a plateau?
- If the ministry is plateaued, do we know why? How close is it to a decline?
- If the ministry is in decline, do we know why? How close is it to death?
- If the ministry is near death, is it time to shut it down?

The Performance Audit

The performance audit will assess the church's strengths, weaknesses, and limitations. Some areas you may critique are the property and facilities, location, convenience of location, ministries (worship, evangelism, preaching, teaching, Christian education), staff, attendance, commitment, and so on. Fill in a chart similar to the one on page 65 to have a picture of your strengths, weaknesses, and limitations.

Strengths

The strengths are what the church does well—its core competencies. Identifying the core competencies will help the church focus its energy and know where to make needed adjustments.

The following questions will surface your ministry's strengths. You may simply discuss them together or use an appropriate tool from chapter 1.

- What are our strengths as a church? What are we good at? What do we do well?
- What are our distinct, unique competencies?
- Why do people attend our church?
- What is our church known and respected for in the community?
- What qualities of the ministry set it off from other ministries in the area? What services do we provide that they do not?

Weaknesses

The weaknesses are what the church does poorly. They represent areas where the church is attempting ministry but for some reason is not doing it well. Scripture challenges us to do our work as to the Lord (Eph. 6:5–8; Col. 3:23–24). Thus if anything is worth doing at all, it is worth doing well. Weaknesses can include ministries that the church should be doing but is not, such as evangelism.

Answer the following questions about your weaknesses:

- What are our weaknesses as a ministry? What are we doing poorly, or what should we be doing that we are not?
- Why do people leave our church? What reasons or excuses do visitors give for not coming back?
- What are people saying about the ministry behind our back?
- What are the weaknesses of the church's staff?
- What are the weaknesses of the laypeople and volunteers?

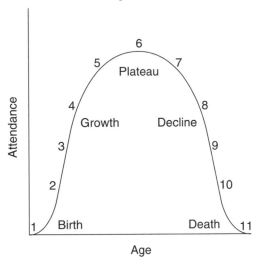

Figure 11

Limitations

No church can do everything well, and there are certain ministries that Scripture does not command and that are, therefore, optional. The ones that your ministry should not attempt are your limitations. Your church may not have enough people or the right kind of people to accomplish them. Some examples are a vacation Bible school, a weekly children's program, a special men's meeting, a handbell choir, an orchestra, a children's choir, and others. The following questions will help you identify ministry limitations:

- What are our limitations as a church? What are we doing poorly that is unnecessary and that we should not even attempt?
- What ministries are we attempting without a qualified leader?
- What ministries are we involved in where the people do not have the talents, gifts, or abilities to do them well?
- How do our facilities (or lack thereof) and/or community limit our ministries?

Strengths	Weaknesses	Limitations

The Direction Audit

The direction audit assesses the church's mission and vision. Every church needs both to survive. The mission determines the ministry's direction. It answers the question, What are we supposed to be doing? The vision is what that looks like in your unique ministry community. The chapters on mission and vision should clarify any questions you may have on these two topics and help you if you find your church does not have a well-defined mission or vision statement.

Answer the following questions about the church's mission and vision:

- Does our church have both a mission statement and a vision statement? If not, why not? If so, what are they?
- Are the stated mission and vision biblical?
- Are the mission and vision statements clear and memorable? How do we know?
- Does the church communicate well its mission and vision statements?
- How well is the ministry accomplishing its mission and vision?

The Strategy Audit

The strategy audit assesses how the church attempts to accomplish its mission and ministry. Though every church may not have a stated mission, it will have a strategy. (However, a strategy without a mission really does not make sense.) The strategy includes the church's programs but is more than programs. The strategy is also the way the programs are arranged and carried out to accomplish the ministry. For example, a typical strategy that many will recognize is the "three-to-thrive" strategy developed in the early twentieth century. It consists of a Sunday morning Sunday school and church service, a Sunday evening church service, and a Wednesday evening prayer meeting.

The following questions will help you assess your strategy:

- Has the ministry clearly articulated and communicated its strategy?
- Does most everyone know what it is?
- Is it working? Is it accomplishing the church's mission?
- If our church does not have a mission, then what is the strategy attempting to do?
- What programs make up the strategy?

- Do any programs overlap in purpose?
- Which programs need to be revamped or ended?

The Congregational Audit

The congregational audit helps the ministry team answer the question, Who are we? It consists primarily of congregational demographics and psychographics. A congregation's demographics concerns its people. It asks, To whom are we ministering? For example, is the congregation primarily Builders, Boomers, Generation Xers, Millennialists, others, or a blend of all? The audit may wave red warning flags. For example, if you determine that the church is made up mostly of Builders (55 and older), it is in deep trouble. Demographics includes gender. In most congregations the women outnumber the men. Demographics includes other information about the congregation, such as education, employment, collar color (blue collar or white collar), family units (singles and marrieds, with and without children), housing, and income.

Psychographics asks, What are our congregation's needs, values, wants, and desires? Congregational demographics tells us who the people are; psychographics tells us why they are in our church and what they want from it. It should be obvious that congregational demographics and psychographics are ministry shaping, yet far too many churches ignore them to their peril.

Answer the following questions about the church's demographics:

- Does the congregation consist primarily of Builders, Boomers, or Gen Xers? If mostly Builders, what does this tell us? If mostly Boomers, what does this tell us? What would it take to reach other generations?
- Is the church made up of more women or men?
- Is this congregation well educated? What difference does this make?
- What do our people do for a living? What does this mean to the church?
- Is the church made up largely of married couples? Are they with or without children? How many singles attend?
- Where do our people live? Do most live in houses, apartments, other? How might this affect the ministry?
- Are our people low, medium, or high income? How might income affect the ministry?

To understand your congregational psychographics, follow all the answers to the questions above with the question, Why? What does this tell us about our people? For example, if more women attend your church than men, ask, Why? Then you might probe the answer. For example, Why are men not attending our church? What would it take to reach men? In addition, ask, What are our people's needs, values, wants, attitudes, and desires?

The Culture Audit

Though the congregation may not be aware of it, every church has a unique culture. The culture audit assesses that culture. I define congregational culture as "the way we do things around here." It consists of such things as its traditions, heroes, expectations, norms, stories, rituals, symbols, rewards, values, and so on. A congregation's culture ties its people together and gives meaning and purpose to its life. It provides a sense of identity and stability and sets boundaries. Leaders gain a sense of the congregational culture when they listen well. They must listen to the talk going on in the church's hallways, parking lots, and rest rooms to gain valuable insight into the culture. Answer the following questions that will help you to articulate your culture:

- Identify some of our church's traditions, both good and bad.
- Who are our church's heroes? (evangelists, teachers, pastor)
- What are our people's expectations? (conversions, good Bible teaching, kids' programs, parking)
- What are the norms and standards? (do's and don'ts)
- What stories do people tell? What are our myths and memories?
- What are the church's rituals? (retreats, vacation Bible school, testimonies)
- What are our symbols? (baptisms, communion, pictures, tapestries)
- What does the church reward?
- Do we support or resist change?

The culture audit could also assess the culture of the church's community. If you desire this information, then ask these or similar questions concerning the church's community.

The Obstacles Audit

The obstacles audit asks, What kind of obstacles do we face? What gets in the way? What is preventing great performance? Two kinds of obstacles are people and organizational.

People Obstacles

One common people obstacle is the way the church thinks. What is thinkable and open for discussion and what is not? Others are the way you solve problems, learn from your mistakes, and what you condone and do not condone. Some leaders condone poor work performance or an abusive employee. The result is terrible morale. Answer the following questions:

- What is not thinkable or even discussable around here?
- Do we face and deal with our problems? What problems do we avoid?
- Do we learn from our mistakes? Why or why not?
- What kinds of behavior do we condone that hurt people?
- Do we have good or bad morale?
- Do we have any traditions that are blocking effective ministry?
- What are other people obstacles that we face?

Organizational Obstacles

A ministry will also have organizational obstacles. Most often they are the source of the people obstacles. There are two types of organizational obstacles: the organization's structures and its systems. Structure affects the church's organization, focus, and flexibility. For example, in a church that is organized vertically, all the decisions are made at the top and handed down to the people. Horizontal organization involves more people in the decision-making process. In a centralized church, the power is invested in a few people. A decentralized system spreads power among many people.

The organization's systems support the structure and make the organization go. Most churches need at least five systems: accountability, information, feedback, recognition, and training.

Answer the following questions about organizational obstacles:

- Is our church organized vertically or horizontally?
- Is the power centralized or decentralized?

- Is the focus inward or a balance between inward and outward?
- Is the church flexible or inflexible? Where is it inflexible?
- Do people know what they are accountable for?
- Does the church effectively collect, manage, and disseminate information? How much is gossip?
- Do people know how well they are or are not performing?
- Does the church reward good behavior? Does it accent the negatives or the positives?
- Is this a learning organization? Does it provide regular training opportunities for its staff and laypeople?

The Spirituality Audit

The spirituality audit seeks to determine how the church is progressing spiritually. The concept of spirituality means different things in different churches. You will need to decide what it means in your church. I use the spirituality audit to explore at least three areas that commonly reflect on an organization's spiritual condition: maturity versus immaturity, carnality versus spirituality, and legalism, liberty, or license.

Using the scale of 1 to 10, rate your ministry by circling a number in each of the following. Add the numbers given by all the evaluators for each category and divide by the number of evaluators to determine an average.

Immature   Mature

1   2   3   4   5   6   7   8   9   10

Comments:

Carnal   Spiritual

1   2   3   4   5   6   7   8   9   10

Comments:

Legalism   Liberty   License

1   2   3   4   5   6   7   8   9   10

Comments:

The Energy Audit

The energy audit assesses the church's energy level. Energy is the degree of effort or intensity that a church exerts in pursuit of its various activities, mission, and ministries. For example, a church that is growing numerically for whatever reason will usually have a high level of energy. Its battery is fully charged. People are more likely to get involved. But a church that is in decline will display a low energy level. A handful of tired people are doing all the ministry while others sit back and watch their efforts. Its battery is drained, and it will likely not survive, depending on where it is on the church life cycle. In this situation, the best thing the leadership could do would be to conduct a loving, caring funeral. This would free people to go elsewhere, serve, and recharge their batteries.

. Using the scale of 1 to 10, circle your church's energy level. Add the numbers given by all the evaluators and divide by the number of evaluators. Also consider whether the energy level is increasing or decreasing.

Comments:

The Emotions Audit

The emotions audit evaluates the emotional level of the congregation. Are the emotions running high or low? In general are the people discouraged or encouraged? As in the energy audit, growing churches tend to be upbeat; whereas dying churches are downbeat. Depending on where it is on the church life cycle, a discouraged church may need to evaluate whether they continue.

Using the scale of 1 to 10, circle the number that best represents the church's emotional level.

Excited		Upbeat		Average		Downbeat		Discouraged	
1	2	3	4	5	6	7	8	9	10

Comments:

The Finances Audit

The finances audit assesses the church's financial health. In Matthew 6:21, the Savior says, "For where your treasure is, there your heart will be also." Most often, you will find congregants' treasures in their purses or wallets. The question is, How much are they willing to give to God and his ministries in the church? The church's bottom line is its budget, and budgeted expenses tell you its values. This audit looks primarily at the budget and its history.

To answer the following questions, you may need the help of the person or persons who are responsible for the finances. They may need time to analyze the budget to supply you with the requisite financial information.

Answer the following about the church's finances:

- Does our church consistently meet its budget?
- Is the church current on all its bills?
- Has the church incurred much debt or is it relatively debt free?
- What are our present giving trends? Are they increasing, plateaued, or declining? For how long? Why?
- Are people giving well in proportion to their incomes? (3–5 percent is average.) What percent do most people give?
- What is the average giving per family unit? Is this good or bad?
- What percent of the giving comes from Builders, Boomers, Gen Xers, Millennialists, and others? What does this tell us about the church's future?
- Is giving evenly distributed across the congregation?
- Are a few people giving most of the money? What will happen if they die or leave the church?
- Are we adequately compensating our pastor and any staff?

The Age Audit

The age audit focuses primarily on two areas. One is the age of the majority of people in the congregation. The other is the age of the facilities. Answer the following questions for the age audit.

- Are the majority of the congregants approaching or over 65? If so, what does this say about the future of the church?
- How old are the facilities?
- Have the facilities been well maintained?
- Are they in need of repair?

Other Ministry Audits

The aggressive church that desires even more information may want to consider other internal ministry audits besides the ones I've suggested. The Readiness for Change Inventory, in appendix A, is a change audit. I have included a values audit in the next chapter on values.

Now that you know how an audit works, you may want to configure several of your own.

The External Analysis

The external analysis looks at what is going on outside and around the church whether good or bad. This is very important for churches that are focused inward because it invites them to discover and learn about the community that lives around them and of which they are a vital part. It consists of three areas: a community audit, a threats audit, and an opportunities audit. A competitors audit is a part of the threats audit.

The Community Audit

The community audit, like the congregational audit, consists mostly of demographics and psychographics. Community demographics asks, Who is our community? Who are the people who live within a certain radius of the church? These are the people who make up your ministry community. You need to understand your community and who in that community you are most likely to reach. Community psychographics asks, What are these people's needs, values, wants, attitudes, and desires?

Answer the following questions about your community:

- Does our community consist primarily of Builders, Boomers, Generation Xers, or others?
- Are we located in an urban, suburban, exurban, or rural community?
- Is the area new or aging? Is it well or poorly kept?
- How many men and women live in the area?
- How are the people in the community employed?
- Are they married, married with children, or single?
- Are they mostly blue collar, white collar, or both?
- Do they live in houses, apartments, or both?
- Are people moving into or out of the area?

For psychographic information, ask why of each of the answers you give above. Why do more people live in apartments or houses? Why are they moving into or out of the area? Also ask what the community's needs, values, wants, and desires are. The answers to all these questions affect how you will reach out to and minister to your community and your effectiveness in doing it. They will also influence other decisions such as relocation.

Usually the church will attract those in the community who are most like it demographically and psychographically. This bothers some. The key, however, is whether the church is willing to accept and minister to people who are different. Even if the church is willing, it does not mean these people will attend the church. Those ministries that truly desire to reach people who are different demographically and psychographically must ask the questions, What are we willing to change to reach people who are different from us? What are we willing to give up? The answer might be changing the worship style or hiring a pastor or assistant pastor who is more like those in the target group.

The Threats Audit

The threats audit signals existing and potential activities or ideas that pose some threat to the church, ranging from minimal to terminal. The question to ask is, What are the immediate and long-term threats to our ministry? Some churches prefer to avoid reality and look the other way. What they see could be too painful. However, a timely discovery could prevent damage and possible ministry demise.

Review the following list of ministry threats. Check any that are or might be relevant to your situation.

- An expanding inner city and a changing, dying community
- Significant numbers of people moving out of the area
- Growing crime rate
- Saturation of churches in the area
- Few, if any, people from the community are visiting or joining the church
- People in the community are different from those in the church
- People in the community are not interested in the church
- Other threats:

The competitors audit looks for organizations or events in the community that compete with the church for the attention of people. (Thus it accompanies the threats audit.) Competitors could be positive competitors, such as a strong church, but most are negative, such as sporting events (the National Football League) or the theater. These compete with the church for the attention of people, either current members and attenders or potential members and attenders.

Circle any ministry competitors:

- Other church or parachurch ministries
- Religious organizations or cults
- The entertainment industry (movies and television)
- Athletics (participative or viewed)
- Health clubs or fitness centers
- Leisure activities
- Recreation opportunities
- Marketplace (shopping malls and department stores)
- Family time
- Other competitors:

The Opportunities Audit

The opportunities audit assesses all the opportunities for ministry in the community and beyond. Some are immediate while others are long term. The church should be aware of these possibilities whether it can address them or not.

Review the following list of opportunities. Check any that might be possible opportunities for your ministry.

- Unreached people (groups) in the community
- New people moving into the area
- Local schools (elementary, secondary, vocational school, university)
- International students attending local schools
- Nearby armed services facilities
- Special people groups (single parents, challenged people, street people)
- Prisons and jails
- Local businesses
- Other opportunities:

Questions for Analysis and Discussion

1. How did your church do on the internal analysis? On the scale of 1 to 10 where would you place it? Circle the number and compare it with the assessment of others on the analysis team.

2. What were your ministry's most glaring faults? What embarrassed you? What frightened you?

3. What were the high points? What made you feel proud? What excited you?

4. If your church is growing, what did you learn that proved helpful? Are you close to a plateau?

5. If your church is plateaued, what did you learn that might help you? Do you understand why you are plateaued?

6. If your church is in decline, what did you learn about your situation? Why are you in decline?

7. Is your church near death? If yes, what do you plan to do? What is in the best interests of God and your people? Would it be wise to end this ministry? How hard would that be? What would keep you from doing this?

8. What are your organization's greatest external threats? Who or what are your worst competitors?

9. What are your church's greatest opportunities? What will it take for you to capitalize on them?

4

Discovering Core Values

Why Do We Do What We Do?

Not only do people have a life cycle—they are born, grow up, age, and die—they also have a soul. That catches only the most robust atheist by surprise, for it is old news. What some do not understand is that churches, like people, have a soul—a collective soul.[1] Congregational or corporate soul is at the very heart of the organization. It is a leadership concept that embraces a combination of the church's unique values, mission, purpose, and vision. What sets successful congregations apart is their discovering and tapping into that soul, making contact at its deepest levels. That is what steps two, three, and five are about.

Ministry Analysis

Values Discovery

Mission Development

Environmental Scan

Vision Development

Strategy Development

Strategy Implementation

Ministry Contingencies

Ministry Evaluation

This chapter is step two of the strategic thinking and acting process. It asks and answers the fundamental ministry question, Why do we do what we do? Once the church has completed the ministry analysis, it is time to take this second step. I have designed this step to help you begin to tap your ministry's heart and soul, specifically what is conceivably the most important element—its core values. They are the answer to the values question.

The Jerusalem church considered core values important, for Luke states that the church "devoted themselves" to core values, which he lists in Acts 2:42–47.[2] After stating that a mission and values are at the foundation of an effective organization, Ken Blanchard and Michael O'Connor write, "Perhaps more than at any previous time, an organization today must know what it stands for and on what principles it will operate. No longer is values-based organizational behavior an interesting philosophical choice—it is a requisite for survival."[3] Lyle Schaller writes, "The most important single element of any corporate, congregational, or denominational culture, however, is the value system."[4] In this chapter we will explore why values are so important. I will provide a definition and then help you discover, develop, and communicate your congregational core values.[5]

The Importance of Values

Just as personal values speak to what is most important in our lives, so a congregation's values speak to what is most important in the church's life. Following are nine reasons why core values are so important to the life of a church.

Values Determine Ministry Distinctives

No two churches are exactly alike. Each is unique in a number of ways. Some churches are very traditional while others have adopted a more contemporary format. Some devote their attention to strong Bible preaching and teaching, others to evangelism, reaching seekers, counseling, or children's ministries. What makes each church unique is its culture, and the most important ingredient in that culture, as Schaller noted in the quote above, is values.

If you examine the values statements or credos in appendix C, you will note many differences. Each one tells you much about the church and its distinctives. You can learn a lot about the church before you walk through the front door. For example, the credo of the church that I pastor, Northwood Community Church, has eleven values. The sixth value—family—is most distinctive. I have not found family listed as a value in any other church credo, and I have collected many.

Family
We support the spiritual nurture of the family as one of God's dynamic means to perpetuate the Christian faith (2 Tim. 1:5).

This value would catch some people's attention, specifically those with a family. It tells them that if their family is important to them, then Northwood is a church worth taking a look at.

Values Dictate Personal Involvement

A ministry's values help people determine what their personal involvement in that ministry can be. A congregant or potential congregant should determine if his or her ministry values align with those of the church. This can be done by simply asking, Do we have the same values? If the answer is yes, then this would be a good ministry match. If the answer is no, the person should look further. The result of a good values match or values alignment is a common cause that leads to ministry involvement and a happy member.

A church revitalization pastor should pay close attention to his values and those of the church. A pastor needs to discover and articulate his core values for a church that he may lead before any involvement takes place. The church planter's values become those of the future church. He merely invites people to involvement.

Values Communicate What Is Important

Core values signal a ministry's bottom line. They communicate what really matters. Clearly articulated values drive a stake in the ground that announces to all, "This is what we stand for; this is what we are all about; this is who we are; this is what we can and cannot do for you." The Jerusalem church communicated what was important through its statement of values in Acts 2:42–47.

A commitment to one's core beliefs or values helps pastors know where to draw the line in the sand. For example, as a result of my ministry at Dallas Seminary, I have come to know many pastors in the Dallas–Fort Worth metroplex. At least once or twice a year a pastor who is having difficulty with his church will come to me, asking if it is time to move on and look for another ministry. My answer is always the same, "Does your situation force you to compromise, deny, or abandon your fundamental ministry values?" If the answer is no, and it usually is, then I encourage them to give the ministry and themselves more time (James 1:3–4). If the answer is yes, then it may be time to leave.

Values Embrace Good Change

This book has already said much about change. The sum of it is that today more than ever before North America is reeling with accelerating, convulsive change. As the country shifts from one worldview to another—modernism to postmodernism—we are experiencing more change than ever before, and it is happening in a shorter time than ever before. No organization, especially the church, is exempt from its effects.

The problem for the church is how to know what is good and bad change. How can we know if a change will help the ministry or harm the ministry? A wrong move could prove disastrous. One answer to this dilemma is our core values. We must ask, Does this change agree with or contradict our beliefs as a ministry? We can embrace that which aligns with our beliefs but must reject that which opposes them.

Values Influence Overall Behavior

A church's values or beliefs are ministry shaping. I have labeled this the values impact. They dictate every decision and influence every action right down to the way we think and the manner in which we execute those actions. They beget attitudes that dictate behavior. They make up the premises of the ministry's policies and procedures. They affect everything about the organization: its decisions, goals, priorities, problems solved, conflicts resolved, spending, and much more.

In the problematic situation of Acts 6:1–7, the Jerusalem church models the values impact. The Twelve faced a potential church split over an accusation of discrimination. The Grecian Jews accused the Hebraic Jews of neglecting the former's widows in the daily disbursement of food. Instead of taking valuable time to wait on these widows, the Twelve assigned this responsibility to seven highly qualified people, while they gave their attention to the higher-value ministries of prayer and the ministry of the Word.

Values Inspire People to Action

A congregation's beliefs are the invisible motivators that move its people toward meaningful ministry. The values of both leaders and followers catalyze—energize—people. For example, you can tell parishioners to evangelize the lost and urge them to support missions. However, if these are not a part of their values mix, then it is not likely to happen. To truly catalyze the greatest amount of energy, to strike a resilient chord in the hearts of its people, to seize the day, each church must penetrate to a deep level. It must touch people at the level that gives meaning to their lives—the values level.

Values Enhance Credible Leadership

Good leadership at all levels is essential to any successful organization. As the leadership goes, so goes the church. Values drive leaders as well as churches. Therefore, leaders must know and articulate what they stand for—their values bottom line. Every bottom line is braced with core values, and it is imperative that these be biblical.

It is most important that leaders model a lifestyle consistent with those values. Leadership that aligns with solid beliefs invites credibility; leadership that violates or contradicts its values quickly loses all credibility and, over time, forfeits the ministry. An example of the former is the Johnson & Johnson Company, the maker of Tylenol. It responded to an episode of product tampering by voluntarily recalling all its product at a cost exceeding a hundred million dollars. It did so because one of its vital beliefs is the health of the customer: "We believe that our first responsibility is to our customers."[6] Consequently, to this day, I prefer Tylenol over any other product.

Values Contribute to Ministry Success

Any organization, Christian or non-Christian, must adhere to a sound set of fundamental beliefs if it hopes to experience success. In order not only to survive, but to achieve success, it must have a solid set of beliefs on which it premises all its policies and actions. It is the organization's ingrained understanding of its shared core values more than its technical skills that make its success possible. This is partly because shared values encourage people to serve longer hours and work harder. An inspired community of believers who are united in a common cause is enthusiastic and exerts a strong influence on its ministry constituents. This seemed to be the key to the effectiveness of the early church (Acts 2:42–47; 4:32–37).

But what is ministry success? A church is successful when through the power of the Spirit it accomplishes its ministry mission (the Great Commission, Matt. 28:19–20) without compromising its ministry values.

Values Influence Ministry Mission and Vision

The church's mission is what it is supposed to be doing. The vision is what that looks like. The mission is a statement of the church's direction; the vision is a snapshot of the same. The first tells us where we are going; the second shows us where we are going. Both are vital to the life of the ministry organization and are located with the values at its very heart and soul.

I have hinted at least twice so far in this book that of all that makes up congregational heart and soul, core values may be the most important. This is because of the effect that the values have on mission and vision. The shared beliefs influence and determine what the mission and vision are. Because evangelical churches value the Scriptures, for example, the mission is the Great Commission, and the vision is what that looks like as people in the church's ministry community come to faith and then grow in that faith. Churches that are not evangelical or that do not value the Bible may have some other mission and vision.

The Definition of Values

Now that we know why core values are so important, it is time to discover what they are. I define core values as the constant, passionate, biblical core beliefs that drive the ministry. This definition consists of five vital elements that we will look at one by one.

Values Are Constant

When I describe a value as constant, I am saying that it is timeless. As a distinct aspect of congregational soul, it remains fixed while almost everything around it is in great flux. When faced with the question of what in the ministry organization should change and what should never change, the answer to the latter is values or beliefs. Properly conceived, they remain fixed. They are the unchanging threads that hold together the constantly changing organizational fabric.

The reason that values cannot change is that they dictate congregational behavior. If they change frequently, this would leave the congregation in a state of confusion. For example, if the church primarily valued evangelism, over time people would share their faith and might even bring lost people to the services. However, if the church dropped evangelism, no longer valuing it, and began to focus more on biblical com-

Nine Reasons Why Values Are Important

1. Determine ministry distinctives
2. Dictate personal involvement
3. Communicate what is important
4. Embrace good change
5. Influence overall behavior
6. Inspire people to action
7. Enhance credible leadership
8. Contribute to ministry success
9. Influence ministry mission and vision

munity or family, people would become confused and frustrated. They would wonder if they were still supposed to share their faith. They would begin to ask if they should invite lost friends to church.

I have said that values should not change. Perhaps a better way to communicate this is to say that they should not change appreciably. A year or so after a ministry has first discovered and articulated its values, the leadership may find they missed a value or two or that one of the values included in the credo should really not be there. So some adjustment can be made over the first few years. After that time, however, the values become relatively fixed. It is possible that with a new pastor who embraces different values, the values may change in time. This is why it is wise for a congregation to know its values and look for a new leader who embraces those values.

Values Are Passionate

Passion is a feeling word. A good core value touches the very heart and soul of the church and elicits powerful emotions. It is more emotional than intellectual. It affects not only what you believe, but how deeply you believe it. It comes with feelings attached. It stirs up those strong feelings that excite and motivate people to action.

This concept will prove most helpful in the next section on values discovery. You can discover your own values by reading a values statement or credo. The ones that you hold will jump off the page at you. They will stand out from the rest because you feel strongly about them.

People who share your values feel the same way about them that you do. If they hear you articulate them or if they read them in a church brochure, they connect with the ministry at a gut level. They sense a kindred spirit that draws them in. These shared values penetrate to the bone and bond people together.

Values Are Biblical

When I say that values are biblical, I mean that most of the values of a ministry are found in the Bible. We all agree that we want whatever we do to be biblical. However, we accept many things in our churches that are not found in the Bible. Some examples are air conditioning, indoor plumbing, computers, faxes, organs, pianos, kneelers, and other helpful things.

Some values are not found in the Bible but they do not contradict or disagree with the Scriptures. Therefore, not all of our values will be articulated in the Bible, but they must not disagree with or contradict it. Even in the marketplace, many of the core values of an organization are biblical. For example, Liberty Bank in Fort Worth, Texas, employed me as a consultant and trainer to help them discover their core values. They embraced five: integrity/honesty, people-orientation, teamwork, excellence, and high performance. Are all of these found in the Bible? Are any unbiblical? Johnson & Johnson's first key value is responsibility to their customers. Is that one in the Bible? Does it contradict Scripture?

Values Are Core Beliefs

Throughout this chapter, I have used the term *belief* as a synonym for value. This could be confusing. What is a belief? Is a core belief any different than the beliefs or doctrines listed in a doctrinal statement?

A belief is a conviction or opinion that you hold as true based on limited evidence. You have faith or trust in that conviction. However, a belief is not a fact, by definition.

A fact is a conviction that a significant number of people hold as true, based on fairly significant and extensive evidence. The doctrines that comprise a church's doctrinal or faith statement are facts based on Scripture. The values that comprise a church's values statement or credo are beliefs. The difference is the number of people who hold a conviction and the evidence that authenticates the conviction. You may find it helpful to compare Northwood Community Church's values statement with its faith statement. Both are in appendix C.

Various churches hold numerous beliefs. When I work with a church as a consultant to help the people discover their beliefs or values, I use the storyboard process that I presented as a helpful planning tool in chapter 1. After we finish the brainstorming portion that attempts to list all the church's values, we may have as many as forty or fifty that are pinned to the storyboard. However, what we are after is the church's core or primary beliefs. These are the values that are central to the organization; those that they believe are at the very heart of their ministry. There may be as few as four or five or as many as ten or eleven. In the storyboard process, I give each participant eight or ten red stickers and ask him or her to place stickers on the eight or ten primary values. When all have finished, I simply look for the values with the most dots to discover the organization's core values. In the discovery phase, I encourage you to follow this procedure.

Values Drive the Ministry

Churches are values-driven, not vision-, mission-, or purpose-driven. People act on their values, not their vision, mission, or purpose. For example, the vision and mission focus people's attention on the goal or objective. A church is vision-focused and values-driven. Most often people do not know their church's purpose. But they are driven by their values. The vision helps people see where they are going, but the values motivate them to begin moving in that direction.

A congregation's primary beliefs function much like a driver sitting behind the wheel of a car. They are the church's shaping force that influences all that its members do as well as how they do it. Primary beliefs determine every decision and dictate every dollar spent. They comprise the bottom line for what the institution will and will not do. They are the deeply ingrained drivers behind all behavior, including decisions made, risks taken, problems solved, goals set, conflicts resolved, priorities determined, and budgets set.

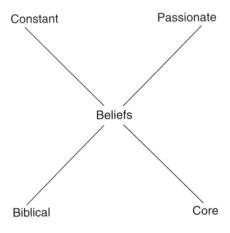

Values-Defining Elements

Figure 12

Kinds of Values

We now have a working definition of a core value or belief. This will help us in the values discovery process. However, before we move to that process, we need to further hone the definition by examining the different kinds of values. We will examine seven that exist in tension.

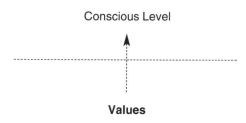

The Values Discovery Process

Conscious Level

Values

Unconscious Level

Figure 13

Conscious versus Unconscious Values

The core beliefs of every church exist at either a conscious or unconscious level. My experience is that most church members are not aware of their values—they exist at the unconscious level. Therefore, it is the leadership's job to move the church's values from an unconscious to a conscious level. This is the values discovery process. When the people in a ministry know and articulate the ministry's values, good or bad, they are aware at a conscious level of what is driving or influencing them. The people will be able to answer the critical question, Why are we doing what we are doing?

Shared versus Unshared Values

Shared values are essential to ministry effectiveness, while unshared values bring ministry demise. The former lead to a common cause; the latter lead away from it. In *In Search of Excellence,* Peters and Waterman write, "I believe the real difference between success and failure in a corporation can very often be traced to the question of how well the organization brings out the great energies and talents of its people. What does it take to help these people find common cause with each other?"[7] Shared values are the key that unlocks the door of common cause. If the leaders and people who make up a ministry share the same values, together they will accomplish their mission and vision.

Personal versus Organizational Values

People have values, and the organizations of which they are a part have values. People hold various beliefs about what the church should be like. These are their personal organizational values, and they use them, for example, whenever they look for a new church. Since churches consist of people, the church's values will be the sum of the people's values.

Common Cause

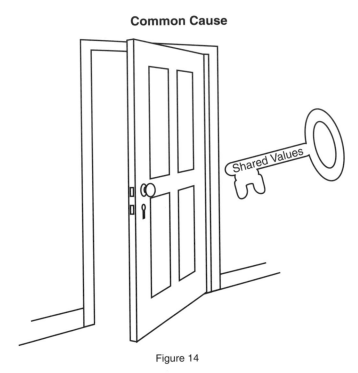

Figure 14

Churches that have dynamic ministries will find that their people share most of the same values. Churches that are struggling most often do not have people who share the same values.

Wisdom teaches that people who are looking for a church should look for one that has their same values. It is much like a marriage. Couples with the same values pull together; those with different values are unhappy and pull apart. Just as it would be foolish for a couple with different values to marry, the same is true of people and the church and of a pastor who is looking for a church. He would be wise to know his core organizational values and those of the church before seeking a position. The church would be wise to know its primary beliefs and keep them in mind when looking for a new pastor. When a pastor marries a church with different core beliefs, either one or both will eventually sue for a divorce.

Actual versus Aspirational Values

Leaders and their ministries have both actual and aspirational values. Actual values are the beliefs people own and practice daily. They are reality. The Jerusalem church's core values in Acts 2:42–47 were actual, for Luke says that they "devoted themselves to" them (v. 42). Aspirational values are beliefs that leaders and their people neither own nor practice. They are wishful thinking. For example, a church may list evangelism as one of its values because it knows it is supposed to be evangelistic. However, its people may have won no one to faith in years. For them, evangelism is aspirational. The proverbial "proof of the pudding" is in the doing not the wishing.

What leaders and their churches must uncover are their ministry's actual values so that they can know what is driving them. In addition, to mix actual and aspirational values leads to a loss of credibility. People know what is and is not a value. To say that a belief is actual when it is aspirational is an integrity issue. This does not mean, however, that you cannot communicate your aspirational values. Just make sure that you distinguish between what is aspirational and what is actual. Northwood Community Church's credo, in appendix C, is one example of how to do this. The aspirational values have an asterisk after them.

Single versus Multiple Values

All organizations have multiple values. They could have hundreds of beliefs. However, it is not unusual for some to have one value that dominates or towers over all the rest. It is called a unifying value in figure 15. It is a single, controlling value that serves to unify the church and communicate its central thrust.

I have charted some of these values for North American evangelical churches in figure 15. Note, for example, that in the classroom church, the single value is information—a knowledge of the Bible. This value, in turn, affects the role of the pastor, the role of the people, the key emphasis, and so on across the chart. For those who are strongly evangelistic, the single value is evangelism. It is justice in many social-conscience churches. I believe that a ministry with a single towering value is using a "niche" ministry approach and this detracts from a Great Commission vision. These churches tend to be biblically imbalanced. For example, little evangelism takes place in most Bible churches, and little biblical information is communicated in many soul-winning churches.

Congruent versus Incongruent Values

Congruent values are those in a congregation's credo that do not contradict one another. Like the pieces of a puzzle they all fit together. Incongruent values do not. An example of a church with two values that are incongruent is one that claims to value reaching all people regardless of ethnicity but targets only a particular group of people such as whites or blacks. It is not wrong to target a particular group of people. Missions and parachurch ministries as well as churches target specific groups of people. Paul and Barnabas targeted Gentiles while Peter, James, and John targeted Jews (Gal. 2:9). What is wrong is to hold two values that contradict one another in some way.

Good versus Bad Values

When I lead an organization through the values discovery process, we are looking for the ministry's good, not its bad, values. However, a ministry would be wise to look for its bad beliefs as well, for they drive the ministry in a different direction from the good values. Some examples of the former are when a church values men above women, the wealthy over the poor, the old-timers over the young "upstarts," especially as concerns congregational leadership, the status quo, mixing politics with religion (liberal or conservative), and many others.

Kinds of Values

Conscious versus Unconscious
Shared versus Unshared
Personal versus Organizational
Actual versus Aspirational
Single versus Multiple
Congruent versus Incongruent
Good versus Bad

The Discovery of Core Values

Once you know why values are important and what they are, then you are ready to identify a set of core operating values. In this section, we will probe two questions. The first is, Whose values? And the second is, How are values discovered?

Whose Values?

The primary thrust of this chapter is to help churches and their leaders discover the overarching, primary beliefs that govern their strategic

American Evangelical Churches

Type of Church	Unifying Value	Role of Pastor	Role of People	Key Emphasis	Typical Tool	Desired Result	Source of Legitimacy	Positive Trait
The Classroom Church	Information	Teacher	Student	To know	Overhead projector	Educated Christian	Expository preaching	Knowledge of Bible
The Soul-Winning Church	Evangelism	Evangelist	Bringer	To save	Altar call	Born-again people	Numbers	Heart for lost
The Social-Conscience Church	Justice	Reformer	Recruiter	To care	Petition	Activist	Cause	Compassion for oppressed
The Experiential Church	Experience	Performer	Audience	To feel	Hand-held mike	Empowered Christian	Spirit	Vitality
The Family-Reunion Church	Loyalty	Chaplain	Siblings	To belong	Potluck	Secure Christian	Roots	Identity
The Life-Development Church	Character	Coach	Ministry	To be	Ephesians 4	Disciple	Changed lives	Growth

Figure 15

thinking and acting. However, organizational values exist on both the personal and corporate congregational levels, and the congregation's values are the sum of each individual's values. Thus we need to look at both.

Personal Organizational Values

Personal organizational values are the actual core beliefs of the people who make up a ministry organization. It is essential to take those values out, dust them off, and take a hard look at them. They exist on three levels. The first level is that of the typical church attenders or members. Their personal organizational values determine whether they are happy at their current church and should dictate where they land if looking for a new church. The second level is the staff, including the senior pastor and any other paid professionals and, in some cases, volunteers. Their core beliefs determine their future at the church, their overall effectiveness, and how well they work together. The final level is the church board. Though it may vary from church to church and tradition to tradition, the board's essential beliefs often affect who is on the pastoral team, how long that team will minister at the church, and ultimately the general direction of the church.

The people at each level would benefit greatly by knowing their values. However, in the real world, only the pastoral staff and boards may realistically achieve this. The typical attender and member, busy with other things, will not make the effort to discover their values. Each person on the staff should discover his or her values. One of my goals as a seminary professor is to help future pastors discover their values while in seminary. I teach them to match their values with those of a potential church to see if a marriage is even feasible. Boards would be wise if they also discovered their authentic, overarching beliefs. Do they as a board share the same values? Are their values the same as the staff's and the congregation's?

Corporate Organizational Values

Corporate organizational values are the actual, not aspirational, values of the entire church. They are primarily what we are looking for in this chapter. Thus far I have never worked with an organization that could not identify a set of shared beliefs. However, the mistake many people make is to assume that a pastor or leader can set a congregation's values or instill new ones. Core values are not something that people simply buy into. They already hold them, and the job of a leader is to discover or identify what they are. It is a discovery process not a sell job. Again, these are actual, not aspirational, values. The leader's task is to discover the actual values, lead the people in pursuing those values, and let those who do not share the values go elsewhere.

Having said that, I do believe that people can change their values. At various times in our lives, we go through a period of values formation when we examine and may change our values. This often takes place when a person attends a university or seminary. Some Christian parents fear this when they send their kids to the public state university. However, changing values is a long process that takes time. Ken Blanchard believes that it takes no less than two to three years to adopt new values.[8] I argue from two to four years. My point is that initially the leader's job is to help the people discover and agree on a set of values that they hold at a gut level. His or her job is not to create or shape new ones. At this time you are discovering what is, not what could be.

How Are Values Discovered?

I use several techniques to help organizations discover their values:

Discuss the Importance and Definition of Values

First, I cover the material in the first two sections of this chapter: the importance and definition of core values. The first motivates people to identify their beliefs, and the second helps them know and understand what it is they are looking for.

Study Other Churches' Credos

Next, I ask them to examine a number of credos from different churches. I have provided some of these in appendix C. As I stated earlier in my discussion of passion, people will identify or connect with certain values and not others. As they come across the values they connect with, those values seem to jump off the page. I ask them to note these in particular.

Do a Core Values Audit

Third, I give them the Core Values Audit. You can find it in appendix D. The advantage of using the Core Values Audit is its objectivity. It is the least subjective of all the techniques I use. It also primes the group for the next technique.

Conduct a Storyboarding Session

Fourth, I conduct a storyboarding session (see the section on strategizing tools in chapter 1). This begins with brainstorming, which involves creative thinking. Prompted by the other techniques, the planning team verbalizes the values, recorders write them on three-by-five-inch cards, and a pinner puts them on the storyboard. Then we do the workout, which involves critical thinking: The team members identify values on the cards that are similar and condense them to one and they discard aspirational values unless they plan to list them as such. During a break I give each person eight to ten red stickers, and he or she places them on the most important (core) values. Here you might ask, "If something went wrong, and someone threatened to penalize you for holding certain of these values, which would they be?" At this point, we simply count the dots to discover what are the critical values and their order of priority. This plus the audit is usually more than sufficient to identify any group's values. However, I have two other techniques that I also use.

Describe the Perfect Church

I ask the team members separately to write one or two pages that describe what they envision as the perfect church. This is a "Have It Your Way" exercise. You ask, If you had an opportunity to plant a church with unlimited resources, what would it look like? What would its values be?

Review the Church's Budget

Finally, I give everyone on the team a copy of their current church budget. You ask them to review it carefully, looking for values. The point is that churches usually give to or set aside funds for what they value.

How Pastors Can Discover a Church's Values

I advise a pastor who is considering a call to a church or is candidating with a church to pursue the following to discover the church's values. First, ask for a credo or values statement, but do not be surprised if they do not know what you are talking about. Second, request a copy of the current budget. Third, visit the church either anonymously or by request and observe and listen. Observe the facilities and the people. If they do not know who you are, observe how well you are treated: Did they greet and welcome you? Are people friendly? Listen to what people talk about as they enter the church and walk its corridors.

How Churches Can Discover a Pastor's Values

I counsel churches that are looking for a pastor to pursue any or all of the following with promising candidates. First, ask them for a core val-

How to Discover Your Values

- Discuss the importance and definition of values.
- Study other churches' credos.
- Do a Core Values Audit.
- Conduct a storyboarding session.
- Describe the perfect church.
- Review the church's budget.

ues statement, but do not be surprised if they do not know what one is. Second, send them the Core Values Audit found in appendix D and ask them to complete it and send you the results. Third, send them a copy of this book and ask them to read this chapter and interact with you over its contents either by phone or face-to-face. Fourth, ask them to describe for you their vision of the ideal church. This will bring their values to the surface. Also ask them what they would not be willing to compromise.

The Development of Core Values

Once the team members have discovered their ministry's core values, the next step is to articulate them for the rest of the congregation. This will take the form of a values statement or credo much like those in appendix C. It involves both preparation and a process.

The Preparation for Developing the Credo

The preparation for articulating the values the team discovered is twofold.

Who Will Develop the Credo?

First, you must determine who will develop the credo. My experience has revealed that the person who should accomplish this is the senior or point pastor on the team. He functions as the draftsman or writer of the statement—at least the first draft. However, any staff people, those on the strategic planning team, and the board may function as his editors. This allows them to provide valuable input and gain ownership.

Why Are You Drafting a Credo?

Second, you should think through why you are writing or crafting a credo. Written values statements benefit the ministry in several ways. One is that it infuses those values with leadership authority. Also writing out the primary beliefs gives them greater clarity. And, in a multi-sensory culture, writing remains fundamental to good communication.

The Process of Developing the Credo

The process of developing the stated values into a credo takes four steps.

Step 1: Determine If It's a Value or a Form

The first step involves making sure that the team is working with the value and not its form. For example, one of the credos in appendix C lists small groups as a value. Actually a small group is a form that expresses or implements a value, but a small group itself is not a value. You may value small groups as a form, but that does not make them a value. Do not confuse what you value with values, themselves.[9] Remember the definition of core values: constant, passionate, biblical core beliefs that drive the ministry. The value behind small groups could be biblical community or evangelism or some other function. Another way to determine this is to ask, Is the item in question an end or a means to an end? Small groups are not an end in themselves—they are a means to an end: biblical community or some other function.

Determining Actual Values

Value	Form
Biblical community	Small group
End	Means to an end

Step 2: Determine the Number of Values

The second step is to decide on the number of values. You will need to decide how many values will be in your statement. If you use the storyboarding process, then you will make this decision before you hand out the red dots because it will dictate how many you give each person. My research indicates that most churches have from five to ten values. The only exception has been Saddleback Valley Community Church near Los Angeles. This church has seventeen. In *Built to Last,* James Collins and Jerry Porras advise that you have no more than six and that most visionary companies have fewer.[10] The rule of thumb is: Having fewer values is better.

Step 3: Decide on a Credo Format

The third step is to determine the credo format. This affects how you state the beliefs. A glance at the credos in appendix C or in the appendix in my book *Values-Driven Leadership* (it has a broader sampling) reveals that the values statement may take several different formats. I suggest that you peruse several credos and determine which you like best. Regardless, you must strive to keep the statements simple, clear, straightforward, and powerful.[11]

Step 4: Test the Credo Format

Finally, test the credo format. Ask the following: Does it attract interest? Is it simple, clear, straightforward, and powerful? Does it have too many values?

Communicating the Core Values

You might develop the perfect credo or values statement for your ministry. However, if the ministry constituency does not see it, or no one ever communicates it, then it dies an untimely death. You should encourage everyone in the ministry to become involved in the values communication process. But it becomes the primary responsibility of the leadership team—board and staff—to see that it is available to all connected with the organization.

The following are some ways that churches have communicated or cast their values:

Life and example of leadership	Training materials
Written credo	Slide-tape presentation
Sermons	Audio- and videotapes
Formal and informal conversation	Skits and drama
	Newcomers class
Stories	Newsletter
Bulletin	Performance appraisal
Framed posters	Cartoons
Church brochure	

I have touched only the tip of the iceberg. The only limit to the communication of the church's values is its creative abilities.

The Values Development Process

Step 1: Determine if the statement is a value
       or a form.
Step 2: Determine the number of values.
Step 3: Decide on a credo format.
Step 4: Test the credo format.

Questions for Analysis and Discussion

1. Can you think of any additional reasons, not given in this chapter, why values are important? What are they? Is any one reason more important than the others? If so, which one?

2. What is the difference between actual and aspirational values? Which is the key to what drives your ministry? Why?

3. Who in your ministry is responsible for discovering the ministry's values? Is it the point person on the ministry team? Who are the key decision makers? What is their role in discovering the ministry's values?

4. Do you know what your ministry's core organizational values are? If so, what are they?

5. Does the church know what its core values are? If so, what are they? Does the church use them in the selection of the staff?

6. Who is responsible in your church for developing the core values? Why? Are any so-called values actually forms and not true values? How many values do you have? What format did you select for your credo? Does your values format pass the test (see page 97)?

7. Who is responsible for communicating your church's values? What methods will be used? Why?

5

Developing a Mission

What Are We Supposed to Be Doing?

In the last chapter, I introduced the concept of congregational or corporate soul. It is a leadership concept that concerns what is at the heart of a ministry organization such as the church. In this chapter I will use the terms *soul* and *heart* interchangeably. Congregational soul embraces not only the church's values but its mission. When leaders communicate a meaningful, biblical mission to their people, it rings true. The people nod and think, *Yes, that is what we must be about.* This is tapping into their congregational heart and soul.

Now that you have completed the first two steps of the strategic thinking and acting process—you have conducted an authentic ministry analysis and you have discovered and articulated the shaping values of your ministry—it is time to take the third step in the strategic thinking and acting process: the development of a core mission statement for the ministry. The Savior believed this to be important, for after his resurrection and before his ascension, he gave the church its mission (see Matt. 28:19–20; Mark 16:15; Luke 24:45–49; Acts 1:8). In *The Seven Habits of Highly Effective People,* Stephen Covey writes, "One of the most important thrusts of my

> Ministry Analysis
> Values Discovery
> **Mission Development**
> Environmental Scan
> Vision Development
> Strategy Development
> Strategy Implementation
> Ministry Contingencies
> Ministry Evaluation

work with organizations is to assist them in developing effective mission statements."[1] That is my goal in this chapter.

The development of an effective, biblical mission statement should be the goal of every church leader as well. Warren Bennis writes, "The task of the leader is to define the mission."[2] In addition, Peter Drucker, in *Managing the Non-Profit Organization,* states, "What matters is not the leader's charisma. What matters is the leader's mission. Therefore, the first job of the leader is to think through and define the mission of the institution."[3] Obviously the church's mission is vital to its ministry. The mission answers the third most basic, fundamental question of the ministry, What are we supposed to be doing? In this chapter we will learn why a mission is so important to a church, define the mission, and show how to develop and then communicate the organization's mission statement.

The Importance of the Mission

Why is the ministry's mission so important? It affects the church in numerous essential ways. Here are nine of them.

The Mission Dictates the Ministry's Direction

Before embarking on a flight, most people want to know where their plane is going. Otherwise, as Yogi Berra, the former New York Yankee catcher, once said, "If you don't know where you're going, you might end up somewhere else." Leaders and their churches must have a direction, and it is the mission that provides that important direction. It answers the directional question, Where are we going? Thus the ministry's mission is directional. It provides a compelling sense of direction, a target for everyone to aim at, and it serves to focus the congregation's energy.

Leaders in the Bible demonstrated a strong sense of direction. Moses pursued with a passion his mission to lead Israel out of bondage to the Promised Land (Exod. 3:10). The same is true of Joshua (Josh. 1:1–5), David (2 Sam. 5:2), Nehemiah (Neh. 2:17), and others. The Savior's mission directed his ministry (Mark 10:45), and Paul was passionate about his direction throughout his ministry (Acts 21:12–14; Rom. 15:20).

The Mission Formulates the Ministry's Function

Besides direction, the mission helps a ministry to formulate or determine its biblical function. It answers the strategic, functional question,

What are we supposed to be doing? What function does the organization exist to perform? What is the primary or main thing that God has called us to accomplish? What are we attempting to do for God and our people? Therefore, the mission is an expression of strategic intent. It summarizes and provides the church with its biblical task and it defines the results that it seeks to obtain.

The Mission Focuses the Ministry's Future

Both the directional and functional questions above address the church's future. That is because the mission, like the church's vision, has everything to do with its future. Though we cannot predict the future (except for biblical prophecy), we can create it, and that is the job of the mission. A clear, biblical mission serves to bring into focus the church's ministry future. The converse is also true: no mission, no future.

In addition, by focusing on the future, the mission helps the ministry not to live in and focus on the past. Paul put his past behind him and pushed forward to experience Christ. In Philippians 3:13–14, he writes, "Brothers, I do not consider myself yet to have taken hold of it. But one thing I do: Forgetting what is behind and straining toward what is ahead, I press on toward the goal to win the prize for which God has called me heavenward in Christ Jesus." We must learn from the past but not live in the past.

The Mission Provides a Guideline for Decision Making

Every day church leaders have to make decisions. It comes with the ministry territory. A dynamic mission or intent not only focuses the church's future, it sets important boundaries. It guides what the church will and will not attempt. It provides direction for when to say yes and when to say no. Mission is to the ministry what a rudder is to a ship, a compass to a navigator, a template to a machinist. It provides a framework for critical thinking, a standard or criterion for all decision making.

Sincere (and sometimes not so sincere) people often approach a church board or pastor with suggestions for new areas of ministry that could potentially lead the church away from its divine direction. However, a clear, shared mission will protect the pastor and the board from involvement in numerous tangential activities. Their response can be, "Thanks so much for your interest, but that would lead us away from our mission."

The Mission Inspires Ministry Unity

Scripture is clear about the importance of unity among Christians. In John 17:20–23, the Savior prays for you and me and all who believe in Christ to be one. The result of this unity is that the world we seek to reach will believe that the Father has truly sent the Son. Paul stresses the importance of Christian unity in the local church. In Ephesians 4:3, he urges the church to "Make every effort to keep the unity of the Spirit through the bond of peace."

Unity is another function of a well-constructed, shared statement of intent or mission. A clear direction communicates a unifying theme to all the members and draws them together as a team or community. It broadcasts "Here is where we are going. Let's all pull together and with God's help make it happen." At the same time, it encourages those with a different intent or another ministry agenda to look elsewhere.

The Mission Shapes the Strategy

A dynamic mission tells the church where it is going. It is the strategy, however, that gets it there. Though both are mutually dependent, the mission leads and shapes the church's strategy. The mission tells what, and the strategy tells how. The mission always comes first—it is found at the front end of the strategy. The strategy is only as good as the mission that directs it. If you do not know where you are going, then any expressway will take you there.

What amazes me is that so many churches today have a strategy, as expressed in their programs, but have no mission. This does not make sense. Peter Drucker writes, "Strategy determines what the key activities are in a given business. And strategy requires knowing 'what our business is and should be.'"[4]

The Mission Enhances Ministry Effectiveness

Drucker has observed the effectiveness of a corporate mission in the marketplace:

> That business purpose and business mission are so rarely given adequate thought is perhaps the most important single cause of business frustration and business failure. Conversely, in outstanding businesses . . . , success always rests to a large extent on raising the question "What is our

business?" clearly and deliberately, and on answering it thoughtfully and thoroughly.[5]

If you should take time to investigate the more effective, God-honoring churches across North America, large or small, you will discover that each has a significant, well-focused mission. They know what business they are in. This is because all good performance starts with a clear direction. People who know where they are going are more willing to go the extra mile.

The Mission Ensures an Enduring Organization

It is rare that any one pastor lasts the entire time that a spiritually healthy church exists. Pastors come and they go. This is not necessarily bad. Once a pastor reaches retirement age, he serves his ministry best by leaving. This may be sad, but it makes room for a younger person who will be more in touch with the current culture and the ministry paradigms that God is blessing.

The goal of every ministry leader should be to leave behind a mission that will continue after he is gone. The mission, like the values, must not change appreciably over time. A biblical, dynamic mission can help ensure the continuity of an enduring and great church.

The Mission Facilitates Evaluation

In 2 Corinthians 13:5, Paul instructs the church at Corinth, "Examine yourselves to see whether you are in the faith; test yourselves." Throughout his second letter to the Corinthian church, Paul subjected both himself and his ministry to close scrutiny.

I have pastored three churches and served as an interim pastor in countless others. I suspect that during those ministries some unhappy congregants examined me and questioned whether I was in the faith. However, few have ever formally evaluated my leadership or the church's ministry. The church that fails to examine its people and its effectiveness as a ministry in light of its mission does itself an injustice. Otherwise, how will the church know if it's fulfilling its mission? How will it improve without formal evaluation? What you evaluate, not only gets done, but it gets done well. While no organization enjoys living under the lens of careful scrutiny, evaluation will improve any ministry and the work of its people.

Why a Mission Is Important

1. It dictates the ministry's direction.
2. It formulates the ministry's function.
3. It focuses the ministry's future.
4. It provides a guideline for decision making.
5. It inspires ministry unity.
6. It shapes the strategy.
7. It enhances ministry effectiveness.
8. It ensures an enduring organization.
9. It facilitates evaluation.

The Definition of a Mission

What is a mission? Let us assume you agree that a mission is important and you desire to develop a clear, consensual one for your church. Precisely what is it you are trying to construct? What is the definition of an organizational mission? When defining a concept, it helps to clarify what it is not as well as what it is.

What a Mission Is Not

People have confused several concepts and used them synonymously with the mission concept. The most common is purpose. For example, Allan Cox defines a mission statement as, ". . . an organization's brief, compelling statement of purpose. . . ."[6] However, the purpose of a church as an organization is very different from its mission in a number of ways.

First, the purpose answers a different question. It answers the *why* question: Why are we here? Why do we exist? What is our reason for being? The mission, however, answers the *what* question: What are we supposed to be doing? What is our divine, strategic intent? What does God want us to accomplish while we are here on earth? You can discover your ministry purpose by asking the *why* question. First, state your mission. It may be to make disciples. Then probe it with the *why* question, Why do we want to make disciples? The answer—to glorify God—is your purpose.

Purpose is different from mission because it is broader in scope. The mission of a church as well as its values, vision, strategy, and other concepts is subsumed under its purpose.

The third difference is that the purpose of the church is doxological: to glorify God (Ps. 22:23; 50:15; Isa. 24:15; Rom. 15:6; 1 Cor. 6:20; 10:31). Thus it is abstract. The mission of the church is practical: to "make disciples" (Matt. 28:19). It is more concrete. When we make disciples (our mission), we glorify God (our purpose).

Fourth, the focus of purpose and mission is different. The purpose focuses on God. He is the object of our glory, not ourselves or another. The mission focuses on people. We are to disciple people.

	Purpose	Mission
Question	*Why* do we exist?	*What* are we supposed to be doing?
Scope	Broad	Narrow
Intent	To glorify God	To make disciples
Focus	God	Man

Every ministry must know its purpose as well as its mission. The purpose is part of the ministry's congregational heart and soul. It is why the ministry exists but it is not the mission. Let's go on to see what the mission is.

What a Mission Is

I define a mission as a broad, brief, biblical statement of what the ministry is supposed to be doing. This definition has five key elements.

A Mission Is Broad

The first element of the definition expresses the expansiveness of a mission. A good mission must be broad, comprehensive, and overarching. It is the primary goal, mandate, or charge that is over all other goals or mandates of the ministry. They are subsumed under the mission. It is the predominate thrust that directs all that the church does. It is the umbrella that is over all the ministry's activities. A mission can be too expansive, however. It is possible to be so broad that you do not say anything. An example is a mission statement that says that the church will glorify God. Glorifying God is the church's purpose, not its mission, and the concept, without explanation, does not communicate what the church will actually do. The average parishioner as well as many pastors do not know what it means to glorify God.

A Mission Is Brief

The statement of the mission should be brief. Cox says that it should be no more than seventy-five words.[7] Others allow for it to be longer.[8] The mission statements in the Bible are short—no longer than a sentence. For example, Moses' mission was to lead God's people, Israel, out of bondage in Egypt (Exod. 3:10). David's mission was to shepherd Israel and become their ruler (2 Sam. 5:2). Nehemiah's mission was to rebuild the wall of Jerusalem (Neh. 2:17). From a hermeneutical perspective, mission statements in the Bible, however, are descriptive, not prescriptive.[9] So Scripture does not mandate this issue.

How short is brief? I believe that the Scriptures, though descriptive and not mandatory, are instructive here. Most mission statements in the Bible are no longer than one sentence. The leadership of a ministry should be able to catch the church's mission statement in a single, concise sentence. Drucker says that the statement should be able to fit on a T-shirt.[10] The leadership at Pantego Bible Church in Arlington, Texas, argues that the mission should be able, therefore, to pass the "T-shirt test." The reason is simple. If the mission is not short, people will not remember it.

A Mission Is Biblical

The third part of the definition means that a mission for a church must be based on the Scriptures. God determines the church's mission. The question is, What does God say the church's mission is? The answer is the Great Commission. In Matthew 28:19, Jesus instructs his disciples, "Therefore go and make disciples of all nations." This was the church's mission in the first century and continues to be its mission in the twenty-first century. Making disciples involves pursuing lost people (Luke 19:1–10), evangelizing them (Mark 16:15), and helping these new Christians to mature, to become like Christ.

A Mission Is a Statement

The fourth element says that the mission is a statement. The church must articulate and communicate its mission edict to the congregation. This takes the form of a statement. Christ expressed the Great Commission in a verbal statement, and Matthew recorded it as a written statement. Mission developers would be wise to express their thoughts not only verbally but in writing. This forces them to think and express themselves clearly. If they cannot write it, then they probably do not yet have a clear, articulate mission.

A Mission Is What the Ministry Is Supposed to Be Doing

The final element focuses on the *functional* question, What are we supposed to be doing? As we discovered above, over two thousand years ago Christ predetermined the church's mission: "Make disciples." That is what the church is supposed to be doing. Research indicates, however, that far too many North American churches have drifted away from or missed entirely Christ's Great Commission mandate.

A good question for a candidating pastor to ask of a church is, What is this church's mission—what is it supposed to be doing? I use it and three similar questions as diagnostic questions when I consult with churches on their mission. Pastors would serve their churches well if they, too, asked these questions. Here are all four that you can use:

1. What is this church supposed to be doing?
2. What is this church doing?
3. Why are you not doing what you are supposed to be doing?
4. What will it take for you to change and do what you are supposed to be doing?

The first question causes leaders to think biblically. They must ask what the Scriptures teach about the church's reason for existence. The second question assumes that the ministry has missed Christ's directive (a reasonably safe assumption). If you are not making disciples, then what are you doing? Some churches function as Christian retirement centers; others are evangelistic ministries; and others are miniseminaries. The third question is very convicting. The room will get silent on this one. The last question is the most difficult and important because the answer reflects the church's willingness to obey Christ and ultimately exert an influence in the community.

The Development of a Mission

Once you see the utter necessity of having a congregational mission and you understand what it is, you are ready to move to the next step. This involves immersing yourself and your team in the crafting of a dynamic, strong statement for your church. It begins with selecting the right personnel to develop the statement and then going through a four-step development process.

The Definition of a Mission

1. A mission is broad.
2. A mission is brief.
3. A mission is biblical.
4. A mission is a statement.
5. A mission is what the ministry is supposed to be doing.

The Personnel for Developing a Mission Statement

Which people in an organization should craft a mission statement for the church? Ultimately, almost everyone can play a role, whether large or small, depending on the size of the ministry. Regardless, I see the involvement of personnel as a "top-down" *and* "bottom-up" process.

A "Top-down" Process

The ministry leaders must support and be involved in the development of the mission. This support begins with the senior or point pastor of the church. He is in the best position to initiate the process, if not write the initial draft. Pastoring a church involves more than preaching and teaching the Bible, as vital as that is. It also includes leading God's church. Mission development is an aspect of that leadership. To hand this baton off to someone else on the staff or board will not work. If this is a difficult area for the pastor, then he should solicit the help of a ministry consultant.

However, once he has initiated the first draft, he would be wise to ask for feedback from the board and staff. He should allow them to serve as editors. Not only will he get some good input, but these influential individuals will feel a part of the process. Their "fingerprints" as well as the pastor's will be all over the statement. This gives them a sense of ownership.

A "Bottom-up" Process

The "bottom-up" process allows people at the grassroots level of the ministry to have some involvement and gain a sense of ownership. This may be easy in a small church, but difficult in a large one. Perhaps one or two "town hall" meetings will help provide congregational input. The downside of congregational involvement is that the squeaky wheels (the disenchanted and special-interest groups) will voice their opinions, and they are usually negative. The advantage is that they will have to acknowledge that they have been given a fair hearing in the process.

The Process of Developing a Mission Statement

When we worked with values in the last chapter, one stage involved discovering the church's core values. That is not necessary when it comes to mission. The Savior did not predetermine the church's values, but he did predetermine its mission. Here is where values have a deep impact on mission. If you value Scripture and believe that it is God's Word, then you must agree that the Bible dictates the ministry mission through the Great Commission (Matt. 28:19–20).

Before you launch into the development phase, you will need to answer an important question, Who is the mission statement for? Who are its recipients? I have discovered in consulting that it affects the process later on if this is not clarified at the beginning. A mission statement is an internal document. It is for those in the church—its members, attenders, and any other people who are considering becoming a part of the church. Though lost people may see it, the mission is not an external document for them.

The mission development process consists of four steps in the form of questions. And each question consists of several additional miniquestions to help answer the initial question.

Step 1: What is the church supposed to be doing?

The first step asks the functional question. The business world asks it this way, What business are you in? and the church is essentially asking the same question, What business are we in? The answer in the business world varies from company to company and will change. The answer for the ministry must neither vary from church to church nor ever change. God has determined what he wants his church to do: Make disciples (Matt. 28:19).

Whom will you serve? The business world asks, Who is your customer? The church is asking much the same question. The first miniquestion focuses the church on its ministry constituency, so that it directs its mission to people, not programs. This is because Christ died for people; thus the church is to be people-directed.

The answer to the question is twofold. The ministry constituency is the church's target group, consisting of the believers who are already part of the ministry (the congregation) and those who could become a part of the ministry (the potential congregation). The potential congregation consists primarily of *unchurched* believers and unbelievers. To target another congregation's believing members is sheep stealing.

I encourage churches to develop a profile person who is typical and representative of their target group. This is an exercise in demographics and psychographics that I will explain in the sixth step of the strategic thinking and acting process. Those whom you will attract to your ministry are like the people who are already a part of the ministry. Therefore, to get an idea of whom you will serve, look at the present congregation, for they mirror your potential congregation. You have already done this to some extent in the earlier ministry analysis (the congregational and community audits). The information you gathered is most helpful in answering this question.

How will you serve these people? The second miniquestion asks, If ministry is people-directed, how will you serve those people? What does God want you to do for them? Here the business world asks, What does the customer want? The answer involves the customer's needs. The primary need of everyone is for a relationship with Christ that leads to a changed life. For the unbeliever it is salvation and for the believer it is sanctification. It is not wrong for the church to address people's felt needs because Scripture does that (Eph. 4:28–29; Acts 2:45; 2 Cor. 8:14; 9:12). But in doing so, the church must point people to their primary or true need: life transformation through Christ.

Two fictitious mission statements are good examples of how to answer the question in step one.

> Our mission is to share the good news of Christ with the people of the New Hope community and beyond so that they may accept Christ and become his committed followers.

This statement answers the question, Whom will you serve? Clearly this church is targeting those in a particular community, New Hope and beyond. So the people know whom they are attempting to reach.

The statement also answers the question, How will you serve these people? The answer is sharing the good news of Christ so that the lost accept Christ and become committed followers.

Here is the second sample statement:

> Our mission is to lead the people of Northern Tarrant County to faith in Christ and growth in Christlikeness.

This statement expresses the church's desire to serve the people located in Northern Tarrant County by leading the lost to faith in Christ and to growth in Christlikeness.

Step 2: Can you articulate your mission in a written statement?

The second step asks you to put your mission down on paper so that it becomes a written statement. In his book, *Learning to Lead,* Fred Smith writes, "In my view, nothing is properly defined until you write it down. Writing forces you to be specific; it takes the fuzz off your thinking."[11] If you cannot write it down, then you probably do not have a well thought-out mission. Three questions help leaders articulate their statement.

What words communicate best with your target group? Mission drafters must be wordsmiths. Their job is to think and rethink, shape and reshape, draft and redraft the statement. They do this with words. Ask, What words best communicate with my congregation? Are they more traditional, contemporary, or a combination? Will older clichés communicate best or fresh, contemporary terms? Also, take into account the part of the country you live in. What terms are native to this locale and would communicate well to these people? Note the following statement as an example:

> Our mission is to colonize the greater commonwealth of Northwest Boston with the gospel of Christ so that it may be liberated from the rule of darkness and adopt a new spiritual constitution that passionately embraces the revolutionary teachings of Jesus Christ.

This statement could serve well the people in and around Boston and other parts of New England. It is regional, however, and would not fit or communicate well in other parts of North America.

Do people understand what you have written? The emphasis here is on clarity. How well do the words that you have selected communicate? Do people understand them? Do they know what you are saying? Some have asked, If the mission statement is the Great Commission, then why not just quote Matthew 28:19–20; Mark 16:15; or Acts 1:8? You could, but many parishioners will not understand the terminology used in the New Testament. These words are not clear to them. For example, the term *disciple* that Jesus uses in Matthew 28:19 may seem ambiguous. What is a disciple? Is making disciples a reference to evangelism only or sanctification or both? Even the average seminarian struggles to answer this question.

Therefore, I would encourage mission crafters to personalize the Great Commission so that it is clear to their particular congregation. We have done this in the mission of my church:

> The mission of Northwood Community Church is to be used of God in helping people become fully functioning followers of Christ.

The words "used of God" imply we cannot do it alone. God is the one who makes disciples. And the words "in helping people" mean that we cannot take all the responsibility ourselves. We can only aid people—they must assume individual responsibility for the process. We have substituted "fully functioning followers" in place of "disciple." Our people understand these words. We define a fully functioning follower as one characterized by the three Cs: conversion, commitment, and contribution. They are converted—they have placed their faith in Christ as Savior (Acts 2:41). They are committed—they have committed their lives to Christ and desire to become more like him as communicated through baptism (Acts 2:41). And they are contributing to Christ—they serve the body, share their finances, and seek the lost (Acts 2:42–47).

Does your format convey well your mission? This miniquestion addresses the format or the way you express the statement. The only possible limit to your construction of the mission statement is your creative abilities. At the risk of stifling your creativity, I will suggest three formats that are common to most of the statements in my collection. If you have difficulty getting started, these should help:

The mission of (name of church) is to _____.

Our mission is to _____.

(Name of church) seeks to _____.

These formats are simple and straightforward. You can use them by simply filling in your church's information.

Step 3: Is your mission statement broad but clear?

The third step focuses on the broadness and clarity of your statement. It attempts to balance or hold two elements in dynamic tension, and you must land between the two. It divides into two miniquestions.

Is the statement broad enough? The mission statement is to be broad, comprehensive, and overarching. It summarizes all you do as a church; it covers all the ministry bases. Here is one that passes the test:

Westbridge Church seeks to assist as many people as possible in becoming fully developing followers of Christ.

If the church is doing something that is not in some way covered under the mission statement, the statement is not broad enough. Note the following:

Developing the Mission Statement

Step 1: What is your church supposed to be doing?
1. Whom will you serve?
2. How will you serve these people?

Step 2: Can you articulate your mission in a written statement?
1. What words communicate best with your target group?
2. Do people understand what you have written?
3. Does your format convey well your mission?

Step 3: Is your mission statement broad but clear?
1. Is the statement broad enough?
2. Is the statement clear?

Step 4: Is the mission statement brief and simple?
1. Does the mission pass the T-shirt test?
2. Is your mission memorable?

> Our mission is to teach the Scriptures so well that people will hunger and thirst for righteousness.

The focus is on teaching alone. Like so many teaching churches, it has missed the Great Commission. What about such areas as worship and evangelism? The statement is too narrow.

Is the statement clear? The expression of the mission must not become so broad that it loses its clarity. The crucial test for clarity is the "people test." As you develop the mission, ask people in the congregation what it means. If they do not get it, then it is not clear. Here is an example of one that lacks clarity:

> Grace Church exists to provide an environment where people can discover a love for God that is real and relevant.

What does this mean? Is discovering the love of God the same as evangelism? or is it worship? Here is one more:

> Our mission is to glorify God by responding to the Savior through exalting him as Lord, edifying his church, and evangelizing the world.

The primary problem here is the use of the term *glorify.* What does that mean? The statement is so broad that it isn't clear.

Step 4: Is the mission statement brief and simple?

The power of the mission expression is in its brevity and simplicity. It is difficult to be both brief and simple. We often want to cram too much into the statement. Two miniquestions help create short, simple statements.

Does the mission statement pass the T-shirt test? Is it short enough to fit on a T-shirt? If not, you have committed the sin of information overload. The most common error is to include a *how* statement along with the mission statement. Here is an example:

> Faith Community Church exists to make disciples by loving Christ, loving one another, and living to reach our world for Christ.

The mission statement is "Faith Community Church exists to make disciples." The *how* statement, signaled by the preposition *by,* is not necessary to the statement of the mission. It provides the strategy for accomplishing the mission. It is important and should be covered, but not in the mission statement.

Is your mission memorable? A good mission expression is memorable. This is because it is well worded and short. You should be able to read it, then turn your head away or close your eyes and remember it. Here is one that is not memorable:

> Trinity Church is a deeply committed community composed of caring men and women who desire to have an impact on southwest Collin County for eternity. We will accomplish this to the glory of God by reaching out to the lost and passionately loving the saved.

Close your eyes and repeat it. Did you remember it? Would someone in your church?

The Communication of the Mission

It is important that you communicate the mission as well as the values. Even though you have a statement that is clear and memorable, if you fail to make it known to your people, it accomplishes little beyond the efforts of the planning and development team.

Many of the methods for imparting the values are the same for imparting the mission: the leader's example, sermons, formal and informal con-

versation, stories, the bulletin, a framed poster, a church brochure, training materials, a slide-tape presentation, audio- and videotapes, skits and
drama, a newcomers class, a newsletter, and the performance appraisal.
You may want to put the mission on a small card that would fit in a man's
wallet or a woman's purse. Or put it on a T-shirt.[12]

Questions for Analysis and Discussion

1. Did this chapter convince you of the need for your church to have
a biblical mission statement? Why or why not?

2. Does your church already have a mission statement? If no, why not?
If yes, what is it? Is it a good one? Does it reflect your congregation's values? Has someone articulated it in a written form? Does the congregation know what it is? Why or why not?

3. What is your church supposed to be doing? Is that what the ministry is doing? Why or why not? What would it take to change what you're
doing and pursue Christ's mission for the church? Where is any resist-
ance to change?

4. Does your church know what its purpose is? If yes, what is it? Are
the mission and purpose statements the same? If you do not have a purpose statement, will you develop one? Why or why not? How will it be
different from the mission statement?

5. If you have an existing mission statement, use the four-step development process to evaluate it. Will you need to make any changes? If so,
what?

6. If you need to develop a mission statement, or if you have decided
to revise the current one, who will be involved in the process? Will you
invite evaluation of the mission expression? Whom will you ask for this
evaluation?

7. If the church has no mission statement, are you ready to craft one?
If not, why not? If so, when will you begin?

8. Which methods for communicating the mission statement appeal
to you? Why? Will you use them to propagate your mission? Why or why
not?

6

Scanning the Environment
What Is Going on Out There?

Far too many evangelical churches have assumed the ostrich position when it comes to knowing and understanding the world that Christ commands us to reach. They have buried their heads in the sand. They have no idea what is going on in this technologically driven twenty-first-century world. Some prefer not to know what is going on. They view this planet as a frightening, somewhat overwhelming, place in which to live, much less minister. Others are so preoccupied with their own internal problems that they have no time to think beyond the boundaries of their properties. Still others apply John's charge not to love the world or anything in it (1 John 2:15) to exploring and understanding this world. They want nothing to do with it, so they ignore it, presuming God's blessing.[1]

If our churches want to relate to and obey the Scriptures, they must spend much time exegeting the Scriptures (the skillful application of basic Bible study methods to the Bible to discover its meaning). If our churches want to relate to and reach our culture, they must spend time exegeting the culture as well as the Bible. In short, they must be culture watchers. We find culture watchers among God's people in the Old

Ministry Analysis
Values Discovery
Mission Development
Environmental Scan
Vision Development
Strategy Development
Strategy Implementation
Ministry Contingencies
Ministry Evaluation

Testament. The writer of 1 Chronicles provides his readers with the number of those who had decided to join David in his battles against Saul. When he gets to the men of Issachar, he describes them as those "who understood the times and knew what Israel should do" (1 Chron. 12:32). How can the church use the Scriptures to address the world that its people live and work in if it does not know what is going on? How can the church know

Figure 16

what to do if it does not know what is happening? Church culture watchers understand the times and know what their churches should do.

This chapter is the fourth step of strategic thinking and acting. It asks and answers the basic ministry question, What is going on out there? In the first step, ministry analysis, the leaders look inward and ask, What is going on in here? A number of church audits answered that question. In this step, the church looks outward. It seeks to discover what is taking place in the world around it and what the future may hold. Once begun, this step never ends but must continue throughout the life of the ministry. The church will always need to know what is taking place "out there" because that information affects what it does, especially its strategy (step six).

In his book, *On Becoming a Leader,* Warren Bennis reacts to our present state of recurring, disruptive change and writes, "For this reason, before anyone can learn to lead, he must learn something about this strange new world. Indeed, anyone who does not master this mercurial context will be mastered by it."[2] He calls this the "Gretzky Factor." He explains, "Wayne Gretzky, the best hockey player of his generation, said that it's not as important to know where the puck is now as to know where it will be. Leaders have the sense of where the culture is going to be, where the organization must be if it is to grow."[3] What is true of the marketplace is true of the church. This chapter seeks to challenge and instruct leaders and churches in how to be self-confessed culture watchers, how to exegete the culture of a radically changing world and then respond strategically.

The rest of this chapter presents an environmental scan that consists of two parts based on 1 Chronicles 12:32. The first, Understanding the

Times, scans the general environment in search of what is going on in our changing world. The second, Knowing What the Church Should Do, scans the church environment in search of how God is working through churches around the world to minister in response to our changing world. This knowledge will, in turn, help churches think and act strategically to minister to and win their world or community for the Savior.

Understanding the Times

The general environment includes the world and all that is taking place in it, whether on an international, national, or local level. Since we now live in a global community, the church should track all three levels. Scanning the general environment involves examining five specific environments or subenvironments. The church accomplishes this with the help of various culture watchers in the congregation.

The General Environment

When the church exegetes the general environment, not only does it seek to discover what is taking place now, but it is looking for future trends or major shaping forces in five generic environments that will affect its future. They are the social, technological, economic, political, and philosophical environments.

Social Environment

The social environment is all that is taking place or will take place internationally, nationally, or locally in the social world that could affect the universal church in general and the local church in particular. It includes all people from every generation—Builders, Boomers, Gen Xers, Millennialists, and others. (For example, a major social issue in North America over the next twenty-five years will be the gap between people of working age and the growing number of older, retired people.) The social environment encompasses

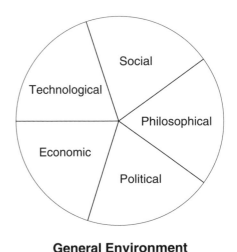

General Environment

Figure 17

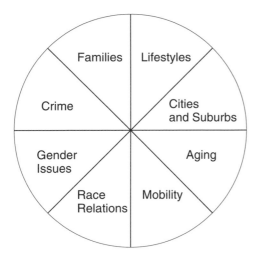

Social Environment

Figure 18

families, marriages, singles, divorce, alternative lifestyles, the cities and suburbs, urbanization, population growth and decline, mobility, ethnic groups, race relations, gender issues, crime, those who are in some way challenged (blind, deaf, hearing impaired, and others), lifestyle issues, collar color (blue and white collar issues), the birth rate, aging, dying, and other social factors.

The church would be wise to gather enough information on this environment so that it is informed and up-to-date on what is happening and what will take place. Two most helpful tools are demographic and psychographic studies. As we saw in chapter 3, demographics tells us who people are, and psychographics explains why they do what they do.

Strategic thinkers should probe each topic and trend with numerous questions. What are the characteristics of the generations? How are they different, and how will we reach and minister to them? Who are the future generations and what must we do now to reach and disciple them? How will we minister to the growing number of older, retired people? Where are our families struggling, and how can we serve them most effectively? How can we serve singles? How will the general population's movement from inner-city urban areas to the suburbs affect our ministry at our location? Can we realistically attract and combine different ethnic groups into one congregation? Do our present facilities make physically challenged congregants feel welcome?

Technological Environment

The technological environment is all that is taking place in the technological world, both now and in the future, that could affect the church. The technological revolution is at the forefront of change in the world. There are five basic technologies—computers, telecommunications, biotechnology, energy, and nanotechnology—that have vast impact on nearly every aspect of life, including the information revolution, transportation, electronics, entertainment, engineering, robotics, artificial intelligence, genet-

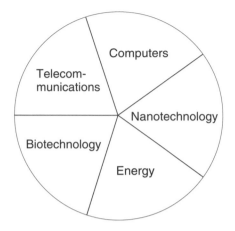

Technological Environment

Figure 19

ics, and medicine. In the area of medicine and genetics, for example, Michael Fossel, author of *Reversing Human Aging,* holds that humans are on the verge of achieving indefinite life spans, suggesting a range of hundreds of years of additional life.[4]

Culture watchers should be asking, How will these technological advances help or hinder the work of the ministry? How can the new communication technology, such as e-mail, cellular phones, faxes, and other such devices, help the church? Would it be possible to have board meetings using a conference call or interactive video conference so that board members would not have to leave their homes? How might these technologies keep the church in contact with its missionaries? How could the revolution in video technology affect preaching and teaching? Should churches incorporate computers into their Christian education programs? Should computer terminals be available to those who wish to take notes during the sermon or a Bible study? Could robots serve as Sunday school teaching assistants or teacher aides? Should churches install and then transform liquid-crystal-display windows into stained glass for effect?

Economic Environment

The economic environment includes all that is happening in the world of finances—international, national, and local economies. It encompasses debt, deficits, trade, taxes, inflation, downsizing, profit and nonprofit organizations, the poor versus the rich, purchasing power, budgeting, spending, saving, investing, debt retirement, and other economic factors.

Leaders who think strategically will need to ask several questions. What is the future of the church's tax-exempt status? What is the church's responsibility to its people who are affected by downsizing? Should the churches replace the Social Security system in meeting the social and economic needs of Americans? What should churches do if Social Security goes bust? As the gap between them increases, what are the respon-

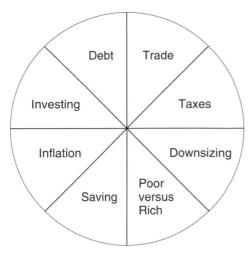

Economic Environment

Figure 20

sibilities of rich Christians toward poor Christians? Is it okay for a Christian to be wealthy? Is it okay for a church to be wealthy? Should wealthy congregations subsidize poor congregations? What are the new trends in raising funds for ministries and building programs? Should churches break even every year or should they try to save and invest their funds? Should churches start credit unions to loan money to other congregations as well as to their own people? Should they charge them interest?

Political Environment

The political environment is all that takes place in the political and legal arenas. It includes legislation, the courts, political candidating, law enforcement, civil rights, activism, the environment, church-state issues, zoning, wills, church discipline, litigation, hiring and firing, facilities issues, and other factors that can affect the church.

Strategic planners might ask the following: Should the church become more involved in politics? How should it be involved? If the church should relocate and build a new facility or add to the present facility, what environmental obstacles might it face? What can the church do now to protect itself against future lawsuits? As the country shifts from an age of belief to one of unbelief and becomes less Christian, what kind of treatment can churches expect from the legal and justice systems? What zoning and environmental restrictions will be established that churches will encounter over the next few years?

Philosophical Environment

The philosophical environment concerns all that is taking place in the philosophical realm, including religion and history. It encompasses such areas as worldviews, religions, cults, secularization, pluralization, privatization, relativism, naturalism, pragmatism, the influence of the church, churched and unchurched peoples, and other related factors.

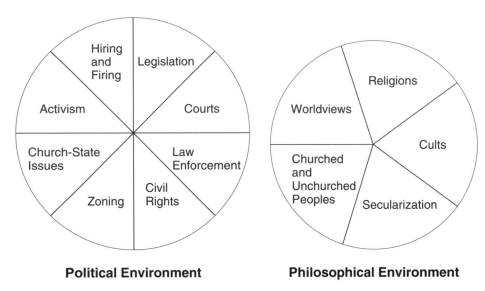

Political Environment   **Philosophical Environment**

Figure 21   Figure 22

Cultural exegetes should ask various questions such as: How will the growth of the number of unchurched and increasing secularization affect the future of the church in North America? What changes will the church have to make to reach the unchurched and unreached people groups? What effects will increasing pluralization have on the church? How will churches reach those who embrace the new postmodern worldview? How can churches counteract the growth of new religions and cults? What role does church planting play in the future of the church around the world?

Culture Watchers

The five environments supply the raw material that strategic thinkers exegete or explore, discovering what is happening and looking for trends and shaping events. But who are the culture watchers and how do they collect and analyze all that information?

Who Watches the Culture?

The senior pastor and his staff should be culture watchers. They need to remain as current with what is taking place in the world or general environment as possible. This involves reading the daily paper, watching the news, and visiting the local newsstand to scan the various periodicals and new books. Church leaders should subscribe to a magazine or two that deals with current events and culture. And maintaining up-to-date folders for each of the environments covered above is essential to effective culture watchers.

The pastor should not depend on himself or his staff alone for this information. A wise pastor will recruit other culture watchers from the congregation. Most congregations have a number of people who attempt to keep current on what is taking place in the world. Not only can a number of congregational culture watchers scan more material than a pastor or his staff, they will probably have an advantage over the church staff because they have more daily contact with the people of the world.

How Do They Watch the Culture?

In the book *Flight of the Buffalo,* James Belasco and Ralph Stayer suggest a system called scan, clip, and review that they borrowed from the CIA.[5] Academic circles know this system as content analysis. Using this idea, people in the church who have agreed to be culture watchers scan newspapers and a certain number of periodicals and books every month. Each clips articles that he or she deems important to what is taking place now and what signals future trends and shaping events and collects them in a file folder. Some culture watchers could review books by futurists such as John Naisbitt, Faith Popcorn, and Alvin Toffler. They are looking for any information that has the potential to affect the church now or in the future, no matter how far-fetched it may seem.

Once a month they could meet at lunch to review what they have found. At this time, they would look for recurring trends and common themes, such as the growing number of unchurched people or the need for strong family values. They would also eliminate all but what they think is the most important material. Then once a quarter they would bring this information to the pastor and staff, who would ask themselves the following three questions:

1. What are the one, two, or three future events that will have the greatest impact on our church?
2. What will happen when those events occur?
3. What can we do now to prepare for them?[6]

Knowing What the Church Should Do

Understanding our times is only half the battle. The rest is determining what the church should do in response to what is happening in our

Job Description:
Congregational Culture Watcher

- Regularly scan, clip, and review newspapers, journals, and books
- Meet monthly to review findings
- Meet quarterly with staff to present findings

times. Remember, the men of Issachar not only understood the times, they knew what Israel should do (1 Chron. 12:32). The information about the current culture will strongly influence the church's strategy (step 6, see chapter 8). Knowing what the church should do is part two of the environmental scan. It involves scanning the church world internationally, nationally, and locally to see what God is doing.

The Church Environments

In spite of growing secularization, God is still working in our world. In Matthew 16:18, the Savior says he will build the church and not even the gates of Hades will overcome it. The church scan simply scans the churches all around the world and asks, What is God doing? What strategies and programs is he using to minister to people who live in this changing world and are affected by it? This is lateral learning. I call it "cross-pollination" or church lateral learning "bumblebee style." Each local church can look at its particular circumstances as affected by our world and then ask, What specifically are other churches in the community, the state, the region, the country, or in some other part of the world doing that could help us minister more effectively in our situation?

Community Churches

Broadly speaking, community churches are those located in your neighborhood, town, or metropolitan area. You should be aware of them and study those that God is blessing. Perhaps some will hold church conferences in which they present the way they conduct their ministry. They will be your best sources of information because they are in your part of the world and may have more in common with you than any churches in other places. In my file, I have collected information, for example, on

Generation X, African American and Hispanic churches, as well as Anglo congregations located in the Dallas–Fort Worth metroplex.

State Churches

State churches are those located in the same state or province that your church is in. Here you ask, What churches in this state is God blessing? They will be relatively close, so you can visit these churches to observe as well as read about what they are doing. You can interview leaders, talk to workers, and observe their programs firsthand.

Regional Churches

Regional churches are those located in the same large geographic area. Churches located in these areas may have more in common than they would with those in other regions. For example, the Pacific Northwest has more unchurched people than the rest of America. Churches in the Northwest thus have a common problem—What can we do to reach our higher proportion of unchurched people? What can we learn from one another?

National Churches

National churches are those located in the same country. They may be similar to your church or very different. What they share is participation in the same country and political system, and probably the same language.

International Churches

Churches located in one country may learn much from churches in other countries. For a long time, international Christians traveled to America to study in its seminaries and to learn from its great churches that have sent missionaries all over the world. However, currently the largest churches are located outside North America. For example, Korea has six churches with more than thirty thousand members in each. Santa Fe, Argentina, has one church of eighty thousand. Buenos Aries has a church of seventy thousand. Lagos, Nigeria, has a church of seventy thousand. Santiago, Chile, has one of fifty thousand, and Manila in the Philippines has one of thirty-five thousand. The largest church in America, Willow Creek Community Church, has around fifteen to sixteen thousand people. Clearly the focal point of Christianity has shifted away from Europe and America to the third world.

The question we must ask is, What can we learn from these international churches? What are they doing to reach so many people? The largest church in the world, Yoido Central Full Gospel Church in Seoul, Korea, ministers primarily through small-group communities. Are small-group ministries the key to reaching more people for Christ? It is difficult to learn from international churches, however, because little information on what they are doing is available.

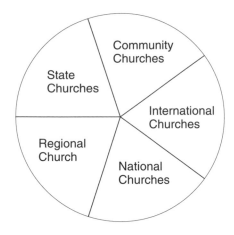

Church Environment

Figure 23

Emerging Characteristics

As I have studied churches in North America and beyond, I have noted some fairly common emerging characteristics of churches that God has blessed in the 1990s and now early in the twenty-first century. One is ministry through small groups, especially in larger churches. The slogan in these churches often is "the bigger we get, the smaller we get." A second characteristic is the use of contemporary Christian music in the worship service. What we must remember, however, is that the adjective *contemporary* is relative. What is contemporary today is traditional tomorrow. There is often a return to the arts in these churches. It is common to find churches ministering through drama, orchestral music, and even dance. Churches are also offering choices or options in terms of their programming because people want choices in the churches they attend. Strong children's and youth ministries are present in many of the churches God is blessing. Churched and unchurched people alike demand quality programs for their children. Many churches have become more evangelistic and try to minister to seekers. Another characteristic of these churches is growing lay involvement. Churches are implementing programs that help members discover their divine designs, train for ministry, and then deploy. There is a trend away from formal dress to a more casual style. An increasing number of pastors, staff, and men in the congregation are not wearing coats and ties at services. Women are comfortable in slacks, and both men and women wear shorts in some churches.

Some additional characteristics of churches God is blessing are an emphasis on life change, nondenominationalism, culturally indigenous ministries, an acceptance of creativity and innovation, the use of marketing techniques, an accepting and nonthreatening environment, indigenous and often nonseminary-trained staff, visionary and proactive pastors, ministry excellence, and practical preaching that addresses people's needs.

Christian Schwarz has written *Natural Church Development: A Guide to Eight Essential Qualities of Healthy Churches*. In this book he claims to present the results of a study of more than one thousand churches in thirty-two countries on five continents. That would make it the most comprehensive study ever conducted on the causes of church growth.[7] Schwarz found that growing, healthy churches around the world exhibited eight characteristics. They have an empowering leadership that equips, supports, motivates, and mentors other Christians for ministry. They have a gift-oriented ministry that emphasizes Christians serving in their areas of giftedness under the power of the Holy Spirit. There is a passionate spirituality that asks, "Are the Christians in this church 'on fire'? Do they live committed lives and practice their faith with joy and enthusiasm?" These churches have functional structures that affect how the church is organized. There is an inspiring worship service that leads to an inspiring worship experience. Holistic small groups help Christians study the Bible and learn to serve others. These churches participate in need-oriented evangelism—they focus on the questions and needs of non-Christians. Showing hospitality, laughing together, being aware of personal problems, and sharing in loving relationships are common. Schwarz further comments that no one single factor leads to growth, rather it is the interplay of all eight characteristics.[8]

A Warning

Churches must be careful, however, not simply to find a church somewhere that God is using and blessing and adopt the model in its entirety. I believe that no church should mimic entirely what another church is doing. This is because each church has unique leaders who minister in different ways with their personal gifts in churches that are located in different communities around the world. These churches, in turn, serve through people who, themselves, have unique gifts and talents. No two churches are alike. Every church is wonderfully unique. God sovereignly directed this diversity because it takes all kinds of churches to reach all kinds of people.

Mimicking other churches is the mistake that numerous new-paradigm churches made in the 1980s and 1990s. They tried to be like Willow Creek Community Church near Chicago or Saddleback Valley Community Church near Los Angeles. When they failed, they did not understand why. They wondered, *If God is blessing them using their strategies, why did he not bless us when we copied those same strategies?*

**Emerging Characteristics
of Twenty-first-Century Churches**

Small-group ministries
Contemporary Christian music and worship
Use of the arts in worship
Programming options
Strong children's and youth ministries
Increased evangelism
Growing lay involvement
Casual dress
Emphasis on life change
Nondenominationalism
Culturally indigenous ministries
Creativity and innovation
Use of marketing techniques, such as mailers
Accepting and nonthreatening environment
Nonseminary-trained staff
Visionary and proactive pastors
Ministry excellence
Practical preaching

What leaders and churches should be asking is, What are churches like Willow Creek, Saddleback, and others doing that God might use and bless in our communities given our circumstances? They probably have little in common with those churches but might be able to adopt one or two programs they are sure will work. They may decide to take a risk and adopt others they aren't so sure of. Either way, the church and its leadership understand what they are doing as they seek to reach their area of the world for Christ.

The Church Watchers

The culture watchers consist of staff and people from the congregation. However, the church watchers are more likely to be staff and congregants who have a high interest and involvement in ministry. They are those with their fingers on the ministry pulse, who are aware of what is taking place in churches around the world as well as at home. Most often they are pastors and staff people who are exposed to this kind of information through seminars and professional books and periodicals.

They may use the same methods as for gathering information about the general environment. The primary method is the scan, clip, and review

Eight Essential Qualities of Healthy Churches

Empowering leadership
Gift-oriented ministry
Passionate spirituality
Functional structures
Inspiring worship services
Holistic small groups
Need-oriented evangelism
Loving relationships

process presented earlier. The senior pastor and those on staff not only attend church conferences, but they scan as many periodicals and books as possible. Helpful periodicals are *Christianity Today, Leadership,* and missions bulletins. Occasionally someone will write a book that supplies much information, such as Russell Chandler's *Racing toward 2001: The Forces Shaping America's Religious Future.*[9] In addition, books written by missiologists can provide information on the international scene.

Recording and Reporting the Information

As church leaders observe trends that affect the general environment and the church and discover how churches at home and abroad are addressing these trends, they will use this information in various ways to make decisions about the church's future direction. They may develop various scenarios of what could happen and how to respond in each case, using the scenario concept from chapter 1 and appendix B as a strategizing tool.

Church watchers need a convenient way to record and communicate the information they gather, for their own use and the use of the congregation.

I record my findings on a piece of paper marked off in two columns. The left column is labeled "Understanding Our Times" and the right column is "What the Church Must Do."[10] For practical purposes and ease of communication, the leadership will need to identify only the primary or most important trends and controlling factors that they observe. I suggest that they limit them to five or six over a period of one to five years. These they write in the left column. In the right column list how the leadership has decided that the church will respond to the trends.

The following is a sample format that Rick Warren presented at a meeting of the California Southern Baptist Convention:

Agenda for a Decade of Destiny
California Southern Baptist Convention
Rick Warren

> "The men of Issachar understood the time
> And they knew what Israel should do."
>
> 1 Chronicles 12:32

I. Understanding Our Times

1. Our state is becoming more diverse.

2. The rate of change is increasing.

3. Time is becoming more important than money.

4. Our population is growing older.

II. What We Must Do

1. We must develop multiple styles of ministry. "I have become all things to all men so that by all possible means I might save some." 1 Cor. 9:22

2. We must change methods without changing our message. (Jesus) "New wine must be poured into new wineskins." Luke 5:38

3. We must streamline our schedules and structures. "Be careful how you walk, not as unwise men, but as wise, making the most of your time, because the days are evil." Eph. 5:15–16 (NASB)

4. We must mobilize mature adults for ministry. "God has given each of you some special abilities; be sure to use them to help each other, passing on to others God's many kinds of blessings." 1 Peter 4:10 (LB)

▶

---

5. The church's influence is declining.	5. We must model Christian discipleship. "Each of you should look not only to your own interests, but also to the interests of others. Your attitude should be the same as that of Christ Jesus." Phil. 2:4–5

I suggest that leaders update this scan as major trends similar to those reflected in Warren's format surface in their cultural environment locally or nationally.

Finally, these trends and factors will affect leaders' visions. That is why I place the environmental scan before the vision in the strategic planning process. The scan provides the current cultural context to which the vision responds.

Questions for Analysis and Discussion

1. Name one or two social trends that could have a major impact on your church. What are one or two technological forces that might affect the ministry? Identify one or two economic trends that could influence the church.

2. Name several political forces that could have a significant impact on your church. What are some philosophy-shaping events that could affect your ministry?

3. Identify the most important five or six trends and forces given in your answers to the two questions above.

4. Who on the church's staff reads broadly? What are they reading and why? Who would be good culture watchers?

5. Who in your church reads broadly? What books do they read? What periodicals are they reading? Who would make good culture watchers?

6. Identify some churches that God is blessing in the international, national, and regional arenas. What are some trends that characterize

these churches? Which trends would help your church have a greater impact for God?

7. Which churches in your state or community is God blessing? How is he blessing them? What are they doing that could help your ministry?

8. Are you attempting to mimic or pattern your church after another church's ministry? If yes, which church? If no, why not? If yes, why might this be harmful? Which church are you tempted to mimic?

9. What could your church do to respond to the five or six forces that you identified in question 3?

7

Developing a Vision
What Kind of Church Would We Like to Be?

The fourth and final element of congregational or corporate soul is the church's vision. Like the ministry's core values, mission, and purpose, vision is essential to the organization. However, unlike the values, mission, and purpose, the vision is more subject to change. It is dynamic, not static. Over time, the vision must be renewed, adapted, and adjusted to the cultural context in which the congregation lives. The change takes place only at the margins of the vision, not at its core. The core—the Great Commission—does not change. The details of the vision and the words used to convey them will change. The vision provides us with a picture of what the mission will look like as it is realized in the community.

The vision concept is not new to the Scriptures. You will find visions sprinkled throughout the Old and New Testaments. For example, God caught Abraham's attention with his vision for him in Genesis

> Ministry Analysis
> Values Discovery
> Mission Development
> Environmental Scan
> **Vision Development**
> Strategy Development
> Strategy Implementation
> Ministry Contingencies
> Ministry Evaluation

12:1–3 (the Abrahamic covenant). God used Moses to communicate his vision for his people, Israel, in Exodus 3:7–8 and Deuteronomy 8:7–10. It is possible that the "joy" that Jesus looked forward to while enduring the cross was the vision of his return to the presence of his Father in heaven (Heb. 12:2).

This chapter is step five in the strategic thinking and acting process. It follows the environmental scan step because the scan sets the context in which the vision is developed. The scan monitors a changing, adapting world, and vision reflects that changing world to some degree. The purpose of step five and this chapter is to help leaders understand the vision concept and how to develop a unique, compelling vision for their ministry. It answers the fundamental question, What kind of church would we like to be? If we could have it our way, what would we look like? Whereas the ministry analysis, step one, uncovered reality, the vision step probes what the church wants to be.

This chapter consists of four sections. The first covers purpose or why the vision is so important to a church. The second provides a definition of a vision so that we know what it is we are talking about and are attempting to develop. The third section helps visionary leaders develop a vision for their organizations, and the last presents several practical ways they can communicate their visions to their people.[1]

The Importance of a Vision

The limited information that is available indicates that pastors and congregations are struggling with the vision concept. For example, in commenting on pastors and their visions, George Barna writes, "But when we asked these pastors, 'Can you articulate God's vision for the ministry of your church?' we found that roughly 90 percent of them could articulate a basic definition of ministry. But only 2 percent could articulate the *vision* for their church."[2] David Goetz writes, "In *Leadership*'s study, however, pastors indicated that conflicting visions for the church was their greatest source of tension and the top reason they were terminated or forced to resign."[3] Clearly, vision is of utmost importance to leaders and their ministry. Here are seven reasons why.

A Vision Encourages Unity

In a ministry a shared vision changes people's relationship to one another. When a leader casts a vision in a church, it is no longer "their church," it becomes "our church." The ministry's vision encourages and allows people to come together and work together. It creates a common identity in two ways. First, it signals to all where the ministry is going. It says that if you want to go where we are going, then climb on board— let us go together. Second, it fosters the retention of congregants and staff. A common vision says that we are working together toward the same goals. We need each other if anything significant is going to happen for Christ. This, in effect, mirrors such passages as 1 Corinthians 12:20–22 and Ephesians 4:15–16.

A Vision Creates Energy

Not much happens without an inspiring, compelling vision. Not much was happening in Nehemiah's day. The people had no vision. Jerusalem lay in ruins, and no one was motivated to do anything about it (Neh. 1:3). Then along came Nehemiah with a vision from God to rebuild the gates and walls of the city. Visions are exciting and they energize people. They strike a spark—the excitement that lifts a ministry organization out of the mundane. They supply the fuel that lights the fire under a con- gregation—leaders are able to stop putting out fires and start igniting a few. A vision from God has the potential to turn a maintenance mental- ity into a ministry mentality. And when your vision resonates with your values and mission, it generates the energy that fuels the accomplish- ment of the ministry task.

A Vision Provides Purpose

The right vision creates meaning in people's lives. It gives them a sense of divine purpose in life. They are a part of something great that God is accomplishing at this time and place in history. With a shared vision, people see themselves not just as another congregant or a "pew warmer" but as a vital part of a church that is having a powerful impact on a lost and dying world. They are not simply in a church; they are on a crusade. They are part of a revolution that has the potential to change this world, to have a wonderful impact for Christ. For example, a wide gap exists in terms of commitment and dedication to God and a sense of personal sig- nificance between one member who, when asked what he or she does, replies, "I am a teacher" and another, who may have the same ministry, but answers, "I am changing the life course of a class of adolescents who will someday accomplish great things for Christ."

A Vision Fosters Risk Taking

A shared vision fosters risk taking by a congregation. This is especially true in church-planting situations. When the point person or lead pastor casts the vision, everyone knows what needs to be done. That is not the question. The question is, How will we do it? Sometimes we know the answer, but most often we do not. Consequently, ministry for Christ becomes an exciting adventure into the world of the unknown. We attempt something for Christ and it does not work. We attempt something else and it does work. Though much of what we are doing is experimental, it is not ambiguous. It is perfectly clear to all why we are doing it. It is for God and the Savior. People are not asking for guarantees. They all know that no guarantees exist, yet people are committed anyway. The risks are great, but so is the God they serve, and the vision he has given them. How else can we explain the early church and what God accomplished through them or those believers that make up the faith hall of fame in Hebrews 11?

A Vision Enhances Leadership

Developing a vision and then living it vigorously are essential elements of leadership. I define a leader as a godly servant who knows where he or she is going and has followers. That describes not only the Savior, but his disciples and those who ministered in the early church as recorded in Acts. Godly servants are people who display Christlike character throughout the ministry organization. They exhibit the fruit of the Spirit, given in Galatians 5:22–23. They know where they are going and where they are leading their ministry. They have a dynamic mission and, most important, a clear, energizing vision that paints a picture of the future. The consequence of character and vision is followers. When a congregation has a leader who owns a vision and lives that vision in a Christlike manner, they will follow that leader to the ends of the earth.

A Vision Promotes Excellence

God desires that his church minister and serve well on his behalf. This calls for ministry excellence. Whatever we do for Christ must be done well, not sloppily or haphazardly. In the Old Testament God required that people give their best when they brought animals for sacrifice (Lev. 22:20–22). This was excellence in worship. In the New Testament Paul

Seven Reasons Why Vision Is Important

1. Encourages unity
2. Creates energy
3. Provides purpose
4. Fosters risk taking
5. Enhances leadership
6. Promotes excellence
7. Sustains ministry

explains that God expects us to put forth our best efforts in our work. He says to perform as if we are working for him (Eph. 6:5–8; Col. 3:23–24). This is excellence in the marketplace.

A shared organizational vision promotes a standard of excellence. Deep down, people want to do a good job, to have a sense that they are effectively and powerfully advancing God's program through their ministry in the church. The vision casts a picture of what that looks like. It provides a visual, mental measure by which staff and congregation can evaluate how well they and the ministry are doing.

A Vision Sustains Ministry

Ministry can be very difficult, even painful. Discouragement and disappointment often lurk in the ministry hallways and boardrooms of the typical church. It is not beyond the enemy to incite persecution against Christ's church (Acts 8:1). Spiritual warfare comes with the ministry territory (Eph. 6:10–18). Many have risked or given their lives for the Savior and the furtherance of the gospel. The list of martyrs for the cause of Christ is extensive. Why? What has sustained Christians from the beginning of the church in the Book of Acts up to today? One answer is a biblical, compelling vision. It encourages people to look beyond the mundane and the pain of ministry. It keeps a picture in front of them that distracts from what is and announces what could be. All the trouble and grief that we experience in this world while serving the Savior are trivial compared to the importance of what we are attempting for him. That picture, carried in our mental billfolds, is one way God sustains us in the worst of times.

The Definition of a Vision

Now that we know why a vision is important, a natural question to ask is, What is a vision? If it is that important, what is it? First, let's determine what it is not.

What a Vision Is Not

Leaders mistakenly confuse values, purpose, dreams, goals, objectives, and mission with vision. I have already defined values and purpose in earlier chapters, so there is no need to elaborate on those. What is important to remember is that a vision, while not the same as core values and purpose, may contain a church's values and purpose. They are often found in a church's vision statement and will affect that statement.

The Differences between Values and Vision

	Values	Vision
Presence	In all churches	May not be in all churches
Function	Drive the ministry	Focuses the ministry

Though some of us use the term *dream* synonymously with vision, they are different. A dream is much broader than a vision. A dream might ignite or catalyze the development of a vision. In fact most great visions are the result of great dreams. Often when working with pastors, I ask them what they dream about. If they do not dream about God's using them to accomplish great things for the kingdom, then I suspect that they are not visionaries. The vision, unlike a dream, is grounded in deep insight into people, the church, and God's Word. Dreams are based more on a blinding flash of inspiration, and visions are based on a solid factual foundation of biblical truth and God's application of that truth to the life of the leader and to his ministry.

The Differences between a Dream and a Vision

	Dreams	Vision
Scope	Broad	Narrow
Basis	Inspiration	Biblical truth

A vision is not the same as goals or objectives. Goals and objectives are cold, abstract things that do not warm the heart. Vision, however, is warm and has the potential to melt even the coldest congregant's heart. A vision is much bigger than a goal or objective. The latter usually follow the vision and are integral parts of the ministry strategy that ultimately accomplishes the vision.

The Differences between Goals or Objectives and Vision

	Goals/Objectives	Vision
Scope	Narrow	Broad
Effect	Cold	Warm

Finally, a church's vision is not the same as its mission. I have saved mission until last because the concepts of vision and mission are confused more than any of the above concepts. Most frequently, people ask, What is the difference between a vision and a mission? They are similar in some ways. They both are based on the Scriptures, focus their people on the future, are directional (tell people where the ministry is going), and are functional (they address what the church is supposed to be doing). However, the differences are greater than the similarities.

I make nine distinctions between a vision and a mission. The mission is a statement of what the church is supposed to be doing, while the vision is a snapshot or picture of the same. The mission is used for planning where the church is going; the vision is used for communicating where the church is going. A mission statement must be short enough to fit on a T-shirt. The vision statement, however, goes into detail and can range from a single paragraph to several pages in length. The purpose of the mission is to inform all of the ministry's function. The purpose of the vision is to inspire people to accomplish the ministry's function. The mission involves knowing. It helps your people know where they are going. The vision involves seeing. It helps people see where they are going. If people cannot see it, it probably will not happen. The mission comes from the head—it is more intellectual in origin. The vision comes from the heart—it is more emotional in origin. Logically the mission precedes the vision. In their development, the vision grows out of and develops detail around the mission, fleshing it out. The mission has a broad, general focus, while the vision has a narrow focus. It singles out the details and specifics of the ministry community. Mission development is a science—it can be taught. The vision, however, is an art—it is caught. You either catch it or you will miss it all together.

Mission and Vision Distinctions

	Mission	Vision
Definition	Statement	Snapshot
Length	Short	Long
Application	Planning	Communication
Purpose	Informs	Inspires
Activity	Doing	Seeing
Source	Head	Heart
Order	First	Second
Focus	Broad	Narrow
Communication	Visual	Verbal

What a Vision Is

I define a vision as a clear, challenging picture of the future of the ministry as you believe that it can and must be. This definition contains six elements.

It Is Clear

We cannot expect people to act on information that they do not understand. My paraphrase of Paul's words in 1 Corinthians 14:8 is, "If the bugler muffs the call to arms, what soldier will know to prepare himself for battle?" Then we will have lost the battle before it has begun. A vision accomplishes nothing if it is not clear and precise. If the congregation or people who make up the ministry do not know what the vision is, the ministry has no vision, only empty words on a piece of paper or vague sounds—a noise—proceeding from the leaders' lips. It is much like Alice's destination in *Alice in Wonderland:*

> "Would you tell me, please, which way I ought to walk from here?"
> "That depends a good deal on where you want to get to," said the Cat.
> "I don't much care where____," said Alice.
> "Then it doesn't matter which way you walk," said the Cat.
> "____so long as I get *somewhere,*" Alice added as an explanation.
> "Oh, you're sure to do that," said the Cat, "if only you walk long enough."[4]

Apparently Nehemiah's vision for Israel and the rebuilding of Jerusalem was clear and specific. He and his followers must have seen in their heads new walls with gates hanging from them. Note the people's response in

Nehemiah 2:18, "They replied, 'Let us start rebuilding.' So they began this good work."

It Is Challenging

Visions often face a quick, untimely death. A pastor hears that he is supposed to have a vision for his church, so he quickly develops something that he hopes will do. However, he is only going through the motions. He may not be convinced in his heart. He has not read the section above on the importance of vision. Consequently he conceives and births something he calls a vision only to see it quickly die and be placed in some ministry graveyard such as a church filing cabinet. If your vision does not challenge your people, you have no vision.

The challenge that emanates from the vision is what excites people and gives birth to ministry action. People need a challenge. It is that challenge that penetrates the deep resources of the mind and touches the human spirit. The challenge serves the vision by pulling people out of the pews and into the arena of effective, passionate ministry.

It Is a Picture

Whereas passion is a feeling word that plumbs the depths of our emotions, vision is a seeing word that probes the imagination and creates visual images. Our vision is our ministry snapshot. It is the photo you carry around in your mental wallet. It is what you see when you envision your ministry two, five, ten, or twenty years from now, the picture of the future you believe that God is going to create. Visionary church planters will tell you that from the very beginning, they had a picture of what the church would look like when it was up and running, when the dream—their vision—was in place.

I suspect that in the waning chapters of Deuteronomy, when God took Moses up on Mount Nebo, he was showing this great leader the reality of what he had carried around and seen in his head for all those years of wandering in the wilderness—a land flowing with milk and honey. It was assurance that, though Moses would not enter the land, the dream was about to become reality.

Vision affects not only what leaders see, it affects what their people see as well. You must ask, Do my people see what I see? If they cannot see the vision, it is not likely to happen.

It Is the Future of the Ministry

The vision is a picture of the future we seek to create. It depicts the church's preferred future. While outside of biblical prophecy, we cannot predict the future, we can create the future. That is the function of the vision. It pictures the end of the ministry at the beginning.

The vision also serves to bridge the past and the future. The right vision provides the all-important link between what has taken place, what is now taking place, and what the organization aspires to build in the future. A strong vision changes the orientation of the church from the past to the future. It takes people's eyes off the greatness of the church in its prime and helps them see how great it can be.

It Can Be

A good vision drips with potential because it is constructed on the bedrock of reality. The dream involves seeing something that is not yet but is possible. The visionary leader is convinced that the vision is attainable. It is what Robert Kennedy had in mind when he said, "Some people see things the way they are and ask why; I see things the way they could be and ask why not."

It Must Be

The vision goes beyond what can be. It concerns what must be. Somewhere toward the end of the "can be" stage, it grabs hold and will not let go. Now the visionary believes not only that it can be, he is convinced that it must be. A critical sense of urgency drives him in his quest for the vision. It may keep him awake at night.

Three things have happened. First, the leader is convinced that God is in the vision—that God himself has placed it in his heart. It is a "God thing"; it is God's doing, not his. Thus he will not find rest until the church has embraced the vision. Second, the leader believes that he is God's person to see the vision through. God has chosen him to pilot the vision ship through his church's ministry waters whether they are smooth or choppy. Finally, he is certain that the vision is the very best thing for people—both lost and saved. Because the leader cares about people, he knows that they will be so much better off when they embrace and own the vision. They will experience eternal life and spiritual renewal. Martin Luther King Jr. knew that his vision "had to be" if black people across America were ever to experience deliverance from racism and intolerance.

The Development of the Vision

It is imperative that leaders not only carry their vision around in their head, but put it in writing. One of the elements in the definition of vision

The Definition of a Vision

1. A vision is clear.
2. A vision is challenging.
3. A vision is a picture.
4. A vision is the future of the ministry.
5. A vision can be.
6. A vision must be.

above is clarity. Writing a vision statement forces clarity from the vision pioneer. This process requires the right people to create a unique product—the vision.

The Vision Personnel

Developing a vision statement, like the mission, is both a top-down and bottom-up process. It begins at the top of the church with the senior or only pastor. He should be a visionary who is convinced of the need for a powerful, inspiring vision. If he is not a visionary, then a vision statement will probably not be developed. The next responsible person, an associate or assistant pastor, cannot substitute for the primary leader. The congregation looks to the point person, the one who stands in the pulpit, for the vision. It can't come from anyone else.

A leader knows whether he or she is a visionary. Visionaries see the ministry's possibilities. They are focused on what the church could be, not on what it is. If a leader is not sure that he is a visionary, he should take the *Myers-Briggs Type Indicator* (MBTI) or the *Kiersey Temperament Sorter*.[5] These tools measure whether a person is sensing (S) or intuitive (N). Sensing-type people are the practical, hands-on realists. They can have a vision; however, they go about it in a different way. Whereas intuitive-type people see the vision naturally in their heads, sensing types have to see it literally with their eyes. They perceive it through their five senses. Thus, they "catch" a vision by actually visiting a church where they can see, smell, and touch the vision. They are able to form the vision as they walk the church's corridors and experience its ministries.

The intuitive types are the abstract, imaginative, natural visionaries. For them, vision is a sixth sense. They seem to carry one around in their head.

If leaders who are senior pastors discover that they are not visionaries, they should not necessarily vacate their position. And I would not advise all visionaries to become senior pastors. This is because there is more to leadership than just vision. For example, leadership gifts and skills are essential. However, nonvisionary senior pastors and their churches will struggle with a general lack of clear direction. I have found that often nonvisionary leaders discover that they function better and are happier in support positions rather than point positions. This is because people do not expect them to have a vision; whereas they do expect the senior person to have one.

However, leaders cannot simply announce the dream or vision from on high and expect universal compliance. I suggest that they write the original vision but let significant others get their fingerprints all over it. This is the bottom-up or middle-out process that results in ownership or a shared vision. The significant others are what Fred Smith calls the "driving wheels." He writes:

> There's a difference between people who provide the momentum in a group and those who go along for the ride. Wise leaders know that if they get the driving wheels committed, they will bring the others along. Without the commitment of the driving wheels, the organization moves unsteadily.[6]

The key is that pastors and the driving wheels agree or share the same vision. This assumes that they share the same personal organizational visions for the church. If the pastor ignores their personal organizational visions, his vision will fail to catalyze energy and commitment. It becomes a shared vision when it connects with the visions of the driving wheels. That is why a pastor must let his key people act as editors and get their hands on the vision.

When it comes to a shared vision, the visionary pastor in an established church will deal with three groups of people. Picture the following as a continuum moving from left to right. On the far left are the people who already share his vision. They are already on his team. In the middle are those who do not share the vision but are winnable. They make up the majority of the congregation in most situations and are likely to join the pastor's team. On the far right are those who do not share the pastor's vision. Most have a vision that is not the pastor's vision. They are the unwinnable people. They will either leave the church, or stay and become inactive, or stay and cause problems. If they never physically leave, they have emotionally left the team.

Won People	Winnable People	Unwinnable People
Already on the team	Join the team	Leave the team

How does the visionary pastor woo and win people to the final vision product? He must be intent on constantly casting his vision before the winnable people. This will involve lovingly pointing out how the church, like many other churches across North America, may have missed God's best for the people and their lost but interested friends. He also needs to point to all the opportunities for ministry in general and outreach to the lost in particular. Once they begin to take note and agree, the pastor must regularly invite them to join him in his efforts to take advantage of the opportunities. He must be prepared to ask them to follow him.

The Vision Process

It is not enough to have the right personnel in place. The vision process is also critical to the product. The process has seven aspects.

Envisioning Prayer

The visionary leader must bathe the entire vision process in prayer. Envisioning prayer must be at the beginning of the development process and remain a part of it throughout. As the leadership prays, God will open their eyes to his Word and its application to the people in the world.

In Nehemiah 1:4–11, Nehemiah prays an envisioning prayer. Word got back to him about the desperate plight of his people and their city, Jerusalem. His response was to fall to his knees for confession and prayer. And it was during this time that God placed his vision on Nehemiah's heart. God wanted him to return to Jerusalem and lead his people in rebuilding the city (Neh. 2:5).

Expanding the Mission

At this point in the process, the leader should return to the mission statement that he developed in step three (see chapter 5). The vision statement is an expansion of that mission statement—make disciples! (Matt. 28:19–20). The visionary immerses this disciple-making mission in the ministry community, where the vision will be implemented, and asks, What do I see? The vision involves developing and adding details to the mission, fleshing it out. It could begin with the mission statement and expand on it, adding the church's purpose, some core values, and later the ministry strategy. Again, the question that is repeated through-out is, What does this look like? Give yourself permission to explore, dream, be creative, and be daring. Get away from it all and spend some relaxed time dreaming and imagining what could be.

Thinking Big

In Matthew 28:19–20, Jesus challenged a small band of itinerant, non-seminary-trained disciples to reach their world with the gospel. As you examine the scope of Jesus' Great Commission from its first proclamation after the resurrection, through the Book of Acts, and up to today, you quickly realize that he was a person of no small vision. He was the visionary of visionaries.

Consequently, visionary pastors should not hesitate to think big. Do not let current realities constrict your dreaming. Someone has said, "Make no small plans, for they have not the power to stir the souls of men." In his doxology in Ephesians 3:20, Paul challenges the Christian community at Ephesus, and us as well, to ask (pray) and think (envision) big: "Now to Him who is able to do exceeding abundantly beyond all that we ask or think, according to the power that works within us" (NASB). Indeed, this seems to be a light slap on the wrist for not asking and thinking big enough. Paul says that God is able to do much more than we are asking or even thinking about. Therefore, vision developers must ask, Is this vision big enough?

Written Brainstorming

As the visionary pastor prays, expands his mission, and thinks big, he needs to begin to write his thoughts down on paper. A point comes when it is time to start writing things down. I call this written brainstorming, writing on paper what God is writing on your heart. Do not wait too long. Whenever thoughts and ideas are exploding in your mind, write them down.

The problem is that these thoughts can come at any time and any place. It happens when you are sitting on the freeway in five-o'clock traffic; it happens as you are lying in bed attempting to fall asleep. Wherever you are, try to write them all down. Carry with you some three-by-five-inch cards or a notepad. You could set aside a regular time to do your dreaming, but innovative ideas generally can't be restricted to a certain time frame. The creative juices tend to flow on their schedule, not ours; it can be difficult to turn them on and off. For morning people, they flow better early in the day; for evening people, they seem to flow better at night.

Organizing the Dream

As you write your thoughts down, begin to organize your material. You can do this in several ways. First, look for a natural progression in what you have recorded. Perhaps you put the mission down first followed by the church's purpose. Then you may have expanded on it. That is a natural progression that you can see in some of the sample vision statements in appendix E.

Another approach is to peruse the vision statements in appendix E first. Look for any that seem to communicate a kindred spirit with your ministry. As you read them, the content and format strongly appeal to you on an emotional level. They seem to jump off the page at you. Then use the format to shape your organizational vision statement, much as a contractor uses wooden forms to shape concrete when pouring a foundation for a house.

Questioning the Dream

As you write the statement, probe it with numerous vision questions. You may use the definition of the vision as a test of the quality of the vision statement. First, ask, Is it clear? Do I understand it; is it clear to me? As Professor Howard Hendricks says, "A mist in the pulpit is a fog in the pew!" Then ask, Will it be clear to my people? The only way to know the answer is to ask. Present it to a random sampling of your congregation and note their answers.

Then ask, Is it challenging? Does it challenge me? And if so, Will it challenge my people? You'll know the answer if you watch the emotional response of your people as you present your vision to them.

The next question is, Is the dream visual? Does it create mental pictures of the future of the ministry? Then, Do I believe this vision can be realized? Is it feasible? Finally ask, Am I convinced that it must be?

Demonstrating Patience

You must be patient with the vision-development process. You cannot rush it, but give it whatever time it takes. Sometimes a vision will pop fully formed into the visionary's head in a matter of days. Nehemiah's vision in Nehemiah 1 came to him fully formed. However, he did not have much time. More often, a vision takes weeks and even months to develop fully. A vision could even take years of cooking on the back burner of the leader's mind.

However, visionary thinking tends to be a way of life for visionaries. They spend much of their waking time envisioning their future and that of their ministry. For most, when it comes time to develop a written state-

A Summary of the Vision Process

Envisioning prayer
Expanding the mission
Thinking big
Written brainstorming
Organizing the dream
Questioning the dream
Demonstrating patience

ment, they simply record what has been on their mind since they first began their ministry.

The Vision Product

Someone has said that a picture is worth a thousand words. I suspect that it was Adam while in the Garden of Eden. Whoever said it must have been a visionary. Pictures and visions walk hand in hand. That is because a vision is a picture or image in one's head. Not only are mental pictures important to vision, but actual vision statements are as well. They help people picture the vision. The culmination of the work of the vision personnel through the vision process is a unique product—the vision statement.

Examine Other Vision Statements

Just as we learned much about values by looking at values statements and about missions by looking at mission statements, we can learn about visions by examining vision statements. Paradoxically, visions are seldom original. It is rare that even the most visionary person was the first to conceive his or her vision. Most often, while perusing several vision statements, one will catch your attention and it will influence the writing of your own statement. Also you may pick up bits and pieces from other sample statements.

Therefore, I have placed several vision statements in appendix E. Before you begin developing your own vision, you may wish to look at these. Note their contents, how their authors structured them, and their wording.

Articulate Your Vision in a Written Statement

In this section I have challenged leaders and their ministry to articulate their vision in a written statement. This is a valuable experience that encourages ministries and leaders to discuss and come to agreement on their vision for the organization even before they write it for public scrutiny. A vision, however, is so much more than a written statement; it is an ongoing conversation. It is the way we think, individually and collectively, about the community that God is using us to build. It is what is important to us. It is why we want to be together.

The Communication of the Vision

It is most important that you communicate to the people the vision, as well as the mission and values. I refer to it as casting the vision. Like a fisherman who casts a lure into the water, hoping that as he reels it in, some fish will follow, so the visionary casts the vision into the congregational waters, hoping that when he reels it in, his people will follow. Vision casting is fishing for men. However, nothing happens if the vision isn't cast, if nothing is communicated.

The Leader's Example

The leader's example is critical to communicating the vision. His or her actions must reflect belief in the vision. If the leader does not live the dream, no one else will. People watch what leaders do as well as what they say.

The Sermon

The sermon is the primary means for casting the vision. Whereas the mission communicates well on paper or written on a T-shirt, the vision is best expressed through spoken communication. The power of the vision is in hearing it preached, not reading it. You can discern this by reading Martin Luther King Jr.'s great vision message and then listening to it. He communicates with great enthusiasm and conviction. Today's preachers who believe in their visions should demonstrate these same qualities.

Other Methods

Most of the methods used for communicating the values and mission can be used for casting the vision. They include the following: formal and informal conversation, stories, the bulletin, a framed poster, a church brochure, training materials, a slide-tape presentation, audio- and videotapes, skits and drama, a newcomers' class, a newsletter, having the congregation vote on it each year, and the performance appraisal. Each ministry will need to discover which method is best for them. What works well in one context may not in another.

Questions for Analysis and Discussion

1. This chapter presented seven reasons a vision is important. Did any one reason seem more important than the others? If so, which one? Would you add any other reasons to the list? If yes, what?

2. Does your ministry already have a vision statement? If no, why not? If yes, what is it? Does it meet the criteria in the definition of the vision statement? (Is it clear, challenging, a picture of the future of the ministry, feasible, a must?)

3. Is the senior pastor a visionary? If yes, how do you know? If no, how do you know? Has he taken the Myers-Briggs Type Indicator or the Kiersey Temperament Sorter? If he is not a visionary, what problems does this present for the ministry?

4. Who else on the staff is a visionary? Are there any visionaries on the board? If so, who? If not, how might this affect the ministry and the leadership of the pastor? Who are the ministry's "driving wheels"? Are any of them visionaries?

5. Have you spent any time praying for a vision? Why or why not? If no, when will you start? If yes, what thoughts have come to mind?

6. Do you tend to think big or small? How do you explain this?

7. Peruse the vision statements in appendix E. Do any excite you or elicit some kind of emotional response? If so, which ones? How might they help you structure and develop your vision statement?

8. What methods for casting the vision appeal most to you? Why? Which will work best with your congregation?

Developing a Strategy

How Will We Get to Where We Want to Be?

In their book, *Flight of the Buffalo*, Belasco and Stayer assert, "Thinking incrementally is an American disease."[1] Though I suspect that other countries struggle with it as well, Americans have been seriously infected with this disease from early in life. Our eager parents encouraged us to eat just a few more carrots and peas and then they would dismiss us from the dinner table. Our patient teachers urged us to exert a little more effort, and the coveted A would be ours the next time. Out on the practice field, the football coach admonished us to play harder next week, and we might win the close one. Belasco and Stayer indicate that thinking incrementally is not bad, but when you think incrementally, you will not be thinking in terms of the new vision and the mission. Thinking incrementally is thinking with no mission or vision or with poor ones. Thinking incrementally can also mean that you begin with the old strategy and its methods and attempt to move toward the new vision and the mission. The problem is that you bring all the problems and limitations of your present paradigm with you, clouding your vision of what could be.[2]

Leaders who think strategically look forward. They begin with their mission and

Ministry Analysis
Values Discovery
Mission Development
Environmental Scan
Vision Development
Strategy Development
Strategy Implementation
Ministry Contingencies
Ministry Evaluation

vision because both articulate and paint a picture of where the ministry should go. Next, they look backward only in the sense that they ask, Now that we know (mission) and see (vision) where we are going, what will it take to get there? How will we have to act? "Looking back" here means developing an entirely new strategy, not returning to the old one. Belasco and Stayer add, "It's the looking back from tomorrow that gives thinking strategically its power, because that perspective helps you escape the limitation of today's situation."[3]

We conduct a careful ministry analysis as the first step in the strategizing process. The analysis serves not to authenticate or perpetuate what is but to show its inadequacies and to motivate us to think about what could be. We leave the ineffective behind and move on to what could be. Then we ask the strategy question, How will we get to where we want to be? If we are to think strategically and not incrementally, it is imperative that we manage backward from the future, not forward from our past.

The purpose of this chapter is to teach leaders how to develop a strategy to realize the missions they have articulated and the dreams they see. Leaders in both the Old and New Testaments led and ministered according to a strategy. Moses strategically led the Israelites through the wilderness (Exodus 3), though they wandered somewhat, due to disobedience. Nehemiah revealed his strategy to rebuild the walls and gates of Jerusalem in Nehemiah 3–6. Jesus led and ministered according to a strategy when he selected the disciples, trained those disciples, and sent them out to minister. In Matthew 28:19–20, he gave the church its mission, and Luke, in the Book of Acts, shows how the church strategically carried it out.[4]

In this step of the strategic thinking and acting process, the fundamental ministry questions are, How will we get to where we want to be? How will we realize our ministry dream? How will God use this ministry to accomplish his ends? The answer is a biblical, strategic architecture that will provide guidance for the operational and strategic decisions that daily affect the life and direction of the church. First I explain five reasons a strategy is important to your church. Next I define what a strategy is and then I take you through the strategy development process.

The Importance of a Strategy

Before you develop a significant, high-impact strategy, you and others on the ministry team should be convinced that a strategy is important and that you need one. Otherwise, the effort will be halfhearted at best. A strategy is important for numerous reasons. Here are five.

The Strategy Accomplishes the Mission and Vision

Every church has a strategy. The question is, Is it a good one? A bad strategy often does not have a vision or a mission to implement. It is easy to spot—people are going through the ministry motions, but not much is happening beyond maintenance.

A good strategy is the vehicle that enables the church to accomplish the mission (the Great Commission) and vision. That is the purpose of the church, why it exists. The strategy moves the congregation from wherever they are spiritually (lost or saved) to where God wants them to be (mature). Therefore a good strategy delivers; that is, it helps the church accomplish the biblical mission that God has set for it.

The Strategy Facilitates Understanding

More than one person in the congregation has thought, Why are we involved in these programs? Why sit in a Sunday school class, a small group, or a worship service? What are we doing here? In some of our older, struggling, established churches, no one has thought through the answers to these questions. The response often is, "We have always done it this way." The ministry programs of these churches have much in common with the white paint on the outside of their building—layer exists on top of layer. No one has taken the time to scrape any old layers off. But eventually the bottom layer will come loose, affecting the entire finish.

The ministry strategy is the thread that runs through all the church's programs, tying them together and giving them meaning. As you will see, leaders build programs around strategies. They design the programs to contribute to and accomplish some aspect of the strategy. For example, at Northwood Community Church the core of our mission and vision is the Great Commission. Each of the programs that make up our strategy contributes to realizing that commission. Our small-groups program provides biblical community. The Sunday school exposes our believers to the deeper teaching of the Bible, and the worship service provides a worship opportunity and a place for the lost and saved to hear a word from God. It is our desire that all our people understand this and know what each contributes to the whole.

The Strategy Provides a Sense of Momentum

As we saw in chapter 2, Bob Gilliam, in his "Spiritual Journey Evaluation," made the startling discovery that the people in the churches he

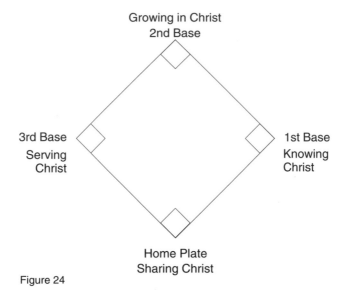

Figure 24

studied were not growing spiritually and they knew it. They had no sense of moving on with the Savior. People who understand their church's strategy to make disciples and who get involved in that strategy will experience a sense of momentum or progress in their walk with God.

Pastor Rick Warren uses a baseball diamond to illustrate his church's strategy. The church encourages each member to work their way around the bases from first base to home plate. First base represents faith in Christ and membership in the church. Second base represents spiritual growth and maturity. Third base is the discovery and use of one's gifts and abilities for ministry. Home plate is involvement in the worldwide mission of sharing Christ. As members realize the requirements of each base, they experience not only a sense of accomplishment but movement. They are not "sitting and soaking" or treading water, but are moving forward in their walk with Christ. At the same time, they know where they are spiritually and precisely where they need to go. That is ministry momentum.

The Strategy Properly Invests God's Resources

God's resources are his people, specifically their talents, time, and treasure. While God is not dependent on people, he has chosen to accomplish his purposes through people. First, he uses our talents. He has given each of us a unique design (Job 10:8–9; Ps. 119:73; Isa. 29:16; 64:8). This design consists of such things as spiritual gifts, talents, a passion, temperament, and other factors (Romans 12; 1 Corinthians 12; Ephesians 4). God can use these characteristics for ministry.

Second, God uses our time. None of us feels that he or she has enough time to accomplish all that should be done each day. We always seem to be running out of time. However, God controls our time and provides us with the amount necessary to accomplish his program (Prov. 16:3).

Finally, God uses our treasure. All that we have comes from his gracious hand (2 Cor. 9:10). And he gives us the privilege of investing our finances in building his kingdom and church (2 Corinthians 8–9).

So what? To invest our talents, time, and treasure in a ministry that has no disciple-making strategy and, thus, is not going anywhere may not be the best use of God's resources. God may want to close a church that has no strategy to free the members for ministry elsewhere. Investing one's blessings in such a church may serve to hinder God's plan by keeping the doors open. Perhaps we need to close some of our older, struggling ministries and use the gifts, time, and money to start new churches where people are excited and have a passion to make disciples.

The Strategy Displays What God Is Blessing

At the end of chapter 2, I wrote about the theology of change. I want to return to that concept and apply it to the importance of a well-thought-through strategy. There I argued that the church's functions such as evangelism, worship, fellowship, and others are timeless and should never change. They are as valid in the twenty-first century as they were in the first century. The forms that those functions take, however, that make up and flesh out a church's strategy, are time-bound and must change for the functions to be most effective. God used the camp meeting, for example, as an effective strategic form or method of evangelism in America during the 1800s. He also used the altar call that Charles Finney popularized and evangelists used with success up to the 1940s and 1950s.

At the end of the twentieth century and the beginning of the twenty-first century, these forms are not as effective in North America as they once were. And we observe that other more effective forms of evangelism have replaced them. Why is this? One answer is the changing times and culture in which we live. The fact is people are different and things change. Thus as times change, it takes a variety of methods to reach all kinds of people. The best answer, however, is that this is the way God has sovereignly chosen to work. The environmental scan helps and encourages us to study churches and ministries that God is using to win people to the Savior so that we can discover what strategic methods he

Five Reasons Why a Strategy Is Important

1. Accomplishes the mission and vision
2. Facilitates understanding
3. Provides a sense of momentum
4. Properly invests God's resources
5. Displays what God is blessing

is blessing and using in the present. This may help us to strategize better and reach people in our ministry community.

The Definition of a Strategy

I define a strategy as the process that determines how your ministry will accomplish its mission. This definition relates to the mission, the process, and the answer to the question, How?

A Strategy Has a Mission

As I said earlier, every strategy needs a mission. A strategy without a mission is like a plane without a destination, and what pilot would even take off if he does not know where he is going? While every church will have a strategy, good or bad, it may not have a mission. This seems strange, but if you studied many of the churches across North America and beyond, you would discover that most do not have a clear mission or a strong sense of direction. Some confuse the strategy with the mission. For example, if you asked the *function* question, What are you supposed to be doing? they might answer, Study the Bible. Studying the Bible is very important, but it is a part of the strategy, not the mission of the church.

As covered under the mission development step, Christ has already predetermined the church's mission in Matthew 28:19–20; Mark 16:15; Luke 24:45–49; and Acts 1:8. It is the Great Commission—make disciples! Therefore, every church must regularly ask itself three critical questions:

1. What are we supposed to be doing?
2. Are we doing it?
3. If not, why not?

My view is that far too many churches in North America have become "niche churches" that specialize in some aspect of the Great Commission (they have good Bible teaching or good counseling or great fellowship), but have missed the Great Commission as a whole. An important part of my personal mission is to call churches back to what Christ has commanded them to do.

A Strategy Involves a Process

A strategy is the process of moving people from spiritual prebirth to Christlikeness or maturity (Matt. 28:19–20; Eph. 4:11–13; Col. 1:28; 2:6–7). This involves moving any person, wherever he or she is spiritually (lost, saved, and immature) to where God wants that person to be (spiritually mature). This process is a part of one's spiritual life journey. It does not take place over a short time, but over one's lifetime. Moving people from prebirth to maturity takes them through the following phases:

Phase 1: Prebirth (unconverted)
Phase 2: New Birth (converted)
Phase 3: Maturity (committed)

When pastors and parachurch leaders speak of discipling people, it usually involves taking a few believers—often young, new, and energetic—through these phases or steps on a one-to-one or one-to-two basis. The strategic purpose of this book and section, however, is to take not a few, but the entire church through the disciple-making process. The strategic process will attempt to put together a churchwide program (not "a" program, but "the" program of the church) that encourages and makes it possible for all the people to become Christ's disciples.

A Strategy Answers the How Question

A good strategy answers the *how* question. The mission and vision of the church answer the *what* questions, What are we supposed to be doing? and What kind of church would we like to be? The strategy tells how we do what we're supposed to do. It is the overall process that enables a church to accomplish its mission. It is the ministry means that accomplishes the ministry end. If the church's mission is to make disciples, the strategy directs how that church will make its disciples. It explains to all involved how the church plans to move people from prebirth to maturity.

The Kinds of Strategies

When defining a strategy, it is also helpful to note that different kinds of strategies exist. One is a personal strategy. Christians should have a personal strategy to accomplish God's purpose for their life. The church's strategy does not relieve the individual Christian of his or her responsibility to become mature. Another kind of strategy is departmental or programmatic. In addition to the church's overall strategy, each ministry, department, or program of the church needs a strategy. The worship, evangelism, or youth ministry, for example, each needs a strategy to accomplish their particular ministry mission.

This chapter is focusing primarily on two types of strategy. One is the church's broad, general organizational strategy that I have been addressing so far and will cover in the next section. The other is the specific working strategy that is a part of the broader, organizational strategy.

The Strategy for Your Ministry

Now that you know why the strategy is important to your ministry and what precisely a strategy is, it is time to develop a general, overall strategy that is tailor-made for your unique ministry situation.

The prior steps in the strategic thinking and acting process will have a significant impact on the strategy. The ministry analysis, for example, evaluates the effectiveness of the old strategy and so influences the new one. Your core values will dictate what does and does not go into the strategy. The mission directs the strategy—it is what the strategy seeks to accomplish—and the vision provides a fresh picture of what that will look like. Also, the vision will energize the strategy. Finally, the environmental scan provides information that affects the strategy in two ways. First, it informs or keeps the leaders apprised of what is taking place in the world all around the church, good or bad, and how those trends and events affect the lives of the people to whom the church will minister. Second, it informs or keeps leaders abreast of other churches that God is blessing and what they are doing that might be included in or influence the church's strategy.

The Impact of the Prior Steps on the Strategy

Steps	Impact
Step 1: Analysis	Evaluates the strategy
Step 2: Values	Dictates contents of the strategy
Step 3: Mission	Directs the strategy
Step 4: Scan	Informs the strategy
Step 5: Vision	Energizes the strategy

As we have seen, the values, mission, purpose, and vision are at the church's very heart and soul. They make up its congregational or corporate soul. They are timeless and do not change appreciably, although the vision may change but only at the edges, not at the core. The same is not true of the general strategy. It should both change and be in tune with the times. To carry out the mission of the church in a changing world, the general strategy—including its practices, structures, systems, and policies—should be changing all the time. When a ministry freezes its strategy, it becomes brittle and begins to decay.

The Ministry Concepts and Change

Timeless (Unchanging Concepts)	Timely (Changing Concept)
Values Mission Purpose Vision	Strategy

The general, overall strategy includes five specifics: the ministry's target group, its working strategy, its personnel, its facilities, and its finances. And each of these asks key strategic questions.

The Target Group

The general strategy begins with the church's target group. The question that the church attempts to answer is, Whom are we trying to reach? To whom are we ministering? The answer involves four steps.

Identify the Target Group

Identifying the target group involves asking several questions. Will you target lost people, saved people, or both? Most congregations land on the third—they want to reach both. But most established churches are ministering more to saved than to lost. Newly planted churches are better at attracting lost people—especially unchurched lost—and then bringing them to salvation and spiritual maturity. Knowing whom you are reaching answers the question of whom you are targeting.

Gather Information on the Target Group

For an established church to know its target group, it simply needs to examine its present congregation. This was accomplished back in step 1 (chapter 3) when the church conducted both a congregational and a culture analysis. Church plants will initially target Christians who desire to be part of a core group that will reach lost people as well as minister to saved people. The church-planting core group needs to ask itself several questions:

1. Will we target lost people?
2. Will we target unchurched or churched lost people?
3. Will we target people like or unlike ourselves?
4. Will we target receptive people?
5. Will we target needy people?

The core group will need to learn much about its target group. This was also done in step 1 when the church conducted a community analysis. The core group can learn much about its target through up-to-date demographic and psychographic studies.

Construct a Profile Person

Some find it helpful to construct a profile person. This person can be either a cartoon character or a real-life man and woman who are typical of your target group. Saddleback Valley Community Church created Saddleback Sam for this purpose. Willow Creek Community Church came up with Unchurched Harry and Mary. The advantage of such a creation for an established or planted church is that it helps the church's people know whom they have targeted.

Determine the Kind of Church Necessary to Reach the Target Group

Once you have identified your target group, you need to decide what kind of church it will take to reach that group. Answering the following questions should accomplish this:

1. What kind of meetings will work best—large, small, and/or medium-size groups?
2. What kind of worship—contemporary or traditional?
3. What kind of programs do we need—Sunday school, men's meetings, and others?
4. What kind of sermons are appropriate—topical exposition, book exposition, both?
5. What kind of pastor will be able to minister best—young or middle-aged, wife and family, seminary graduate, strong leader, gifted evangelist, and so on?[5]

The Working Strategy

The narrow, working strategy is the second specific of the general, overall strategy. It answers the question, How will we reach those in our target group? What is the process that our church will take people through as they become Christ's disciples? You can view coming to faith in Christ as God's moving a lost person across a continuum from one extreme (no knowledge about Christ) to the other (maturity in Christ). Conversion happens somewhere in between. A good strategy will take into account this process.

No knowledge of Christ   Maturity in Christ

Conversion

The recipe for the working strategy consists of four ingredients: mission statement, strategic goals, action steps, and a visual. The strategy for Northwood Community Church is in appendix F. You will want to refer to it as you examine each of the following ingredients.

The Mission Statement

The first ingredient of the working strategy is the church's mission statement that you developed back in step 3 (chapter 5). One of its primary uses besides direction (telling people where the church is going) and function (what it is supposed to be doing) is planning. Thus it is key to the strategy. If the strategy is to accomplish the church's mission, then the first item that must be in the working strategy is the mission statement. Since Christ has predetermined that the church is to make disciples, then the rest of the strategy is how your church will accomplish this. At Northwood Community Church our personalized mission statement says, "Our mission is to be used of God in helping people develop into fully functioning followers of Christ." We have defined disciples as fully functioning followers. They have three characteristics (the 3 Cs): They have been converted to Christ, they are committed to Christ, and they are contributing to Christ. You will see the importance of these characteristics as they become goals or steps in the second ingredient of the working strategy.

The Strategic Goals

The second ingredient is the church's strategic goals. To discover them, we look back to the mission statement. The goals flow naturally from the mission statement. The mission statement breaks down into several specific goals. There should be at least two and no more than six or seven, because then they become unwieldy and hard to remember. The goals summarize and present the natural progression, steps, or levels (or whatever you may wish to call them) that your people move through on the way to becoming mature, Christlike disciples. The key to determining what these goals are is to ask what you believe are the biblical characteristics of a mature disciple—the object of every church's mission statement. As I look at the strategies of various churches that are making disciples, they all seem to have this in common. For example, Willow Creek Community Church has the five Gs (grace, growth, group, gifts, good stewardship). If you examine Saddleback Valley Community Church's baseball diamond, illustrated on page 154, you will note four characteristics of a mature disciple represented by each base path (knowing Christ, growing in Christ, serving Christ, and sharing Christ. Northwood Community Church has three strategic goals—the three Cs—that flow from the mission statement. Each represents and communicates the stages in becoming a fully functioning follower of the Savior.

1. To see people converted to Christ (to interest in becoming a disciple).
2. To bring people to a commitment to Christ (to become a committed disciple).
3. To equip people to make a contribution to Christ (to become a contributing disciple).

The Action Steps

The third ingredient of the working strategy is the action steps that accomplish the strategic goals. Thus they represent the steps your people take to realize each goal. Northwood Community Church developed three action steps that move our people from prebirth to conversion. We use a visual—a three-legged stool—as a memorable way to communicate these steps to our people. Each leg of the stool presents a level of commitment.

First Leg: Conversion to Christ
Second Leg: Commitment to Christ
Third Leg: Contribution to Christ

Included under each action step is one or more strategies or ministrategies to accomplish that step. These strategies consist of various programs or ministries, such as small groups, Sunday school, children's ministries, men's and women's Bible studies, and many others.

The Visual

The fourth ingredient is a visual representation or diagram of the working strategy. Many people are visual learners and most people remember ideas better if some type of visual or diagram helps it stick to the ribs of their mind. In general we remember pictures better than words. Saddleback Valley Community Church, for example, developed the baseball diamond visual to communicate Saddleback's strategy (see figure 24 earlier in the chapter). This has proved to be an excellent visual for a North American church. Understandably, it does not communicate as well in other parts of the world where baseball is not played.

Since my training ministry takes me out of the country, I have found that Northwood Community Church's visual has served well to communicate our strategy internationally. We have adopted the typical three-legged stool that dairy farmers all around the world use when milking their cows or goats (figure 25). The three-legged stool is a metaphor for discipleship that I like for two reasons. First, a three-legged stool is stable no matter how rough or uneven the ground is on which it rests. It will not topple over. In the same way, this disciple-making strategy can serve the church in many different situations and circumstances, the bad as well as the good. Also the strength of the stool depends on all three legs resting on the ground. The one who wishes to become a fully functioning follower (disciple) must have all three legs in place to minister properly. A person can function with only one leg (conversion), but the stool is wobbly at best. A person can function much better with two legs (conversion and commitment). A person can serve Christ best, however, when all three legs (conversion, commitment, and contribution) are in place.

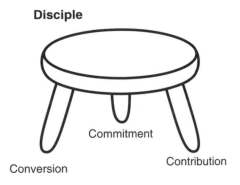

Disciple

Commitment

Conversion

Contribution

Figure 25

The Ministry Personnel

We have seen that the general ministry strategy must include the target group and a working strategy. The third specific of the general strategy is the ministry personnel. Here the question is, Who will be involved in reaching our target group? Who makes up the ministry team? The vital point to remember is that your church will only be as good as the people who make up the team. The personnel principle is that it takes good people to lead and build good churches.

When you develop a ministry team strategically and not incrementally, you need to examine all staffing from the perspective of your vision and mission, not on the basis of who happens to be available or already on the ministry team. This could mean releasing people who do not fit the team well. As painful as that is, the church does not exist to provide jobs for people, but to provide ministry through people in the right positions. Somebody is not better than nobody. The stakes are too high for this kind of thinking. While no one is perfect for any position, put simply, the challenge is not finding people, it is finding the right people—the people God wants on your team. To accomplish this, you should ask the following five questions.

1. What positions does your strategy call for? To get the right people in the right ministry positions, you start with the position. Every church begins with a pastor. Many churches have one pastor, and he may be only part-time. I question if part-time is better than no-time. It may depend on the circumstances. My pastoral experience has taught me that pastoral ministry is a full-time venture. Part-time ministry most often results in a maintenance ministry at best. Rarely do part-time pastors lead growing ministries.

The best ministry takes place in a team context. New Testament ministry is team ministry. When you find the apostle Paul's name in the New Testament, it is usually one among several others, such as Barnabas, Silas, and Timothy. Team ministry can exist in numerous contexts. One person has to be the primary leader or point person for the team. Some advocate a coleadership approach where there are two equal, primary leaders. My experience is that coleadership is not especially characteristic of biblical leadership and most commonly results in no leadership. Additional members on a team could be a worship leader, an administrator, a Christian educator, a youth leader, a family minister, a small-groups pastor, a counselor, and others.

2. What kind of people will it take to fill these positions? Once a leader has determined the necessary positions, the second step is to select the best people for those positions. Because you are so busy, the temptation will be to rush this process. Just remember that a mistake here has the potential of undermining not only your character but the entire ministry. When unkind, misplaced people are released from a church, they can be vindictive and spread false rumors, affecting the entire church.

You will discover that no perfect candidates exist. Recruitment and selection of ministry personnel usually involve trade-offs. Even Paul and Barnabas had their difficulties (Acts 15:36–41). On the one hand, you will need to construct the perfect profile for the position. On the other hand, you will need to accept the fact that no one will fit the profile perfectly. You must consider the balance of a person's ministry potential with his or her personal flaws. You are looking for godly interpersonal skills. You should ask, Can we get along well with this person as well as minister with him or her?

The profile for a ministry position identifies several requirements:

1. Character. This is the first and most important requirement. Insist on it. (A good standard for staff is that set in both 1 Timothy 3:1–13 and Titus 1:6–9.)
2. Agreement with core essentials of the ministry. These essentials are the ministry's values, mission, purpose, vision, and strategy.
3. A divine design. This includes specific gifts, passion, and temperament that align with the needs of the position. (Ask, Has God "wired" this person for the position?)
4. Competence. The best predictor of future behavior and competence is past behavior and competence.

5. People skills. The ability to get along with people is essential. Fifteen percent of ministry is technical, but 85 percent involves working with people.
6. Seeing the ministry as a holy cause. Those in this ministry are on a crusade, a mission for God.
7. Doctrine. Where is there disagreement and how will that affect the working of the ministry team? For example, is there disagreement on such issues as the charismatic gifts, divorce and remarriage, women's role in ministry, and politics and ministry?
8. Pastoral loyalty. This is an inner conviction that the lead pastor is clearly God's man for the church. He will be supported and his leadership followed within reason.

Where will you find people who meet these requirements? Some look to evangelical Bible colleges or seminaries. However, a growing number of churches feel that these colleges and seminaries are out of touch with the real world and the newer ministry paradigms. Some argue that seminaries provide good biblical and theological training but little in the area of leadership training that is so important to pastors and staff persons.

So where do churches find their leaders? Many recruit those with proven leadership character and abilities from within their own or other congregations. However, a major disadvantage of this approach is that these people may not be well grounded in the Bible and theology. The best of both worlds is balance: a seminary graduate with a good ministry track record.

3. How will you structure your personnel? Here the questions are, Where do our people fit? How will they relate to one another? Who is responsible to whom? In theological circles, this involves a church's polity. We need only to talk with people from several different denominations and churches to discover that divergent opinions exist on polity.

Basically there are three forms: episcopal (government by bishops), presbyterian (government by elders), and congregational (congregational rule). Those who hold each view argue that Scripture supports their form or structure of government and can provide scriptural documentation. My own position is that those who hold these three views wrongly assume that Scripture prescribes only one structural form and that all the early churches embraced that one correct form. The reason for the different forms of polity is that the early church did not embrace only one form, but practiced different forms as they adjusted their polity to their particular situation. That is why churches are able to marshal biblical support for their particular position.

Also I believe that this is a function versus form issue (see chapter 2). Church government is the function that takes many different forms, such as congregational, episcopal, and presbyterian. My point in all this is that, with exceptions, a church has the freedom to select the form that best fits its particular ministry context. Should circumstances change, another form could be adopted if it better serves the people and purpose.

The corporate world holds that because of change, organizations must be innovative and agile and that rigid, pyramidal organizations do not permit this. Some even argue that the best organization is no organization. However, people do need to know who reports to whom, their authority, their boundaries, as well as their roles and responsibilities. This is the purpose and value of job or ministry descriptions. For example, at Northwood Community Church, we needed a minister of Christian education. However, the man we wanted for the position was most reluctant because we had no job description. He wanted to know all the above regarding this position. What were our performance expectations? Exactly what were his responsibilities? For what would he be held accountable? To whom did he report and who reported to him? He was a wise young man.

The answer for us at Northwood was twofold. First, we developed job or ministry descriptions for every position (I have provided one example in appendix G).[6] Second, we developed three organizational charts. This helped us immensely. I have discovered that a church functions as a cause, a community, and a corporation.[7] Our structures reflect these three functions.

The cause reflects the church's leadership structure. Our desire is that Christ be our leader (1 Cor. 11:3). Under Christ is the senior pastor, who, as primary leader and visionary, works mainly with the board and staff in large churches. With them, the pastor sets the direction for the church, and the board and staff lead and work with the congregation. In smaller churches the pastor works with the board, staff, and congregation.

The community function reflects how the church relates to one another as family. This represents the church as an organism. As family we are all brothers and sisters (Heb. 2:11–13). Therefore, we are equals in Christ (Gal. 3:28).

Finally, the corporation function reflects the business and legal side of the church. Some do not like to acknowledge that a church has a business side, but it does. It is necessary for legal and other purposes. For example, most churches incorporate to protect individuals in the church from any lawsuits brought against the church. Ministries, like businesses, also enter into legal contracts such as when buying and selling a facility or property.

Figure 26

Community
(Family)

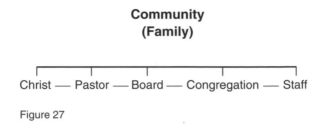

Christ —— Pastor —— Board —— Congregation —— Staff

Figure 27

4. How will you train your people? Constant training must be a hallmark of the strategy of any church ministry. This includes everyone on the staff. It answers the important question, How will we get better? Ken Blanchard notes that, "The second most common reason, after unclear goals, why people fail in their jobs is lack of training."[8]

Those on the staff may bring a certain amount of training to the position. For example, a pastor may have a seminary degree, or an administrative assistant may have completed a business degree. However, they must not rest on the laurels of a diploma on the wall. Our world and the ministry are changing so rapidly that all staff must pursue regular training or they will quickly fall behind. Each day the team's level of skills is either increasing or decreasing. We must not assume that our people will have

Corporation
(Accountability/Responsibility)

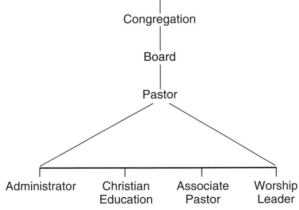

Christ

Congregation

Board

Pastor

Administrator   Christian   Associate   Worship
                 Education   Pastor   Leader

Figure 28

the time to keep up with the changes that are taking place in their particular ministry areas or will find out on their own—they are simply too busy.

How might staff obtain further training? Several possibilities exist. One is to find a coach or mentor. A secretary, a youth minister, or the senior pastor should be able to find someone in the area who is excellent at doing the same job. The secretary or pastor or whoever should ask to meet with the mentor once a month for coaching for a designated time. (This is mandatory for inexperienced leaders who are planting churches or pastoring their first church.)

Various seminars that come to your area of the country, whether specifically dealing with ministry or from the business sector, can offer further training. Or you can take courses that you deem helpful from a nearby college or seminary. For example, here in Dallas, Southern Methodist University's business school offers special short-term courses on executive leadership for those who have a bachelor's degree.

Pastors may choose to pursue a ministry degree through a good doctor of ministry program in an area that will benefit them. Pastoral staff should visit twice a year at least two other churches that God is blessing to discover what they are doing that might prove helpful to the home church. Also church conferences are beneficial, such as the one that Willow Creek Community Church sponsors three times each year. Take as many people as possible with you to such a conference so that all understand and catch the vision of what these ministries are attempting. Finally, bring in various consultants to train your people in some important ministry area on site.

5. *What will you do for your people?* This last question concerning the ministry team focuses on how the church will take care of its personnel. Those involved in working for churches, whether custodians, secretaries, or pastoral staff, are generally paid less than in most other professions. This may reflect a congregation's poor giving habits (they do not have the funds), unrealistic expectations, poor or inexperienced leadership, or a lack of biblical knowledge about adequate compensation for personnel. Scripture makes it clear that the church is to take care of its people: 1 Corinthians 9:13–14; Galatians 6:6–7; 1 Timothy 5:17–18.

What should a church do for its personnel? The percentage of most church budgets designated for pastoral compensation ranges between 30 and 60 percent, depending on the size of the church. The ministry may base pastoral compensation on what they think is fair, the experience and education of the staff, or the salary of those in comparable positions in the community (schoolteacher, principal, store manager). Gary McIntosh suggests that churches use the base-salary method. The church would set a

Staff Training

- Find a coach or mentor.
- Attend area training seminars.
- Take courses.
- Pursue a ministry degree.
- Visit other excellent area ministries twice a year.
- Attend church conferences.
- Use the services of a consultant.

base salary for the senior or only pastor and then calculate any other positions as an index of that standard. For example, if the senior pastor's salary is $35,000, it is an index of 1.0. Then an associate pastor's salary is indexed as .85 or 85 percent of the senior pastor's salary: $29,750. The youth pastor's salary may be .75 and so on. The church could provide supplements to the base salaries for education, experience, and other factors.[9]

How does a church determine the senior pastor's base salary? McIntosh believes that a fair base salary is approximately three times the annual mortgage payment for buying an average home in the community where the church is located. He bases this on a study that showed that the average mortgage in America has consistently been around one third of a family's household income.[10] The church then adds salary supplements for experience, completed education, ordination, and other factors.[11]

The church can provide other help for its personnel. One is benefits such as paid sick leave, holidays, vacation, personal days, time off for jury duty; insurance packages; retirement; long-term disability; and so on. Another benefit is reimbursements for expenses associated with ministry such as travel expenses, books and subscriptions, continuing education, and others. Regardless of its compensation package, the church should review this package at least twice a year to take into account any changes in the pastor's or church's situations.

The Ministry Facilities

Once you have determined your target group, designed a specific, working strategy, and recruited your ministry personnel, you are ready in the general, overall strategy to examine the ministry's facilities. The question you are addressing is, Do we have the best facilities for reaching our target group?

The Ministry Personnel as Part of the Strategy

1. What positions does your strategy call for?
2. What kind of people will it take to fill these positions?
3. How will you structure your personnel?
4. How will you train your people?
5. What will you do for your people?

A major distinction that has taken place over the last thirty years in the shifting of church paradigms is where they meet. In the past, people—usually Builders—have wanted their church buildings to look like a church. Since the early church did not meet in structures like today's traditional churches, that means something similar to the churches in Western Europe from the 1400s or 1500s to the present.[12] However, the typical new-paradigm church prefers commercial space to "churchy" facilities. For example, such a church may meet in a converted warehouse, a rented school auditorium and classrooms, leased space in a shopping mall, storefront, grocery store, or a public meeting room in a bank, hotel, or movie theater. These facilities, of course, have no stained glass windows or religious symbols.

New-paradigm churches offer several reasons for this shift. First, considering the cost of land and new construction, it is considerably less expensive to meet in such places. Second, they are attempting to distance themselves from the traditional forms that so many of the people in their target group have abandoned. Third, a building can pose a significant constraint to a growing church. As Pastor Rick Warren advises, "Do not let the shoe tell the foot how big it can get!" Fourth, new-paradigm churches prefer to invest their finances in people and staff rather than costly buildings. And fifth, often these churches desire to locate in the center of American life where the people are, especially in shopping malls.[13]

However, in time most churches do invest in a permanent facility. But these facilities still do not resemble the European churches of past generations. For many of the reasons given above, churches often relocate to modern facilities that could also be used by a commercial organization. Ministries have realized that only other churches are in the market for a church building that looks like a church and have found it wise to invest in a building that could be sold either to a business or to another church, should there be a relocation.

A number of established churches are discovering that their target group is no longer living in the community. They have moved elsewhere. Thus the question Do we have the best facilities for reaching our target group? is moot. As we saw earlier, these churches can respond in several legitimate ways. One is to redefine their target group, to target the new people who have moved into the neighborhood. Few succeed at this. Another is to relocate to where the church's target group is located. They sell their facility to a church that is targeting the people in their present neighborhood and purchase or build a new facility in the new area. A third is to stay put, change nothing, and die.

The Ministry Finances

The last item in the general, overall strategy is finances. The obvious question is, How much will it cost to reach our target group? Few churches in the early twenty-first century have an abundance of money for ministry. Expenses and expectations are up while contributions are down. The church is primarily dependent on the support of its people for survival. In most situations, one out of three adult attenders donates nothing to the church, and those that do contribute, give less than 3 percent of their aggregate income, despite Jesus' warning in Matthew 6:21: "For where your treasure is, there your heart will be also."

The Importance of Vision

The key to raising finances for your church's ministry is vision. My experience is that people are not that interested in paying the light bills, nor do they respond well to guilt trips, negativism, or needs. People give to big, dynamic visions. They are more willing to invest in "what could be" (future possibilities) than "what is" (present reality), especially if "what is" is floundering or in the red. The exception is when "what is" is obviously blessed of God and growing spiritually and numerically.

The Biblical Teaching on Giving

Pastors also need to preach and teach what the Bible says about giving. Some shirk this responsibility, fearing what their people or "seekers" might think. Many pastors want to please their people and be liked. That is normal; however, a significant difference exists between being liked and being respected. Jesus did not hesitate to address people in the area of their finances (Matt. 6:19–24), and pastors must not either. Most people really do want to know what the Bible teaches about money because it is an issue that is so close to their heart. Many know that their finances are not pro-

The Development of an Overall Strategy

1. The Target Group: Whom are we trying to reach?
2. The Working Strategy: How will we reach them?
3. Personnel: Who will be involved?
4. Facilities: Do we have the best facilities for reaching them?
5. Finances: How much will it cost?

viding true happiness and they want to know the truth. Pastors must be truth tellers. Some set aside one month each year for biblical instruction on giving. Pastors who preach two or more messages in a series usually note a better response than those who preach only once a year or several messages spread out over the year.

Fund-Raising Organizations

A number of churches are using fund-raising organizations to conduct capital campaigns for them. Usually this is the case in the purchase of property and new construction, facility relocation, facility renovation, debt reduction, and annual budget campaigns. Many of these churches report that after the campaign, general giving remains higher than before. Thus churches should consider using a fund-raising organization as a viable option.

Once you have thought through and developed a general, overall strategy for your church, you must continue to think strategically and work through all five areas: target group, working strategy, personnel, facilities, and finances. Resist the urge to set the general strategy in concrete, because about the time you have finished with the process, it will be time to tweak it some. Remember, strategizing in the twenty-first century is not a onetime deal. It is an ongoing process, dictated by the needs of your people and the community of those you seek to reach with the gospel of Christ.

Questions for Analysis and Discussion

1. Can you think of some additional reasons why a strategy is important to a church? If so, what are they?

2. Most churches are trying to reach anybody and everybody. Is this true of you? Is this realistic? Does your church have a target group? If so, who? If not, whom are you reaching in general or who are your people? Are they representative of your target group?

3. What is your mission statement? Does it contain the term *disciple(s)* or its equivalent? Can you break it down into the characteristics of a disciple? If so, what are they? Do these become the steps or levels in your disciple-making strategy? What kind of visual would best communicate the working strategy to your people?

4. Who are the church's current ministry personnel? Are they the best people to reach your target group? Who does not fit? What do you plan to do about him or her? What if that person is the senior pastor?

5. How well is the church taking care of its personnel? Is the compensation package adequate? Why or why not? On what is the pastor's salary based? What benefits does the church provide? Does it reimburse its staff for personal money spent on ministry? Why or why not?

6. Are your facilities right for reaching your target group? If yes, why? If no, why not? If your answer is no, what do you plan to do to make your facilities more conducive to reaching your target group? Should your church consider a relocation to another community? Why or why not?

7. How would you rate your people as givers? Why are they giving or not giving well? If they give poorly, what do you plan to do? Does the pastor ever preach on giving? If yes, how often? If no, why not? Would you ever consider using an outside capital funds consultant or campaign organizer? Why or why not?

Implementing the Strategy

Where Do We Begin, When, and with Whom?

Most experts on planning and strategic thinking have identified implementation as the greatest problem in the strategizing process. Leaders as strategists develop good general, overall strategies, as we saw in the last chapter (step six), but they do not know how to implement them. Having a strategy in writing is one thing, turning it into action is quite another. Having developed a good organizational strategy, we must now take action; we must make it happen. The temptation is to spend all your time on vision, mission, or strategy and none on implementation. At some point you have got to move. To fail here is like moving the ball the entire length of the field in American football but not scoring, or going to the altar without getting married. This is the failure to follow through. It is what Moses and God's people in the Old Testament experienced when they made it to the Promised Land the first time but failed to enter (Deut. 1:19–46). The result is the same. The strategy dies for lack of implementation.

Ministry Analysis
Values Discovery
Mission Development
Environmental Scan
Vision Development
Strategy Development
Strategy Implementation
Ministry Contingencies
Ministry Evaluation

This chapter presents step seven in the strategic thinking and acting process. It follows naturally the development of the general strategy in step six, for its purpose is to communicate how to implement that strategy or how to transform it into the very fabric of the organization. It teaches you not only to announce the church's destination and how it will get there, but to do something—to follow through on the details. It answers the core ministry questions, Where do we begin, when, and with whom? Step seven consists of five parts.

Formulate Implementation Goals

The very first part of the implementation step is to formulate the specific goals needed to effectively implement the ministry strategy. It answers the question, Where do we begin? You cannot implement the entire strategy all at once. That would be overwhelming. Therefore, you must determine what specific goals you must take right now to afford the greatest impact.

A Church Plant

The church-planting team will need to look at its disciple-making strategy and ask, Given our present size and financial situation, what must we put into place first to start making disciples? The church may begin as a small group that over time grows and divides until it is big enough to begin large-group meetings for public worship and evangelistic preaching.

A Revitalization Project

The leadership team in a revitalization context will need to compare the organizational strategy for their church, developed in step six, with their church's current situation. Determine where the discrepancies lie by asking, What is missing? What do we need to implement now to make this dream a reality? What ingredients are missing that are necessary for us to make disciples? To illustrate how to do this, I have included in appendix H the implementation process that we instituted at Northwood Community Church. You will need to turn to appendix H now to understand what follows.

Northwood Community Church is a revitalization project that was dying when I became its pastor in 1996. I led it through the strategic thinking and acting process presented in this book. When we came to the implementation step, we developed some of the implementation goals you see in appendix H: the development of a Christian education program, the development of one to another groups, the assimilation of newcomers, a ministry assessment program, and other actions not listed, such as the development of a newcomers class, the fine-tuning of the Sunday morning worship service, and the upgrading of the church's sanctuary.

We did not attempt all of these at once. We began with the four given in appendix H and then, as we accomplished them, we added the rest over time. Note how we organized them. We identified each one as a certain priority: priority one, two, three, and so on. Under each we explained the implementation goal, such as: "Develop a Sunday school program, nursery, and children's church . . ." under Priority One. Then we listed the specific actions that it would take to realize that goal.

Priority One: Christian education program

Develop a Sunday school program, nursery, and children's church that provide Christian education for all the people in our church.

Actions
1. Recruit pastor of Christian education.
2. Recruit teachers, helpers, and a director.
3. Train teachers, helpers, and the director.
4. Remodel rooms where necessary.
5. Implement Christian education program.

Identifying Misalignments

Identifying misalignments means taking a close look at the ministry organization, talking to your people, gaining input, and asking, If these are our core values and this is our vision and strategy, what are the obstacles that are in our way? Ask yourself and your team, What in our present system of things is holding our people back from becoming mature disciples? Where are the ministry snags, the ministry misalignments?

These misalignments exist not because people are intentionally trying to sidetrack the ministry or do not want to be or make disciples. They occur because over the years, the church has institutionalized ad hoc traditions and practices that obscure its values and vision. For example, if the people of a church have associated only with other, familiar members, they may decide to adopt a more friendly stance toward visitors. A church that values prayer but limits its practice to a Wednesday night prayer meeting may be wise to emphasize prayer in its small-groups ministry as well.

Implementing Change

This may sound simple but it isn't because it involves change, and organizations resist change. This is because people get comfortable with the way things are. They prefer what is familiar. Ken Blanchard suggests dealing with the following "people concerns" to help your church make the necessary changes.[1] I have added advice that will help you deal with these concerns.

Information

Congregants' first concern is for information. They want to know what change you have in mind and they want to ask many questions about it. So you will need to hold frequent meetings after church or during the week, write letters, and meet with your people one-on-one so that they get the correct information. Keep your ears open for any misinformation and deal with it quickly.

Personal

Their second concern is personal. They want to know if they will be able to survive the changes and where they will fit in the new scheme of things. Assure them that they will survive and that the changes are best for the church. Show them how others have gone through similar changes and not simply survived, but prospered, and assure them that there is a significant place for them in the future.

Implementation

Their third concern is implementation. Now that they know what you are talking about and feel they can live with it, they want to know how it is going to be accomplished. This is a strategy and implementation issue. In your communications with them, carefully and repeatedly go over the strategy and its implementation until it "sticks."

Impact

The final concern is impact. They want to know the result of the changes and how the changes will benefit them and the church. Since so many churches going through the change process are plateaued or in decline, you have a distinct advantage. Give your people the facts. They must face reality. Reality for many is that the church will not survive if it does not change. Paint a picture of what can be—a strong, growing church that brings glory to Christ.[2]

Helping Congregations through Change

Concerns	Response
Information	*Communicate*
Question: What do you plan to change?	Meetings Letters One-on-one meetings
Personal	*Assurance*
Questions: Will we survive? Where will we fit?	Others have done it—we can too! We will be better off! We will always have a place for you!
Implementation	*Repetition*
Question: How will it be accomplished?	Cover implementation repeatedly.
Impact	*Reality*
Questions: What will be the results? How will they benefit us and the church?	Give people the facts. Cast the vision for what can be. Discuss the benefits of change.

Determine Specific Priorities

Once you have formulated the specific implementation goals, you must next prioritize them. Ask, Which will we do first, second, third, and so on? The highest priorities are those things that need to be done right away, if not yesterday. Determining strategic priorities allows the church to focus all its resources—people, energy, finances, creativity, and so on—on what needs to be done now. To fail to set priorities means that *everything* will become a priority. When everything is a priority, then nothing is.

How do you determine what is and is not a priority? The answer is threefold. First, you must bathe your situation in prayer. Ask God to show you the priorities, remembering that he may have already done this, and they are obvious. Second, determine what goals will have the greatest impact on the church's ability to accomplish its mission and implement its strategy. Third, determine which of these will have the most immediate impact. Ask, Which will bring quick but significant, enduring results?

Determining specific priorities is not easy. You have to make reasonably quick decisions and take risks. If you are a slow decision maker, and

Three Steps That Determine Priorities

Step 1: Pray and ask God to show you the priorities.
Step 2: Determine which goals will have the greatest impact on the church.
Step 3: Determine which goals will have the most immediate impact.

you are a reluctant risk taker, setting priorities will be a struggle. Get help from those in the congregation who do it for a living and are good at it.

At Northwood we made the development of a Christian education program our first implementation priority. This was because our target group consisted primarily of Boomers and Generation X who, in Dallas, insist on significant, quality programs for their kids. As an established church, we had a Christian education program, but it needed much work. People had already left the church because of it. Consequently it was imperative that we improve the quality of our Christian education program as soon as feasible. For us it meant survival.

Articulate Specific Actions

Once the ministry formulates its implementation goals and prioritizes them, the third step is to articulate the specific actions that will realize these goals. For example, the specific actions that are necessary to implement Northwood's Christian education program are five: recruit a pastor of Christian education, teachers, helpers, a director, and several other workers. You should list these in chronological order, asking which action is taken first, second, and so on.

Decide on Deadlines

The fourth step is to decide when the action items must be accomplished. I have discovered that in ministry like almost everything else, some people are doers, but most are procrastinators. The motto of the latter is "Never do today what you can put off until tomorrow." I suspect that everybody has a little procrastinator in them. And that means we all need deadlines, for they signal not only when we have to be finished, but when we have to begin.

To do their best work, some people need much advance time. They prefer not to be rushed. They like plenty of time to think and be creative. Others do their best work when under pressure. When things come down to the final out in the final inning, they can step up to the plate and hit the ball out of the ballpark. In either case, a deadline is essential.

Deadlines can be broad or specific. Usually a year and a month should be specified. The day can be given also. Make sure that you note these deadlines on the implementation sheets (see appendix H).

Assign Responsible Persons

Assign responsible people to accomplish the priorities. This presents a problem for which I have a solution.

The Problem

Sometimes we operate under the false assumption that somebody will pick up the slack and accomplish our implementation goals. If we simply let people know what needs to be done, then surely someone will rise to the occasion. This is not reality. The kinds of people who rise to the occasion have already risen to the occasion and are already "up to their eyeballs" in ministry's alligators. The rest simply do not rise to the occasion. And most things do not get done on their own. It takes people—qualified, passionate people—to accomplish them.

The Solution

In an earlier chapter, I said that a ministry is only as good as the people who lead and operate that ministry. Therefore, every ministry will need a ministry assessment and development program that places the best people in each position. This addresses the fundamental question, With whom do we begin? At Northwood our fourth priority was assessing our members for ministry, but some churches may need to make this priority number one. The idea is to help our people discover how God has designed them for ministry and then place them in positions that fit their design.

Most people have a profound inner desire to accomplish something of significance with their life. Our job as leaders is to assist our people in accomplishing this for Christ. We do this by helping them discover their gifts, passions, and temperaments. I have written *Maximizing Your Effectiveness* to help Christians in this process.[3]

Spiritual Gifts

The spiritual and natural gifts that people have provide them with the tools or abilities to accomplish certain ministries well. Every Christian has at least one gift (1 Cor. 12:7, 11; Eph. 4:7; 1 Peter 4:10) and possibly several (2 Tim. 1:11). You will find the gifts listed in four books of the Bible: Romans 12; 1 Corinthians 12; Ephesians 4; and 1 Peter 4. How can you discover your gifts? One way is to take a spiritual gifts inventory.[4] Another is for Christians to look for these gifts in themselves and others and call attention to their presence.

Passion

Christians also have a passion. Their passion is the emotional aspect of their divine design—what they feel strongly about. Passion serves to focus our spiritual gifts and motivate us to use them. Most people have a passion for ministry to a certain group of people. For example, some have a passion to minister to college students, others to minister to children. Their passion motivates them to exercise their gifts in ministry to these people.

Temperament

Each Christian has a unique temperament. Your God-given temperament provides your unique personal characteristics and tendencies for ministry. Temperament primarily has to do with one's behavioral style. Nine times out of ten, given the same or a similar situation, a person will behave the same way. A knowledge of temperament helps Christians know who are leaders and who are followers. It also helps in the development of ministry teams and numerous other ministry roles.

When you and the people in the church know each other's divine design, you have a greater chance of getting the right people into ministry positions. In the long term, this will determine whether the specific action will be accomplished or not. Make sure these names are written down on the implementation sheet so there is no question as to who the responsible person is for each action (see appendix H).

Communicate the Implementation Plan

On the one hand, you must know your goals, priorities, actions, and so forth. On the other hand, they will not get done unless others know them as well. You must communicate this information to the church in general and those involved in particular. This facilitates "partnering"— bringing together all interested parties, those who have a role or stake in the outcome, even before any action is taken. It, too, answers the "with whom?" portion of the ministry question.

The Reason for Communication

People need to know the strategy before they can commit to its implementation. It is important that as many as possible understand and commit to making the strategy happen. The implementation process should read like an open book. Keeping people informed of what is taking place will build trust—the vital ingredient in anyone's leadership recipe. The people must not feel that the leadership is trying to hide something from them. Unfortunately many Boomers and Gen Xers feel this way. They are naturally suspicious of people in authority.

Informed people feel that they have a greater stake in the church. They tend to take more responsibility and work harder to make the strategy happen. So the three keys for the success of implementation are communicate, communicate, and communicate. Even when people do not agree—and there will always be somebody—if you communicate and listen (a missing ingredient in much communication), these people will feel that they have been heard, which will also result in a certain amount of trust.

The Responsibility for Communication

Communication is the responsibility of those on the leadership team, especially those who have a direct role in implementation. And it is to be an ongoing process. Once it begins, it never stops. This involves conveying information not only through strategy information sheets (like the one in appendix H), but through sermons, meetings, small-group leaders, bulletins, newsletters, brochures, announcements, and word of mouth.

Establish MIR Meetings

The final aspect of the implementation process is the MIR meeting. MIR stands for monthly implementation review, which describes what the meeting is about.

The Frequency of the Meetings

At least once a month the staff and the responsible persons take whatever time is needed—an hour or more—to follow up and make sure that the strategy is on track for implementation. This makes it the most important meeting of the month. At Northwood it is one of our required monthly staff meetings. Making it a staff meeting gives it a priority that other meetings don't have. Since the MIR meeting occurs only once a month, the leadership must make sure that it does take place and that the responsible people are present.

The Focus and Purpose of the Meeting

Implementation is the specific purpose and focus of the monthly review. This meeting is held to review the implementation step, not some other aspect or business of the ministry. Handle the latter at the other staff meetings during the month. People should come with their implementation sheets in hand, so that the meeting can be focused and effective.

The Content of the Meetings

The MIR looks primarily at two areas: progress and problems.

Progress

First, it asks a number of questions that allow the leadership team to monitor what is taking place and the progress that the staff and other people have or have not made in implementing the strategy. They would ask, How are you doing? Have the various responsible people taken charge of their action steps? Are you making progress? How do you know? Does it look as if you will meet your deadlines? Obviously the review will lead to a certain amount of accountability. What will be reviewed is most likely to get done. Those who come unprepared to this meeting will have to account for their lack of progress. And those who are progressing well should be affirmed.

The Implementation Process

Formulate implementation goals.
Determine specific priorities.
Articulate specific actions.
Decide on deadlines.
Assign responsible persons.
Communicate the implementation plan.
Establish MIR meetings.

Problems

One purpose of the MIR is to surface and deal with problems that implementors are facing. It asks, What problems are you facing? Do any seem insurmountable? How can we help you with your problems? You and the team will need to become aware of any resources that will help you handle the problems.

Questions for Analysis, Discussion, and Implementation

1. What implementation goals will you need to formulate to implement your strategy? Make a list. What current goals or practices will you need to eliminate to better implement your strategy? Will this be difficult for your people? How so? What can you do to help them through the change process?

2. Look over your list of goals. Which will you attempt to accomplish first, second, third, and so on? Have you prayed about the order? Which will have the greatest impact? Which will have the most immediate impact? Once you have made these priority decisions, then place the resulting goals on an implementation sheet.

3. What are the deadlines for each goal? Have you put them down on the implementation sheet? How specific do you intend to be? Why?

4. Does the church have a ministry assessment program in place for its people? If no, why not? Who are some of the responsible people in your church? How do you know? What are their gifts, passions, and temperaments? Which actions should they attempt to implement?

5. How important is it that you communicate the priorities and actions to your people? How will you accomplish this?

6. Do you sense the need to have MIR meetings? Why or why not? When could you schedule these meetings? How will your people, staff, and others respond to them?

10

Preparing for Contingencies

How Will We Handle Pleasant
and Not So Pleasant Surprises?

It was approximately 4:00 A.M. in late March of 1979 when the alarm bells pierced the early morning calm surrounding the massive cooling towers of two nuclear reactors at Three Mile Island. Before the sun set that day, the reactors had released a deadly cloud of radioactive steam into the air. Had the reactors exploded, they would have blown Three Mile Island and a substantial chunk of Pennsylvania off the map. What happened is that a series of events—compounded by equipment failures, inappropriate procedures, and human errors—escalated the incident into the worst crisis yet experienced by our nation's power industry. This crisis sent shock waves not only through nearby Harrisburg, Pennsylvania, but through the rest of America and the world.

Israel—God's people of the Old Testament—were poised to go into the Promised Land. God had described it as a good land, a land flowing with milk and honey, "a land with streams and pools of water, with springs flowing in the valleys and hills; a land with wheat and barley, vines and fig trees, pomegranates, olive oil and honey; a land where bread would not be scarce and

Ministry Analysis

Values Discovery

Mission Development

Environmental Scan

Vision Development

Strategy Development

Strategy Implementation

Ministry Contingencies

Ministry Evaluation

you will lack nothing" (Deut. 8:7–9). Yet the majority report had just come in. Ten of the twelve leaders of the tribes, who had spied out this wonderful land, brought back a bad report, saying that the enemy's cities were huge with walls surrounding them that reached to the sky. To make matters worse, they reported that giants, who made them look like grasshoppers, inhabited the area. God must have been mistaken about their living in this land. As fear of their enemies replaced God's promises to them, their leader, Moses, wondered what God would have him do.

In May of 1993 a fifteen-year-old parishioner accused the music minister of St. Andrew's Episcopal Church in Kansas City, Missouri, of molestation. The minister confessed, and the church terminated him after seventeen years of ministry. Though neither the boy nor his parents filed suit against the minister or the church, the incident tore deeply into the very fabric of the church's life. Before it was over, nearly fifteen families had left the church, and many of those who remained felt anger, confusion, and mistrust.

Each of these crises represents contingencies that some organization or group of people had to face. According to one survey, at least half of all businesses and most churches read about these crises and, though thankful they didn't happen to them, do little or nothing to prevent or preclude such events from taking place and wreaking havoc with their own organization.[1] The safest assumption that a business or church can make is that a crisis looms on its horizon. This does not have to be bad news, but it is reality. However, in these complex and difficult times, many crises prove as devastating as the three examples above.

What can a church do, if anything, to prepare for ministry contingencies? Given the unpredictability of such events, are churches not at their mercy? Churches can do a great deal in preparing for and handling various contingencies. It is called contingency planning. This is step eight in the strategic thinking and acting process. Once the church has developed and is implementing its strategy, it is time to plan for any contingencies that could neutralize or destroy the strategy. However, before we pursue contingency planning, we must understand the nature of ministry contingencies. This will help us deal effectively with them.

The Nature of Ministry Contingencies

Ministry contingencies are those unforeseen events, good or bad, that take place in the life of every ministry and have the potential to help or hurt the ministry. This definition contains several key ingredients.

Unforeseen Events

Ministry contingencies are unforeseen events. Contingency situations, such as a church fire or the theft of church property, are usually unforeseen and unexpected. They happen before you know it. They appear from nowhere and catch almost everyone involved in the ministry by surprise. For example, everyone at St. Andrew's Episcopal Church was surprised that the minister of music was molesting a fifteen-year-old parishioner. People do not expect this kind of thing to happen in churches. The unsuspecting Christian public as well as unchurched non-Christians assume that most churches carefully screen applicants for ministry before hiring them. Unfortunately most do not.

This does not mean that no warning signs exist that some contingency is about to happen. In most cases there are many warning signs. The problem is that we do not see them because we are not looking for them. We have not been trained to see or look for them. Contingency situations bring the church or ministry into a crisis that usually consists of four distinct stages:

1. The crisis stage
2. The acute crisis stage
3. The chronic crisis stage
4. The crisis resolution stage[2]

The first or crisis stage is the warning stage. It is marked by warnings that a crisis is imminent. If the organization misses the warning signs, the event can happen with such swiftness and impact that it can render the ministry helpless. Therefore, a key to the proper handling of contingencies is sharpening our awareness of the warning signals during the warning stage. Then we may be able to spot the coming crisis and manage it more effectively in the early stages. How? A major step is simply becoming aware of what is happening around us. For example, has someone stopped attending? Does another appear unhappy? We must be observant and sensitive to what is going on in the church.

Contingencies Can Be Good or Bad

Contingencies are unforeseen events that can be either good or bad. The general assumption is that contingency situations are all bad—the opening examples reflect this, and most of those that get our attention leave that impression. However, the examples below will demonstrate that good contingencies can exist. Contingencies, good or bad, are characterized by a certain degree of risk and uncertainty that cause most people surprise or alarm. However, with proper handling, it is possible that even a bad situation can result in a highly desirable and positive outcome.

Good Contingencies

Good contingencies are unexpected events that have the potential to help a church or its ministries in a positive way. One example is a large gift of money, a facility, or land. Another is sudden growth or a large influx of people. The attendance of a celebrity, such as an athlete or film star, could be a positive contingency. Celebrities who are committed Christians influence others to come to church and grow in the faith. I observed this in a church where I was an interim pastor. Two Dallas Cowboy tight ends attended. One had led the other to Christ and encouraged him to attend the church. That they decided to come to this church imbued it with a sense of significance. The church felt that it was making a difference in the community.

Positive publicity is a good contingency. On occasion the newspaper will feature an article on a newly planted church or write a story about an established church that is making some contribution to the community. This amounts to free advertising that can alert potential attenders—lost or saved—to the church's presence in the community. A revival or spiritual awakening is also good. Some unforeseen event occurs, such as the public confession of sin, and God's Spirit uses this to precipitate a revival throughout the congregation. On occasion, these have spread through an entire community.

Bad Contingencies

Bad contingencies are those unexpected events that have the potential to undermine the ministry of the church. They may cause a small amount of damage or they may cause the church's demise. The result often depends on how the leadership handles the event and how the church and the community react.

One example of a bad contingency is a church split. This occurs in spite of the biblical plea for unity (John 17:20–23). A church split is usually the result of internal problems and it leaves no winners. Another bad contingency is the resignation of the senior or only pastor. This may be due to a forced termination or what this person perceives as a better situation at another church. Regardless, it leaves the church feeling disappointed or rejected.

Examples of Good Contingencies

- A large gift of money, a facility, or land
- Sudden growth or a large influx of people
- The attendance of a celebrity
- Positive publicity
- A revival or spiritual awakening

An affair involving someone on the church staff will send a shock wave through the church and the community. The unbelieving community and the church's critics view it as proof of hypocrisy. Meanwhile, the church is devastated and often blames itself for not seeing what was going on.

Embezzlement of church funds, involving a treasurer or staff person, will cause alarm, even when the leadership attempts to handle it quietly by terminating the employment of the guilty person.

A fire, whether arson or an accident, is a catastrophe that can work out for good if it causes a church to rethink its mission and purpose in the community and band together to get reestablished. I am aware of several churches that relocated due to a fire, resulting in a better ministry in another area.

Other negative contingencies include a sudden economic downturn that means serious cutbacks in ministries and the loss of staff; power plays, involving a strong board member or influential person in the congregation who decides that the pastor or another staff person must go; existence of a group that does everything possible to maintain the status quo to preserve church life as it was in the 1940s or 1950s; sexual harassment—touching and teasing that may seem appropriate to some will seem inappropriate to others; sexual molestation, usually involving males with young children or teenagers; kidnapping of a child from the nursery, usually a noncustodial parent taking a child without the custodial parent's knowledge or permission; a rape in the parking lot or a deserted classroom during one of the church's services; an accident, injury, or death on the premises during or after a service; attendance by a problem person—someone with an aberrant theology, such as a member of a cult, or someone with an unacceptable lifestyle, such as a gay or lesbian person.

Examples of Bad Contingencies

- A church split
- The resignation of the senior or only pastor
- An affair in the life of someone on staff
- The embezzlement of church funds
- A church fire
- A sudden economic downturn
- A power play
- Sexual harassment, sexual molestation, rape
- A kidnapping
- An accident, injury, or death on the church premises
- Attendance by a problem person

Again, we must remember that as bad as some of these situations may be, God can use them in some way for good. He can bring lost people to Christ and he can bring saved people back to Christ. This truth reminds us of the miraculous nature of Christianity and the wonderful character of our God. It also encourages us and gives us hope in the midst of difficult circumstances.

Contingencies in the Life of Every Church

Contingencies are unforeseen events, good or bad, that take place in the life of every church. Most churches do not prepare for contingency situations because they do not expect them to happen. The safest assumption a ministry can make is that a crisis is just around the corner, if it is not happening presently. This is not necessarily bad news—just reality. It does not have to be a major event such as a church split or someone giving a large sum of money to the ministry. It could be a minor incident such as a disagreement between the pastor and the chairman of the board or a staff member. The problem is that these minor situations, if not handled properly, often escalate into major contingency situations. Regardless, the question is not, Will a crisis event happen? The question is, When will it happen? That they have happened in the past signals that they will happen in the future.

The leaders of most ministries will nod their heads and agree that a crisis is probably imminent. But they must do more than nod their heads. True belief results in action (James 1:22). Wise leaders know a crisis is on the horizon and prepare accordingly. When leaders simply nod their heads in agreement and go about business as usual, they are not prepared for the crisis. They may survive a series of minor crises, but when a big one hits, they are caught off guard and respond poorly. People react poorly under pressure and they make poor decisions that serve only to further aggravate the problem. It is better to prepare contingency plans in an atmosphere of calm and reason, than to wait until a major crisis occurs that forces you to react under emotional and tense circumstances.

The Potential to Help or Hurt a Ministry

Contingencies are unforeseen events, good or bad, that happen in every church and have the potential to help or hurt the ministry. Bad contingencies do not necessarily have to affect a church adversely. They may bring about the church's good. Acts 8:1, for example, tells us that a great persecution broke out against the church at Jerusalem. That was bad because people such as Saul (Paul before his conversion) persecuted the church in an effort to hinder the proclamation of the gospel. However, according to Acts 1:8, the church at Jerusalem needed to take the gospel beyond the confines of the city, and it was the same persecution that ultimately accomplished this (8:4).

What would appear to be good contingencies do not always affect the ministry positively. In Acts 15:36, Paul and Barnabas decided to revisit and strengthen the churches they had planted on the first missionary journey. Barnabas wanted to take John Mark, and Paul thought that to be unwise because once before the man had deserted them. This kind of disagreement can be good. It forces people to deal with issues, especially those not dealt with in the past. Apparently Paul and Barnabas had not worked through this issue and now was the time. The result, however, was such a sharp disagreement that both men parted company and went their separate ways. That was bad.

The obvious key to the outcome of contingencies is how leadership handles them. Romans 8:28 teaches a profound truth that is sprinkled throughout the Bible. Paul states, "And we know that in all things God works for the good of those who love him, who have been called according to his purpose." It is important to note that he is not saying all things are good. He is teaching, however, that in all things—good or bad—God works for the good of those who love him. God has the wonderful ability to turn bad situations into good situations. That is what took place when Saul and others persecuted the church in Acts 8.

Joseph affirms this principle in Genesis 45:4–9. His brothers sold him into slavery in Egypt and that was very bad for him. However, Joseph notes that God is sovereign and used this bad circumstance for good—to save the lives of many people and to preserve a Jewish remnant on earth (vv. 5–7). God orchestrated events so that Joseph became like a father to Pharaoh, lord of his entire household, and ruler of all Egypt (v. 8). Joseph used his position to store up grain so that the Egyptians and his family could survive the great famine that struck the land for seven years.

Wise leaders must realize that Romans 8:28 teaches and Joseph's situation demonstrates that God is sovereignly in control of all events and can turn even the worst contingencies into good situations. One of the ways he accomplishes this good is through the development of good contingency plans before the situations occur.

Contingency Planning

When, not if, a crisis hits your ministry, it is imperative that you have a contingency plan in place to deal with that crisis. This plan answers the fundamental ministry question, How will we handle pleasant and not so pleasant surprises? Step eight of the strategic thinking and acting process involves the crafting of that contingency plan. This has six parts.

Select a Planning Team

First, you must determine who will direct and take responsibility for your contingency plan.

The Pastor

In smaller churches, the pastor will serve at the central core of the planning team. In a larger church with more staff, another person, such as an administrative pastor, could take the responsibility to head up a team. The person who heads the team needs to understand how to develop a contingency plan, be able to coach others in the process, and assume final responsibility for the plan. However, he is not to do all the work. That is the job of the whole team.

Other Members

The other members of the team are the people who lead and are responsible for the various ministries. They have the greatest knowledge and expertise in their areas and can, therefore, do effective contingency planning. For example, the person who is responsible for the church's financial matters would deal with a financial crisis. He or she has the most expertise and knowledge in this area. The worship director or pastor would handle a worship crisis. The person responsible for the nursery would be prepared for a nursery crisis, and so on. Thus when the crisis hits, the persons whose areas are affected will work together with their pastors or some other staff persons to implement the plan that they developed for their area.

Each area of ministry is responsible for coming up with its own plan that will become a part of the final, overall plan. Thus the church contingency plan is the sum of the various contingency plans developed by each ministry.

The team will need to meet periodically to decide on an acceptable format for the plan, encourage those who are procrastinating on the development of plans for their area, and update the plans after a year or more.

The Spokesperson

Another vital person on the team is a spokesperson. This responsibility naturally falls to the pastor as the primary leader of the church and the one who is probably the most articulate member of the team. Choosing a backup is necessary because the crisis could involve the pastor or spokesperson in such a way that they could not function as the spokesperson. The spokesperson's job is to communicate pertinent information to the congregation and any outside people, such as the media.

Identify Potential Contingencies

Those responsible for the various ministry areas, who are the members of the team, will need to identify potential contingency situations for their areas, much as I have done in the examples above. This involves them in scenarios (see appendix B). They and any workers under them must imagine numerous scenarios or ask what-if questions: What if such and such happened? What should I do in such a situation? Try to consider every possible contingency, good or bad, that is realistic for this particular ministry.

Determine the Steps for Each Contingency

As you work through the process for handling the various crises, write this information down in the form of steps to be taken. For example, if someone experiences a heart attack during the worship service, what steps will the team of ushers take to deal with this crisis? Here is a possible plan:

1. One usher will go and sit next to the person to provide whatever immediate help is necessary.

2. Another usher will notify a physician in the congregation and direct that person to the heart attack victim.
3. An usher will call for an emergency vehicle.

Contingency Prevention

As they think through the various steps needed, your people will quickly realize that a contingency may have a preventive as well as a corrective side. They will begin to come up with ways to prevent certain contingencies from taking place. For example, the nursery team could require that only the person who checks a child into the nursery is able to pick up that child, unless he or she leaves different instructions. Such a policy would prevent an estranged spouse or some other person from kidnapping the child.

Legal Aid

You would be wise to ask an attorney to review your contingency plan. It is possible that it could put the church at risk legally in some way. Areas of risk include the termination of a staff person, giving references for former staff and personnel, church discipline, sexual harassment, and sexual molestation. The attorney may also need to instruct the ministry's spokesperson on what to say and what not to say from a legal perspective.

Communicate the Contingency Plan

Each member of the planning team must communicate its contingency plan to those who need to be aware of it. The members should ask, Who needs to know of this plan? Who will be affected by it? They must inform anyone who needs to know the plan but didn't help develop it. In most cases the people who receive the ministry need to be aware of the contingency plan. In the nursery illustration above, the mothers and fathers who check their children into the nursery must know the policies governing the nursery's ministry to them.

You may communicate the plan verbally and in writing. When the nursery team meets, the director can briefly review the plan and any changes. She or he could ask for additional input as well. The director could also pass out a copy of the plan to all who are on the nursery team, post a copy inside and outside the nursery, and mail copies to the parents who regularly put their children in the nursery during the church's services or classes.

Operate with Integrity

It is important that Christian organizations operate like Christian organizations. They must "walk their talk" (Eph. 5:1–21; Phil. 2:12–18).

Those outside the Christian faith carefully scrutinize professing Christian organizations such as churches to see if they live up to their profession. Those in the media seem to take pleasure in exposing the hypocrisy of ministries that fail in some way.

The Proper Response

What should churches do when they have made some error in judgment whether intentionally or unintentionally? Should they come clean and admit their mistake, or should they remain tight-lipped?

The church should first seek the advice of a good attorney in these situations. It is wise not to make any statements before all the facts are in because the church could mistakenly admit to something it did not do. However, if it becomes clear that the church is wrong, then the leadership needs to acknowledge the truth and ask for forgiveness from those who have been affected. Proverbs 28:13 says, "He who conceals his sins does not prosper, but whoever confesses and renounces them finds mercy." God wants to use us to build a Christ-honoring church, not a Christ-detracting church. Not only is truth telling the right thing to do, it also defuses irate people. They want to know the truth, and that is what you must tell them.

How should the church respond to the media in a crisis? Being dishonest with the media will only work to escalate the crisis in a way that is staggering. This will serve to destroy any present and future credibility with the press and the viewing public.

A Positive Example

A good example of holding integrity in such a contingency situation is the Johnson & Johnson Company mentioned earlier in this book. When they discovered that someone had laced some of their Tylenol capsules with cyanide, they did not hesitate to pull the product off every shelf in the country, even though it cost them more than one hundred million dollars. Later they reintroduced Tylenol when they had developed a tamperproof cap. If organizations that do not profess to be Christian operate with integrity, then an organization that represents Christ to a lost and dying world must operate with the same or higher integrity.

Look for the Opportunities

Earlier in the chapter I gave the four stages of a crisis. The third is the chronic or cleanup stage. It is a period of recovery, healing, and self-analysis. Once the ministry reaches this stage, it should look for any potential ministry opportunities arising from the crisis.

Developing a Contingency Plan

1. Select a planning team.
2. Identify potential contingencies.
3. Determine the steps for handling each contingency.
4. Communicate the plan to all who are affected by it.
5. Operate with integrity.
6. Look for opportunities to minister.

Revisit Romans 8:28 and ask, How does God want to use this situation for good? What good can come of it? How might God want to use us to accomplish his good? The answer may or may not be evident. However, if you are not looking for the ministry opportunities, you will miss them, even though they may be staring you in the face.

One opportunity that will always be present is the evaluation of the contingency plan itself. You should view the chronic or cleanup stage as an opportunity for self-assessment, modification, and the fine-tuning of the plan. Ask, What did we do well? What did we not do well? What changes should we make in our plan so that it will work better the next time? This provides an excellent opportunity to make any midcourse corrections that will serve to improve the plan.

Questions for Analysis and Discussion

1. What contingencies has your ministry faced in the last year or two? Were they good or bad? Did they catch you by surprise? How well did you handle them? Did they help or hurt the ministry?

2. Did this chapter or your own experiences convince you of the need for contingency planning? Why or why not? Do you have a contingency plan? Why or why not? If no, do you plan to develop one for the church?

3. Who in the church is the best person to lead the contingency planning team? Why? Will this person also be the spokesperson? Who will be the backup? Who in the church should be a part of the planning team? Why?

4. Make a list of the potential contingencies your church might face in the next five to ten years. Put them under the headings of good and bad contingencies. Do some of the potential crises in this chapter appear on your list? What additional contingencies are on your list that were not in this chapter?

5. What are the steps that your team has developed for each potential crisis? What preventive steps might the various ministry areas take now to head off a potential crisis? Will you have an attorney review your plan or questionable parts of the plan? Why or why not?

6. Who needs to be aware of the contingency plan? How will you communicate the plan to these people? What can be communicated verbally? What should be communicated in writing?

7. How important is it to you and the other leaders that you maintain integrity throughout a ministry crisis? Why? How do you plan to handle "outsiders" such as the media?

8. Identify the last major crisis situation in your church. When was it? What ministry opportunities did this contingency provide for your church? Did you miss them or take advantage of them?

11

Evaluating the Ministry
How Are We Doing?

The idea of having someone evaluate you as a leader and pastor or evaluate the ministry of your church can be frightening and intimidating. Who in their right mind would invite personal or ministry critique? Some would argue that we should not evaluate the church or its people because it is a spiritual, not a secular, undertaking. Only God should appraise a spiritual ministry such as a church. I would argue that we must not allow fear and personal feelings of intimidation to get in the way of honest, objective feedback. That a ministry is a spiritual endeavor is more an argument for than against healthy critique.

Ministry Analysis
Values Discovery
Mission Development
Environmental Scan
Vision Development
Strategy Development
Strategy Implementation
Ministry Contingencies
Ministry Evaluation

Far too many churches have offered up ministry mediocrity under the guise of "it's a spiritual undertaking for God!" Scripture encourages God's people to give and do their best for him. Israel was to bring their best animals for sacrifice (Lev. 22:20–22; Num. 18:29–30). When they did not bring the best, it was an indication that their hearts had wandered from God (Mal. 1:6–8). In Ephesians 6:5–8 and Colossians 3:23–24, Paul teaches that God expects us to give only our best in our work. We are to do our work as if we are working for God. When Jesus turned the water into wine at Cana, it was the best, not mediocre, wine (John 2:10). If God gave his best for us when he gave his Son (John 3:16), how can we not give our best for him?

Even if a church doesn't invite critique, it takes place. It takes place every Sunday on an informal level. People are very discriminating. On the way home from church, a husband naturally asks his wife, "What did you think about the sermon?" Or, "Do you like the new Sunday school class?" Some go so far as to have roast pastor or roast church for Sunday lunch. Seeker church pastors are quick to remind us that when lost people visit our services, they do so with a critical eye. If ministry evaluation takes place on an informal level, why not move it to a formal level so that we can benefit from it rather than be a victim of it?

Every leader should ask, Am I evaluating my ministry effectiveness and do we evaluate the effectiveness of the church? Personal ministry and church ministry appraisal are necessary to refine any work for God. When you avoid honest, objective assessment, you are opting for comfort over courage and ministry mediocrity over meaningful ministry.

Evaluation is not foreign to the Scriptures. While no examples exist in the New Testament of a church passing out some kind of performance appraisal, that does not mean that they did not appraise their people and ministries, nor does it mean that we do not have the freedom to do so.[1] In 1 Timothy 3:1–13, Paul gives the qualifications for deacons and elders. That means that some kind of evaluation was made or such qualifications would not have made sense. In 1 Corinthians 11:28, Paul preached healthy self-examination to the members of the church at Corinth. He encouraged them to examine themselves before taking the Lord's Supper. This would result in the proper proclaiming of the Lord's death (v. 26) and preclude judgment (vv. 29–32). Again, in 2 Corinthians 13:5–6, he tells the people of the church to examine and test themselves to see whether they are in the faith. To fail such a test would have been a calamity. But he seems to indicate that not to test oneself would be an even greater calamity. Just as an unwillingness to measure one's spiritual condition makes spiritual growth nearly impossible, so failure to measure a church's effectiveness makes its growth nearly impossible.

Performance appraisal is the final step in the strategic thinking and acting process. It assumes that the church has analyzed its ministry, discovered its core values, and developed a mission. It regularly scans its environment, has developed a vision and strategy, is implementing the strategy, and is prepared for contingencies. With these in place, the ministry seeks to answer the fundamental question, How are we doing? Without valid critique, the ministry, as well as the process, is quick to go to seed. This final chapter will cover the purposes, personnel, and process of evaluation.

The Purposes of Evaluation

In spite of what I have said above, not everyone is convinced of the need for personal and ministry appraisal. Those who are convinced of the need should have a rationale for careful, objective feedback. The purposes of evaluation demonstrate the need. No fewer than six purposes of evaluation exist.

Evaluation Accomplishes Ministry Alignment

As we have seen, the values, mission, and vision statements of a church are very important, and many leaders will be tempted to spend too much time drafting and redrafting them. It is critical to the organization that they move on to aligning their ministry with the values, mission, and vision. There is a wide gap between a ministry that has drafted statements of values, mission, and vision and a ministry that is visionary and mission directed. Accomplishing alignment bridges the gap, preserving the ministry's core values, reinforcing its vision, and catalyzing constant movement toward the mission.

To accomplish alignment, we must first discover what is out of alignment, and this involves evaluation. Leaders and their people look around the church, talk to other people, gain feedback, and critique what is taking place. A sample evaluative question is, If this is our mission as a church, what are the obstacles that are in the way of accomplishing this mission? Where are we out of alignment?

Evaluation Prioritizes Ministry Accomplishment

I referred earlier to the saying in some ministry circles—what gets evaluated gets done. We evaluate some things and do not evaluate others. What we choose to evaluate sends a message to our people. It says this is important; whereas, something else is not important or not as important. For example, if every Sunday several people in the congregation evaluate the worship service and the sermon, this signals to those involved—the worship team and the pastor—that these are high-priority areas of ministry. The result is that the worship team focuses on the worship service, making it the best it can be.

Evaluation Encourages Ministry Assessment

A third purpose for appraisal is ministry assessment. People need to know the answer to the question, How am I doing? It is not unusual for a person to spend a year or more in ministry, thinking that all is at least okay or even good, only to discover, when he or she is abruptly dismissed, that it was not good. This is unfair to that person. He or she needs an early-warning system.

Some churches respond to poor job performance in another way. They simply refuse to deal with individuals who do not have the abilities to do their job, who constantly show poor work habits, or who may be abusive. These churches feel that they are being nice to these people, or they feel sorry for them, or they worry about what others will think if they dismiss them. The problem with this thinking and practice is that it makes everyone else's job more difficult. Others have to pick up the slack, or, in some cases, take unnecessary abuse. Long-term bending over backwards for and coddling this kind of worker weakens, frustrates, and diminishes the entire organization.

A fair approach in every employment situation is regular ministry appraisal when a supervisor or mentor identifies problems and deficiencies as well as strengths. When this is done, the person knows where the problems lie and what he or she must do to improve. These areas are reviewed again at the next appraisal. If no progress is made or can be made, the church has proper grounds for dismissal, for discipline, or for shifting the individual to another ministry within the church.

Evaluation Coaxes Ministry Affirmation

In my experience as pastor of three churches and as interim preacher in numerous churches across several different denominations, I have learned that the people who make up the average church tend not to affirm those who are serving them well, whether on a pastoral or lay level. They appreciate excellence in ministry but are slow to affirm those who achieve it. I believe that they assume the individuals who serve well are aware of their accomplishments and the impact they are having. However, this is usually not the case. Proverbs 16:24 says, "Pleasant words are a honeycomb, sweet to the soul and healing to the bones." Who does not look forward to the day when the Savior will say, "Well done, good and faithful servant"?

How can we regularly affirm those in our churches who minister well? The answer is regular evaluation. Most turn up their nose at evaluation because it frightens and even intimidates them. However, identifying problems is only one side of evaluation. The other side is affirmation. If we evaluate workers several times a year, then even when no one else affirms them, they will receive needed, valued affirmation during those times.

Evaluation Emboldens Ministry Correction

Affirmation is one side of the appraisal coin; correction is the other. The word sounds ominous and conjures up images of difficult times, times of discipline and chastisement. Some hear the word *correction* and envision a harsh father with a strap in his hand. While correction frightens most of us, it is a much needed but most often neglected aspect of leadership and pastoral ministry. No one wants to do the correcting or chastising or be the object of them, but in a fallen world it has become a necessary fact of life. Scripture teaches that God corrects and even disciplines us for our good (Heb. 12:10).

When assessment takes place, we discover that all of us have areas that need correction. We have blind spots. They are things we may not perceive as problems but they hamper our ministry efforts. These could include a distracting mannerism, tone of voice, or gesture that detracts from a pastor's message; an annoying sense of humor; or inappropriate clothing for the job. Most people can correct these after they are made aware of them, but it will not happen unless some kind of appraisal system is in place to call attention to the problem.

Correction is also needed when the sinful nature, as Paul calls it in Galatians 5:16–21, is allowed to dominate. The acts of the sinful nature indicate that one is not being led by the Spirit (vv. 17–18). This happens far too often in ministry. How do leaders know when the sinful nature predominates in their life? Hopefully someone will confront them. This is not likely to happen, however, unless a regular performance-appraisal system provides the opportunity to surface and deal with the problem.

Evaluation Elicits Ministry Improvement

Inviting and accepting critique is difficult, but the result can and must be learning that leads to improvement. Obtaining objective feedback from someone who is more experienced and qualified in our area of ministry is invaluable for those who desire to be the best at what they do for the Savior.

As hard as it is to hear, we desperately need people in our life who will bravely and honestly tell us when something is not working. This is how we get better at what we do. If we choose to immerse ourselves in a com-

The Purposes of Evaluation

- Evaluation accomplishes ministry alignment.
- Evaluation prioritizes ministry accomplishment.
- Evaluation encourages ministry assessment.
- Evaluation coaxes ministry affirmation.
- Evaluation emboldens ministry correction.
- Evaluation elicits ministry improvement.

fortable, nonconfrontive ministry cocoon, we will likely create ministry that is much less than it could be for Christ. We need people—hopefully but not necessarily loving people—who provide an objective, informed perspective of what we are attempting for Christ.

I cannot emphasize enough the importance of good ministry appraisal. The benefits far outweigh the disadvantages. However, some liabilities do exist, and you must watch for these. First, evaluation has the potential to terrify volunteers, especially those in up-front positions. The thought that someone is critiquing them is often unnerving. Second, in situations where you ask someone to evaluate you, you are giving that person a certain amount of authority over you—be careful whom you choose. Third, too much evaluation can create an environment of constant criticism in the church. Ask, have we become more critical in a negative sense than we were before we started the evaluation process? Fourth, an overemphasis on assessment can destroy enthusiasm, creativity, and spontaneity in the ministry.[2]

The Appraisers

People are the gist of any appraisal system, doing evaluation and being evaluated. The people who do the appraisal can be divided into two groups: the insiders and outsiders.

The Insiders

The insiders are the ministry constituents. They are the people who have shown a long-term interest in the church. They consist primarily of the ministry's members and regular attenders.

Some Potential Appraisal Liabilities

- Can terrify volunteers
- Grants some authority to the appraiser
- Can create a critical environment
- Can destroy enthusiasm, creativity, and spontaneity

Members

The members are the key to the church's present and future. They are the staff, boards, and laypeople who believe in and have committed themselves to the ministry through their membership. They have bought into the church's values, mission, vision, and strategy. At Northwood the board critiques themselves and others. Naturally the staff is heavily involved in assessment. They and the board are the engines that drive all assessment. If they are not willing to critique and be critiqued, we cannot expect others to do what they will not do.

Attenders

Every church also has a number of regular attenders. They are people who have not joined for various reasons. Some, for example, are not sure if they agree with the church's core concepts. Others are slow to commit because they shy away from commitments in general or they have been abused in other churches and need a little time and space before coming on board.

I believe that we should ask them to evaluate the ministry as well. They may view the church in a totally different light than the members. Often members are blind to certain inadequacies that others see clearly. For example, nonmembers may like the pastor's sermons but not want to join a church that does not maintain its facilities. However, the members have become accustomed to poor facilities and no longer notice that they are in such poor condition.

Others

We expect others in leadership positions to appraise themselves and the ministries they lead. The person who leads the nursery ministry, for example, is responsible for personal and departmental critique. The person who leads the youth ministry, staff or otherwise, is responsible to critique him- or herself and those who minister in the youth area.

We also invite other members and nonmembers to critique our ministry. We provide what we call "Com Cards" (communication cards) in the worship service so that our people can easily communicate with us. These cards provide a readily accessible vehicle for feedback of any sort. Periodically we ask certain members and nonmembers to evaluate the worship services or the sermons.

The Outsiders

The outsiders are the church's visitors. They consist of several different kinds of people. Some are churched Christians who have been active in other churches in the area, but for some reason they are looking for a new church home. Others are unchurched people, both Christians and non-Christians.

A phenomenon of the last half of the twentieth century has been the growth in the number of unchurched people across North America as well as much of Europe. In the United States the number of unchurched ranges from 60 to as high as 80 or 90 percent of the population. The south has the highest number of churched people, and the northwest and some portions of the northeast have the lowest number. In Europe the number of unchurched people is even higher. When I ministered in Amsterdam, for example, Christians in that city estimated the unchurched to be 97.5 percent of the population.

Some churches are not only aware of unchurched people, but they have designed their strategies to include reaching out to the unchurched, as well as addressing the needs of the churched. That is a part of our strategy and mission at Northwood. We have found that when unchurched people attend Northwood, they come to the morning worship service. This is because many prefer anonymity, and the worship service provides that.

Since some churches seek to reach the unchurched, they would be wise to ask for their evaluation of the church and all that it does. At Northwood we want to know if we are doing something that needlessly turns lost people off to spiritual things. We must never compromise the gospel. If unchurched lost people are going to stumble over anything, we want it to be the gospel (1 Cor. 1:23) and not a matter of church culture. The only way we can know this is to ask them to appraise what we are doing.

People and Ministries That Are Appraised

The Ministry Personnel

The ministry personnel comprise the members of any boards, pastoral and administrative staff, ministry leaders, and those full- and part-time workers in each ministry area. At Northwood we attempt to assess all of these people at some time during the year. Thus I think that it is important that we apprise them of this when they first agree to be involved in some way on the ministry team. It is not the first thing that I mention, but I do cover this when we recruit individuals for service.

Because appraisal can be most intimidating to people, especially volunteer laymen and laywomen, I suggest that the pastor or senior pastor take some time with the topic of evaluation so the people fully understand its importance and process. Make it the occasional topic of a sermon. Explain its purpose and benefits when you give and receive evaluation. I try to sell our people on evaluation so that they believe in it and will want to be evaluated. I want it to be a positive, growing experience for them. Though all of us feel varying degrees of intimidation before an appraisal, if we are doing our jobs as unto the Lord, then the actual appraisal will turn out to be a time of affirmation more than correction. We should find out more about what we are doing well than what we are not doing well.

The Ministry Products

What gets evaluated? Not only do we evaluate our people, but we must evaluate what they produce in ministry—their ministry fruit (John 15:16). For example, products of the board and staff are the church's core values, mission, vision, and other vital concepts. We must evaluate them. Other products are the various church programs such as the worship, youth, children's, evangelism, and other key programs of the church; the bulletins; attendance; finances; small-groups meetings; and so on.

At Northwood we wanted to know how people—especially visitors—feel about the morning worship service, so we designed a special form that has undergone some revision since the original (the first item in appendix I). We also developed one for our members and regular attenders (second item in appendix I). If our products of ministry are to improve and bring honor to the Savior, then it is imperative that we place them under the microscope of appraisal.

Conducting the Evaluation Process

- Put a qualified person in charge of the process.
- Design good appraisal forms.
- Determine who will evaluate each team member.
- Decide who will review each evaluation with the person evaluated.

The Process of Evaluation

We know why evaluation is important, who evaluates, and who and what is evaluated. But how do we accomplish evaluation and what process is best? In this final section I answer two questions: How do you conduct evaluation and How often do you do it?

How Do You Conduct Evaluation?

A valuable, objective appraisal process has several requirements.

Put a Qualified Person in Charge of the Process

It is important to put a qualified person in charge of the evaluation process. Someone has to be responsible for evaluation, or like so many other good things in ministry, it will not happen. In a small church this often is the pastor. I suggest, however, that he find a gifted, talented layperson who can take full responsibility for the appraisal process and then report the findings to the pastor. People who can do this exist in practically every ministry. They are not always aware of their abilities in the area of appraisal or may not be aware that the church needs their help. Many people experience evaluation and review in their job, and some of these, no doubt, may be responsible for doing it. Find these people, train them to exercise this ministry in the church, and then release them to ministry.

In larger churches a pastor, administrative pastor, or administrative staff person could take responsibility for the evaluation program. Many of the new-paradigm churches have begun to recruit and use pastors for assessment. Using titles such as Pastor of Evaluation and Assessment or

Pastor of Involvement, these people serve in a twofold capacity. First, they help laypeople discover their divine designs and then help them use those designs in service to God. Second, they are responsible for performance appraisal.

Design Good Appraisal Forms

The next requirement is the design of good appraisal forms. At the core of appraisal is the questionnaire. As I noted in chapter 8 on ministry strategy, we use job or ministry descriptions at Northwood. We take time with these and work hard on them so that our people know precisely what our expectations are. We use them for recruitment and guidance in ministry and also for evaluation. At Northwood we simply take the job description and convert it into an appraisal questionnaire. I have placed a sample of the ministry description for our Christian Education Director and his ministry appraisal as the third and fourth items in appendix I. The fifth item in appendix I is the general appraisal of the Christian Education Director. It asks the evaluator to appraise such things as the director's job knowledge, quality of work, productivity, character, and other areas pertinent to the position. Every person evaluated is involved in designing his or her evaluation questionnaire. This has relieved much of the anxiety for some over the appraisal process.

Determine Who Will Evaluate Each Team Member

Next you must determine who will evaluate each team member. At Northwood we use three-hundred-sixty-degree evaluation. This means that a person is evaluated by his or her supervisor, peers, and those who minister under him or her. For example, those on the church leadership board evaluated one another, and the staff, who are under the board, evaluated each board member. The senior pastor evaluated each staff person, the staff evaluated one another, and anyone responsible to the staff evaluated them as well. All team members also complete a self-appraisal, thus they evaluate themselves. We highly recommend three-hundred-sixty-degree evaluation.

Decide Who Will Review the Evaluations

The staff member or layperson responsible for a certain program is usually the best person to review each evaluation with the person evaluated. At Northwood, however, we found that some were uncomfortable with this. Consequently we worked out the following procedure for evaluation review on the board level. The chairman of the church leadership board meets with and reviews the appraisals of all the board members. As the senior pastor, I am an elder and thus a board member of the church. Therefore, the chairman reviewed my evaluation with me as well as the other board members. As pastor, I, in turn, reviewed his with him and reviewed each of the staff.

How Often Do You Conduct Evaluation?

The ministry team must determine the frequency of appraisal. This will vary, depending on the personnel or product evaluated.

At Northwood we opted for the following. We evaluate our ministry personnel (leadership board and staff) twice a year. We agree with W. Edwards Deming, the patron saint of the Total Quality Revolution, who has argued that in the corporate world if managers had to go a whole year before evaluating employees, a review would be ineffective. Instead, he believed evaluation needs to be an ongoing, not merely a yearly process. Workers need immediate feedback when they do something well and when they do something poorly. Waiting a year to tell them is too long. We also asked those responsible for ministry areas such as the small groups and nursery as well as our teachers to assess themselves and their programs twice a year.

The staff and board evaluated the core values, mission, and vision once a year. Much of this involved tweaking a word here and there, especially in the vision statement. However, we reviewed the strategy at least twice a year because we felt that we must regularly update it to remain on the ministry cutting edge.

Frequency of Evaluations

Who/ What	Frequency
Core values, mission, and vision	yearly
Board	twice a year
Staff	twice a year
Program leaders	twice a year
Sunday school teachers	twice a year
Strategy	twice a year
Implementation review	monthly
Attendance, giving, and esprit de corps	weekly
Worship service	weekly

There were several areas that we attempted to scrutinize weekly. Some are what we refer to as our ministry "vital signs": attendance, giving, and congregational esprit de corps. We also asked for weekly feedback on our worship service from selected members and visitors.

Finally, on a monthly basis, we reviewed the implementation of the church's strategy. In chapter 9, I covered the monthly implementation review (MIR) meeting. The primary purpose of this review was to make sure that the responsible persons actually implemented the various phases of the strategy. If we found they had not, we tried to determine why not. Consequently, the MIR also serves to critique the implementation process.

Questions for Analysis, Discussion, and Action

1. Are your present operating ministry practices, strategies, structures, and systems in alignment with your core values, mission, and vision? Why or why not? Do you have some type of formal ministry appraisal currently in place? If yes, what is it? If no, would one enhance the accomplishment of your ministry?

2. What are your personal feelings about having someone evaluate you and the ministry you lead? Why do you feel this way? Will your feelings encourage or discourage the implementation of a performance appraisal system?

3. Do people in your ministry know how they are doing? Do you know how you are doing? Does the church regularly affirm its people? If yes, how? If no, why not? Does the church regularly correct its people? If yes, how? If no, why not? Does your ministry elicit improvement from your members? If yes, how? If no, why not?

4. Having read this chapter and the section on the purposes for evaluation, are you convinced of the need for appraisal in your ministry? Why or why not? Will you follow through and implement an appraisal process in your ministry? Why or why not?

5. Who are the people who might do evaluation? Do you have enough people? Are they insiders, outsiders, or both? Why would you want outsiders to appraise your ministry or certain parts of it, especially lost people?

6. Make a list of whom and what you would like to see evaluated in your ministry. Did you include yourself? Why or why not? Are you

attempting to appraise too much or too little? What are the disadvantages of either extreme?

7. Who would be the best person to take responsibility for performance appraisal? Why? Would some of the appraisal forms in appendix I help you design your own forms?

8. Who will evaluate each team member? Will you attempt to implement a three-hundred-sixty-degree evaluation system? Why or why not? Who will review each evaluation with the person evaluated? Are they the best or only people available?

9. Go back to the list you made in question 5 above. How often will you evaluate each person and product? Is it often enough to make evaluation worthwhile? Is it too frequent and thus unrealistic?

Appendix A

Readiness for Change Inventory

Directions: Each item below is a key element that will help you evaluate your church's readiness for change. Strive for objectivity—involve others (including outsiders) in the evaluation process. Circle the number that most accurately rates your church.

1. **Leadership.** The pastor and the church board (official leadership) are favorable toward and directly responsible for change. Also, any influential persons (unofficial leadership: the church patriarch, a wealthy member, etc.) are for change—score 5. If moderately so—score 3. Only the secondary level of leadership (staff other than the pastor and board, Sunday school teachers, etc.) is for change while unofficial leadership opposes it—score 1.

5   3   1

2. **Vision.** The pastor and the board have a single, clear vision of a significant future that looks different from the present. The pastor is able to mobilize others (staff, boards, and the congregation) for action—score 5. The pastor but not the board envisions a different direction for the church—score 3. The pastor and board have not thought about a vision, and/or they do not believe that it is important—score 1.

5   3   1

3. **Values.** The church's philosophy of ministry (its core values) includes a preference for innovation and creativity. Though proven forms, methods, and techniques are not quickly discarded, the church is more concerned with the effectiveness of its ministries than with adherence to traditions—score 5. If moderately so—score 3. The church's ministry forms and techniques have changed little over the years while its ministry effectiveness has diminished—score 1.

5   3   1

4. **Motivation.** The pastor and the board have a strong sense of urgency for change that is shared by the congregation. The congregational culture emphasizes the need for constant improvement—score 3. The pastor and/or the board (most of whom have been in their positions for many years) along with the congregation are bound by long-standing traditions that are change resistant and discourage risk taking—score 1. If somewhere between—score 2.

3   2   1

5. **Organizational Context.** How does the change effort affect the other programs in the church (Christian education, worship, missions, etc.)? If the individuals in charge are all working together for improvement and innovation—score 3. If some are—score 2. If many are opposed to change and/or are in conflict with one another over change—score 1.

3   2   1

6. **Processes/Functions.** Major changes in a church almost always require redesigning processes and functions in all the ministries of the church, such as Christian education and church worship. If most in charge of these areas are open to change—score 3. If only some—score 2. If they are turf protectors or put their areas of ministry ahead of the church as a whole—score 1.

3   2   1

7. **Ministry Awareness.** Does the leadership of your church keep up with what is taking place in the innovative evangelical churches in the community and across America in terms of ministry and outreach effectiveness? Does the leadership objectively compare the church's ministry

with that of churches very similar to it? If the answer is yes—score 3. If the answer is sometimes—score 2. If no—score 1.

> 3   2   1

8. **Community Focus.** Does the church know and understand the people in the community—their needs, hopes, aspirations? Does it stay in direct contact with them? Does it regularly seek to reach them? If the answer is yes—score 3. If moderately so—score 2. If the church is not in touch with its community and focuses primarily on itself—score 1.

> 3   2   1

9. **Evaluation.** Does the church regularly evaluate its ministries? Does it evaluate its ministries in light of its vision and goals? Are these ministries regularly adjusted in response to the evaluations? If all of this takes place—score 3. If some takes place—score 2. If none—score 1.

> 3   2   1

10. **Rewards.** Change is easier if the leaders and those involved in ministry are rewarded in some way for taking risks and looking for new solutions to their ministry problems. Also, rewarding ministry teams is more effective than rewarding solo performances. If your church gives rewards—score 3. If sometimes—score 2. If your church rewards the status quo and has only a maintenance mentality—score 1.

> 3   2   1

11. **Organizational Structure.** The best situation is a flexible church where change is well received and takes place periodically, not every day. If this is true of your church—score 3. If your church is very rigid in its structure and either has changed very little in the last five years or has experienced several futile attempts at change to no avail—score 1. If between—score 2.

> 3   2   1

12. **Communication.** Does your church have a variety of means for two-way communication? Do most people understand and use it, and does it reach all levels of the congregation? If all of this is true—score 3.

If only moderately true—score 2. If communication is poor, primarily one-way and top-down—score 1.

3   2   1

13. **Organizational Hierarchy.** Is your church decentralized (there are few if any levels of leadership between the congregation and the pastor or the board)? If so—score 3. If there are people on staff levels or boards/committees who come between the congregation and the pastor or the board, then more potential exists for them to block essential change—score 1. If between—score 2.

3   2   1

14. **Prior Change.** Churches will most readily adapt to change if they have successfully implemented major changes in the recent past. If this is true of your church—score 3. If some change has taken place—score 2. If no one can remember the last time the church changed or if such efforts failed or left people angry and resentful—score 1.

3   2   1

15. **Morale.** Do the church staff and volunteers enjoy the church and take responsibility for their ministries? Do they trust the pastor and/or the board? If so—score 3. If moderately so—score 2. Do few people volunteer and are there signs of low team spirit? Is there mistrust between leaders and followers and between the various ministries? If so—score 1.

3   2   1

16. **Innovation.** The church tries new things. People feel free to implement new ideas on a consistent basis. People have the freedom to make choices and solve problems regarding their ministries. If this describes your church—score 3. If this is somewhat true—score 2. If ministries are ensnared in bureaucratic red tape and permission from "on high" must be obtained before anything happens—score 1.

3   2   1

17. **Decision Making.** Does the church leadership listen carefully to a wide variety of suggestions from all the congregation? After it has gath-

ered the appropriate information, does it make decisions quickly? If so—
score 3. If moderately so—score 2. Does the leadership listen only to a
select few and take forever to make a decision? Is there lots of conflict
during the process, and after a decision is made, is there confusion and
turmoil?—score 1.

3   2   1

Total score: _____

If your score is:

47–57: The chances are good that you may implement change, especially if your scores are high on items 1–3.

28–46: Change may take place but with varying success. Chances
increase the higher your scores on items 1–3. Note areas with low
scores and focus on improvement before attempting change on a
large scale.

17–27: Change will likely not take place. Note areas with low scores
and attempt to improve them if possible. Consider starting a new
church and implement your ideas in a more "change-friendly" context.

For additional copies write or call:

Vision Ministries International
3909 Swiss Avenue
Dallas, TX 75204
214-841-3777

Cost: $3.00 per copy (includes postage and handling)

For further help

If you desire further help in understanding and implementing change
in your ministry, read *Pouring New Wine into Old Wineskins: How to Change
a Church without Destroying It* by Aubrey Malphurs. You may order from
Baker Book House by calling 800-877-2665.

Appendix B

Scenario Planning

The Air Force first introduced the world to the scenario concept. It used scenarios in World War II to anticipate what America's opponents might do and to prepare alternative strategies. Herman Kahn later brought the concept over into the business world and developed it further, and Arrie DeGeus of Royal Dutch/Schell popularized scenario thinking through his work with that organization.

Scenarios are not plans but hypothetical sketches or stories of what an organization's future could look like. They are potential or possible futures.

Scenario planning is a disciplined method for imagining and examining in the present a church's different possible futures. It simplifies the data into a limited number of possibilities. Creating scenarios and doing scenario planning allow individuals and churches to be proactive more than passive in dealing with the future. They help leaders prepare for whatever may happen.

Scenario planning is accomplished best in a team context. The various team members represent different perspectives that may add important insights and viewpoints to the overall process. With a team it is also easier to do the work of research and information gathering.

Scenario planning takes more time than storyboarding. Time is needed to gather and interact over the material that makes up each scenario. Thus you must approach and use this tool with patience. If you hurry the process, the tool will not help you make good decisions about the ministry's future.

Scenario thinking is more an art than a science. That means that it is more caught than taught, and some people will be better at it than others. Regardless, anyone can learn to do it with some proficiency and benefit from it. Though it is an art and somewhat intuitive in its development, scenario building does have a recognizable process. In *The Art of the Long View*, Peter Schwartz outlines the following scenario-developing process.[1] I would add that from a Christian perspective, a church should bathe the entire process in prayer and the regular study of God's Word. Divine guidance is essential to any decisions that Christians make.

Step 1: Articulate Your Key Decisions

The first step in the scenario-developing process is to articulate key decisions that your ministry will have to make. Decisions are critical to your life and the future of your ministry. They shape life in the future. To a great degree, your life and that of your ministry is the sum of your decisions. Though various events that are beyond your control will affect your ministry, your decisions and reactions to those events *are* under your control and will affect your future as well.

Leading a church in the twenty-first century involves making numerous decisions about the ministry and its future. For example, a number of churches at the beginning of the twenty-first century are in decline. They face major decisions regarding their future: Should we continue to minister as now? Should we consider relocating to another community for ministry? Should we disband, sell our property and facilities, and give the proceeds to another ministry such as a church plant? Other churches are experiencing numerical growth. They also face major decisions regarding their future: Should we start a new S-curve now or next year? Should we expand our present facilities or move to a new location and build a larger facility at that site? Should we add new missionaries or start an aggressive program of church planting? Scenarios lead to a better awareness of a church's future and to better decisions affecting that future.

You must articulate what decisions need to be made before you can make effective ones. Ask, What decisions will we have to make soon? What decisions will have a short- and long-term influence on the future of this church? Some people avoid thinking about the future because it seems like such a mystery. Others may fear the future and what it may bring. Many prefer to just let the future happen and then deal with it. Like the proverbial ostrich with its head buried in the sand, this is a passive approach that leaves leaders and their ministries most vulnerable.

Several questions will help you articulate and make better decisions: Are you aware of the paradigms that inform your assumptions that, in turn, affect your decisions? What is your mindset and what are the church's paradigms that affect your decisions? Are they flexible? For example, is the congregation locked into an old-paradigm ministry mindset or is it open to new paradigms for doing ministry? Exposure to others on the team should help you question your own mindset. What questions should you be asking to make better decisions? You should ask both specific questions that affect your ministry and broad questions related to the world at large. Whereas the first affects your ministry in the immediate, the latter will affect it long term.

Step 2: Do In-depth Research

The second step in the scenario-building process is to do in-depth research. This involves the team in hunting and gathering information that will affect your decisions. But what are you looking for and where should you look for it?

First, you look for trends and information. Schwartz suggests that you pay attention to the following topics.

1. Science and technology are one of the most important drivers of future events. They literally shape the future. Consider new developments in physics, biotechnology, computer science, ecology, microbiology, and engineering.[2] For example, e-mail has the potential to revolutionize communication within churches.
2. Perception-shaping events influence people's thinking. This concerns not necessarily what is actually happening, but what people perceive is happening. You glean this information from television, various polls, and by interviewing people.[3]
3. Music communicates what people are feeling. For example, are people listening to love songs or songs of anger and rage?[4]
4. New knowledge develops at the fringes. Do not ignore unconventional thinkers. People like Albert Einstein started at the fringes.[5]

Second, you need to know where to look. I attempt to keep up with what is happening in the following general subenvironments: society, technology, economics, the political/legal environment, and the philosophical/theological environment. Schwartz suggests that we specifically look in the following places.

1. Remarkable people (those with a finger on the pulse of change). This would include writers, rock stars, computer scientists, busi-

ness people, especially those who differ with you.[6] These people may not be Christians, but that does not mean that they do not see the immediate future.

2. Sources of surprise. Schwartz advises us to read books, specifically those in other disciplines.[7] For example, a pastor could read Bill Gates's latest book.

3. Filters. Filters are primarily editors and newspeople. He suggests that we scan magazines and view CNN.[8]

4. Immersion in a different, challenging environment. Here he is referring to travel and living in another culture.[9]

Another place to look is the ministry or church environment. Seek to stay abreast of what other churches that God is blessing are doing locally and around the world. Ask which might be of help to you and your ministry.

Step 3: Look for Driving Forces

The third step is to look for driving forces. They are the specific trends or factors that will influence the outcome of events, especially in your ministry. We have little control over these driving forces. Our leverage comes from recognizing them and understanding their effects. Some examples are a key person's vision, interest rates, new technology, unsaved people's response to attending church, and others. Two kinds of driving forces will affect your ministry.

The first is predetermined elements. These are predictable or inevitable trends or events. Demographic studies often recognize and inform us of them. For example, demographic studies inform us that another baby boom will occur in the United States during the first twelve years of the twenty-first century. By 2012 the annual number of births may exceed 4.3 million. The question for the church is, What kind of church will reach these people in the year 2020? Another predictable event is the development of new models for churches. Through research you can spot these now and follow their development. Some models will characterize megachurches and will affect numerous pastors and their churches, regardless of their size.

The second driving force is critical uncertainties. They are unpredictable events and trends that tend to blindside us. You wake up in the morning and discover that they have happened unexpectedly. Examples are the gift of a large sum of money to the building fund, the resignation of the pastor, or the conversion of the village atheist.

Determine which forces are significant or most important to your situation and will influence your people and church events. The way to do this is to look at the decision you have to make and ask: Which trends and events will affect it and which will not? Will they have immediate or long-term effects or both?

Step 4: Develop Scenarios

The fourth step is to develop several scenarios. Again, scenarios are hypothetical sketches in the present of what the church might look like in the future. They describe how the driving forces (trends and events) may behave or not behave, based on how they have behaved in the past and realizing they could act differently in the future.

Here is how a typical scenario session works. A scenario-developing team comes together for a day or two after having done their research on the particular decision they are facing. Schwartz suggests that they wrestle with the following questions:

1. What are the driving forces?
2. What is inevitable (predetermined elements)?
3. What is uncertain (critical uncertainties)?
4. How about this or that scenario?[10]

Construct two or three scenarios. (On rare occasions you may want four.) You should limit the number of scenarios because people can handle only so many. As you construct each scenario, ask, What would happen if . . . ? Mix equal amounts of prediction and imagination with your answers. Keep in mind that the primary purpose of this exercise is not to develop accurate pictures of the future as much as to gain a deeper understanding of the forces, trends, or events that will affect your future. Show how different plots handle the same forces. Finally, be open to diverse points of view.

As an example, the following provides one set of possible scenarios. I have applied them to a recent decision that we had to make at the church I pastor, Northwood Community Church, in Dallas. This church is a revitalization effort located in an older, changing community. None of the members live in the community, and the church over the years has failed to have any impact on the people who live there. A large, low-income housing project sits just south of the church's property. A gang of young kids who live in the housing project is systematically damaging the church facilities, and nothing can be done to stop them.

A growing number of churches who find themselves in a similar situation sell their properties to ethnic churches (who are better suited to reach those who have moved into the community) and relocate to an area closer to the epicenter of where the congregation lives. Last year I began to ask our people if they believe that the future of the church is at this location. All said they believe that it is not. Then I suggested that we consider relocating the church closer to where our people live. This would involve purchasing property in a new, growing area. Then we would meet most likely in a nearby strip mall until we could afford to build a new facility on the property. All this is contingent on the church growing while meeting at the new site.

The first scenario is the worst case. Here you ask, What if the worst happens? For Northwood the question is, What if we relocate the church and we fail to grow? The answer is that we would not survive. For us to meet expenses and build a new facility, we would have to expand our giving base considerably. That means new people would be needed.

The second is the best-case scenario. What if the best happens? What if we relocate and things go very well? What if we grow, construct a new facility on the land, and reach many people in the area for Christ? Our research indicated that this was a real possibility. We knew of no churches in the Dallas area who had relocated and died. All had done relatively well. The answer in all likelihood is that we would become a Christ-honoring church that would reach people for him.

The third is the status-quo or "surprise-free" scenario. In Northwood's case, it asks, What if we choose not to relocate? What if we decide to stay in our present facility in our present community? Our research indicated that though the church was experiencing some growth, it was transfer growth, and the church would soon begin to lose a number of its established people who were driving long distances to attend the services. They said, "If the church doesn't move, we will have to leave." The church would probably last a year.

Schwartz has identified several types of scenarios. One is winners and losers—if somebody wins, then somebody has to lose. Another is challenge and response—there will be problems but we will view them as challenges and, somehow, we will survive them. A third is evolution—that involves slow changes in one direction, either in growth or decline.[11] Then he lists other common scenarios such as revolution (a sudden, dramatic change), cycles (history occurs in predictable cycles), infinite possibilities (things will get infinitely better), and the Lone Ranger (the little guy surprises and defeats the big guy).[12]

The Scenario-Developing Process

Step 1: Articulate the key decisions.
Step 2: Do in-depth research.
Step 3: Look for driving forces (influencing trends/events).
  • Predetermined elements
  • Critical uncertainties
Step 4: Develop two or three possible scenarios.
Step 5: Consider the implications.

Step 5: Consider the Implications

The final step in building your scenarios is to consider the implications of the decisions. Ask, How does our decision look in each of the scenarios? Does it look like a good decision in only a few but not all scenarios? Also, ask, What are the implications and consequences of each variable? For example, should Northwood decide to relocate, who will and will not move with us?

Only time will tell which is the more accurate scenario. You would be wise to monitor the key indicators as the future unfolds. Regardless, you will have given the result some thought and will be aware of the driving factors affecting your ministry.

Now all that remains is to make the decision. Ask, What are we going to do? In light of what we have learned from our scenarios, what decision are we going to make?

Appendix C

Values Statements

- Northwood Community Church
  Dallas, Texas

- The Jerusalem Church
  Jerusalem, Israel

- Northwood Community Church (Faith Statement)
  Dallas, Texas

- Fellowship Bible Church of Dallas
  Dallas, Texas

- Lakeview Community Church
  Cedar Hill, Texas

- Willow Creek Community Church
  South Barrington, Illinois

- Parkview Evangelical Free Church
  Iowa City, Iowa

- Findlay Evangelical Free Church
  Findlay, Ohio

Northwood Community Church
Dallas, Texas

Core Values Statement

The following presents the core values of Northwood Community Church. We desire that they define and drive this ministry in the context of a warm and caring environment.

Christ's Headship

We acknowledge Christ as the head of our church and submit ourselves and all our activities to His will and good pleasure (Eph. 1:22–23).

Biblical Teaching

We strive to teach God's Word with integrity and authority so that seekers find Christ and believers mature in Him (2 Tim. 3:16).

Authentic Worship

We desire to acknowledge God's supreme value and worth in our personal lives and in the corporate, contemporary worship of our church (Rom. 12:1–2).

Prayer

We rely on private and corporate prayer in the conception, planning, and execution of all the ministries and activities of this church (Matt. 7:7–11).

Sense of Community

We ask all our people to commit to and fully participate in biblically functioning small groups where they may reach the lost, exercise their gifts, be shepherded, and thus grow in Christlikeness (Acts 2:44–46).

Family

We support the spiritual nurture of the family as one of God's dynamic means to perpetuate the Christian faith (2 Tim. 1:5).

Grace-Orientation

We encourage our people to serve Christ from hearts of love and gratitude rather than guilt and condemnation (Rom. 6:14).

Creativity and Innovation

We will constantly evaluate our forms and methods, seeking cultural relevance and maximum ministry effectiveness for Christ (1 Chron. 12:32).

Mobilized Congregation

We seek to equip all our uniquely designed and gifted people to effectively accomplish the work of our ministry (Eph. 4:11–13).*

Lost People

We value unchurched, lost people and will use every available Christ-honoring means to pursue, win, and disciple them (Luke 19:10).*

Ministry Excellence

Since God gave His best (the Savior), we seek to honor Him by maintaining a high standard of excellence in all our ministries and activities (Col. 3:23–24).*

*These are aspirational values. While they are not yet our values, we are working hard at making them our core values.

The Jerusalem Church
Jerusalem, Israel

The Core Values of the Jerusalem Church

1. We value expository teaching (Acts 2:42–43).
2. We value fellowship (Acts 2:42).
3. We value prayer (Acts 2:42).
4. We value biblical community (Acts 2:44–46).
5. We value praise and worship (Acts 2:47).
6. We value evangelism (Acts 2:47).

Northwood Community Church
Dallas, Texas

Our Faith Statement

Northwood Community Church is an Evangelical Free Church. Thus, the members of Northwood Community Church have adopted the following twelve-point statement of the Evangelical Free Church of America.

1. We believe the Scriptures, both Old and New Testaments, to be the inspired Word of God, without error in the original writings, the complete revelation of His will for the salvation of men, and the divine and final authority for all Christian faith and life.

2. We believe in one God, Creator of all things, infinitely perfect and eternally existing in three persons—Father, Son, and Holy Spirit.

3. We believe that Jesus Christ is true God and true man, having been conceived of the Holy Spirit and born of the virgin Mary. He died on the cross as a sacrifice for our sins according to the Scriptures. Further, He arose bodily from the dead, ascended into heaven, where at the right hand of the Majesty on High, He now is our High Priest and Advocate.

4. We believe that the ministry of the Holy Spirit is to glorify the Lord Jesus Christ, and during this age to convict men, regenerate the believing sinner, indwell, guide, instruct and empower the believer for godly living and service.

5. We believe that man was created in the image of God but fell into sin and is therefore lost and only through regeneration by the Holy Spirit can salvation and spiritual life be obtained.

6. We believe that the shed blood of Jesus Christ and His resurrection provide the only ground for justification and salvation for all who believe, and only such as receive Jesus Christ are born of the Holy Spirit, and thus become children of God.

7. We believe that water baptism and the Lord's Supper are ordinances to be observed by the church during the present age. They are, however, not to be regarded as means of salvation.

8. We believe that the true Church is composed of all such persons who through saving faith in Jesus Christ have been regenerated by the Holy Spirit and are united together in the body of Christ of which He is the Head.

9. We believe that only those who are members of the true Church shall be eligible for membership in the local church.

10. We believe that Jesus Christ is the Lord and Head of the Church, and that every local church has the right under Christ to decide and govern its own affairs.

11. We believe in the personal, premillennial and imminent coming of our Lord Jesus Christ, and that this "Blessed Hope" has a vital bearing on the personal life and service of the believer.

12. We believe in the bodily resurrection of the dead, of the believer to everlasting blessedness and joy with the Lord, of the unbeliever to judgment and everlasting conscious punishment.

Fellowship Bible Church
Dallas, Texas

Our Values

We have ten core values that guide us. These values describe the culture that we seek to create at FBC. We aspire to be . . .

1. **Biblically Faithful:** We make Scripture the final authority rather than church tradition. We seek to be innovative and flexible as long as we do not violate Scripture.

2. **Culturally Relevant:** We try to adapt our ministry to current needs and trends in American life, without compromising biblical absolutes. We attempt to communicate the good news of Jesus Christ to American society in ways it can understand.

3. **Grace Oriented:** We emphasize God's unconditional acceptance and full forgiveness through Jesus Christ. We attempt to motivate people through love and thankfulness rather than guilt, shame, and duty.

4. **Seeker Sensitive:** We know that many who are not yet committed to Christ are attracted to our ministry; therefore, we desire to create a non-threatening environment in which they are free to explore the Christian faith at their own pace.

5. **Growth Responsive:** We appreciate the advantages of a small, intimate congregation, but also feel we should respond to the numerical growth that often results from reaching out to those who are exploring Christianity. We do not set a particular limit on the size of our congregation, but trust God to show the church leadership what our facilities should be and how best to utilize them.

6. **Relationally Centered:** We stress healthy relationships among Christians. We emphasize small groups as a primary means for Christians to care for each other, develop friendships, and share their lives.

7. **People Developing:** We seek to help people grow spiritually. We provide biblical instruction, and we encourage believers to discover and exercise their spiritual gifts.

8. **Family Affirming:** We seek to provide an atmosphere which strengthens marriages and families. We are committed to strong youth and children's programs.

9. **Simply Structured:** We assign the ultimate leadership of the church to elders and the daily operations of the church to paid staff who are responsible to set up effective programs.

10. **Cross Culturally Effective:** We reach beyond our own culture as we seek to have an effective impact on other cultures with the gospel.

Lakeview Community Church
Cedar Hill, Texas

This statement of principles clarifies the attitudes and approaches which will be encouraged in the ministries of Lakeview Community Church. Most of these are not biblical absolutes, but represent our understanding of how to most effectively accomplish our purpose.

A Commitment to Relevant Bible Exposition—We believe that the Bible is God's inspired Word, the authoritative and trustworthy rule of faith and practice for Christians. The Bible is both timeless and timely, relevant to the common needs of all people at all times and to the specific problems of contemporary living. Therefore, we are committed to equipping Christians, through the preaching and teaching of God's Word, to follow Christ in every sphere of life.

A Commitment to Prayer—We believe that God desires his people to pray and that he hears and answers prayer (Matthew 7:7–11; James 5:13–18). Therefore, the ministries and activities of this church will be characterized by a reliance on prayer in their conception, planning, and execution.

A Commitment to Lay Ministry—We believe that the primary responsibility of the pastor(s) and teachers in the local church is to "prepare God's people for works of service" (Ephesians 4:12). Therefore, the ministry of Lakeview Community Church will be placed as much as possible in the hands of nonvocational workers. This will be accomplished through training opportunities and through practices which encourage lay initiation, leadership, responsibility, and authority in the various ministries of the church.

A Commitment to Small Groups—We are committed to small group ministry as one of the most effective means of building relationships, stimulating spiritual growth, and developing leaders.

An Appreciation for Creativity and Innovation—In today's rapidly changing world, forms and methods must be continually evaluated, and if necessary, altered to fit new conditions. While proven techniques should not be discarded at a whim, we encourage creativity and innovation, flexibility and adaptability. We are more concerned with effectiveness in ministry than with adherence to tradition.

A Commitment to Excellence—We believe that the God of our salvation deserves the best we have to offer. The Lord himself is a God of excellence, as shown by the beauty of creation; further, he gave the best that he had, his only son, for us (Romans 8:32). Paul exhorts servants, in whatever they do, to "work at it with all your heart, as working for the Lord, not for men" (Colossians 3:23). Therefore, in the ministries and activities of Lakeview Community Church we will seek to maintain a high standard of excellence to the glory of God. This will be achieved when every person is exercising his or her God-given spiritual gift to the best of his or her ability (1 Corinthians 12).

A Commitment to Growth—Although numerical growth is not necessarily a sign of God's blessing, and is not a sufficient goal in itself, we believe that God desires for us to reach as many people as possible with the life-changing message of Jesus Christ. Therefore, we will pursue methods and policies which will facilitate numerical growth, without compromising in any way our integrity or our commitment to biblical truth.

Willow Creek Community Church
South Barrington, Illinois

Willow Creek's 10 Core Values

1. We believe that anointed teaching is the catalyst for transformation in individuals' lives and in the church.
This includes the concept of teaching for life change—Romans 12:7; 2 Timothy 3:16–17; James 1:23–25.

2. We believe that lost people matter to God, and therefore, ought to matter to the church.
This includes the concepts of relational evangelism and evangelism as a process—Luke 5:30–32; Luke 15; Matthew 18:14.

3. We believe that the church should be culturally relevant while remaining doctrinally pure.
This includes the concept of sensitively relating to our culture through our facility, printed materials, and use of the arts—1 Corinthians 9:19–23.

4. We believe that Christ-followers should manifest authenticity and yearn for continuous growth.
This includes the concepts of personal authenticity, character, and wholeness—Ephesians 4:25–26, 32; Hebrews 12:1; Philippians 1:6.

5. We believe that a church should operate as a unified community of servants with men and women stewarding their spiritual gifts.
This includes the concepts of unity, servanthood, spiritual gifts, and ministry callings—1 Corinthians 12 and 14; Romans 12; Ephesians 4; Psalm 133:1.

6. We believe that loving relationships should permeate every aspect of church life.

This includes the concepts of love-driven ministry, ministry accomplished in teams and relationship building—1 Corinthians 13; Nehemiah 3; Luke 10:1; John 13:34–35.

7. We believe that life-change happens best in small groups.
This includes the concepts of discipleship, vulnerability, and accountability—Luke 6:12–13; Acts 2:44–47.

8. We believe that excellence honors God and inspires people.
This includes the concepts of evaluation, critical review, intensity, and excellence—Colossians 3:17; Malachi 1:6–14; Proverbs 27:17.

9. We believe that churches should be led by men and women with leadership gifts.
This includes the concepts of empowerment, servant leadership, strategic focus, and intentionality—Nehemiah 1–2; Romans 12:8; Acts 6:2–5.

10. We believe that the pursuit of full devotion to Christ and His cause is normal for every believer.
This includes the concepts of stewardship, servanthood, downward mobility, and the pursuit of kingdom goals—1 Kings 11:4; Philippians 2:1–11; 2 Corinthians 8:7.

Parkview Evangelical Free Church
Iowa City, Iowa

Parkview's Values

1. Scripture
A Biblical Message: We are committed to the clear and accurate communication of God's Word in a way that ministers grace and urges obedience (2 Timothy 3:16–17).

2. Creativity
A Fresh Approach: We are committed to forms of worship and ministry that will best capture and express what God is doing in our generation and culture (Luke 5:33–39).

3. Ministry
A Team Effort: We are committed to a team model for ministry and organization that equips and empowers every family, member, and leader (Ephesians 4:11–16).

Findlay Evangelical Free Church
Findlay, Ohio

Distinctives of Findlay Evangelical Free Church

1. A commitment to creative forms and non-traditional methods of ministry.
2. A commitment to godly leadership.
3. A commitment to encouraging all believers to utilize their spiritual gifts.
4. A commitment to a Bible-centered teaching ministry.
5. A commitment to cultivating a Christ-like and loving atmosphere within the body.
6. A commitment to helping Christians develop a life of godliness in all areas of Christian living.
7. A commitment to meeting the material needs of those in serious need, both within and outside our own body.
8. A commitment to cultivating deep abiding relationships within the Body of Christ.
9. A commitment to unity, love, and forgiveness among believers.

Appendix D

Core Values Audit

What are the core values of this ministry organization? Rate each of the core values below from 1 to 5 (1 being the lowest and 5 the highest). You need not be overly analytical. Work your way through the list quickly, going with your first impression. Try to give as few 5s as possible.

_____1. godly leadership
_____2. a well-mobilized laity
_____3. Bible-centered
preaching/teaching
_____4. the poor
and disenfranchised
_____5. creativity and
innovation
_____6. world missions
_____7. people
_____8. attractive grounds and
facilities
_____9. financially responsible
_____10. the status quo

_____11. visitors
_____12. cultural relevance
_____13. prayer
_____14. sustained excellence/
quality
_____15. fellowship/community
_____16. evangelism
_____17. family
_____18. God's grace
_____19. praise and worship
_____20. a Christian self-image
_____21. social justice
_____22. commitment

___23. giving/tithing

___24. counseling

___25. civil rights

___26. Christian education
     (all ages)

___27. the ordinances

___28. equal rights

___29. compassion

___30. growth

___31. community service

___32. the environment

___33. responsibility

___34. the lordship of Christ

___35. dignity

___36. loyalty

___37. fairness and equity

___38. high tech

___39. efficiency

___40. ethnic diversity

___41. enthusiasm

___42. discipline

___43. teamwork

___44. life (prolife)

___45. authenticity

___46. life-change

___47. Great Commission

___48. humor

___49. optimism

___50. flexibility

51. Other: _____

_____

_____

_____

Write down all the core values that received a rating of 4 or 5 (list no more than what you believe are the 12 most important values). Rank these according to priority (place the number 1 in front of the highest, 2 in front of the next highest, and so on).

Appendix E

Vision Statements

- Moses' Vision
  Deuteronomy 8:7–10

- Northwood Community
  Church
  Dallas, Texas

- Lakeview Community Church
  Cedar Hill, Texas

- River City Community Church
  Louisville, Kentucky

- Saddleback Valley
  Community Church
  Mission Viejo, California

- Crossroads Community Church
  Ontario, Ohio

- Willow Creek Community
  Church
  South Barrington, Illinois

- Dr. Martin Luther King Jr.'s
  Vision
  From *"I Have a Dream"*

Moses' Vision

"For the LORD your God is bringing you into a good land—a land with streams and pools of water, with springs flowing in the valleys and hills; a land with wheat and barley, vines and fig trees, pomegranates, olive oil and honey; a land where bread will not be scarce and you will lack nothing; a land where the rocks are iron and you can dig copper out of the hills."

Deuteronomy 8:7–10

Northwood Community Church
Dallas, Texas

Vision is not about reality or what is. Vision is all about our dreams and aspirations or what could be.

At Northwood Community Church, we envision our sharing the good news of Christ's death and resurrection with thousands of unchurched friends and people in the metroplex, many of whom accept him as Savior.

We envision developing all our people—new believers as well as established believers— into fully functioning followers of Christ through people-friendly worship services, Sunday school, special events, and most important, small groups.

We envision becoming a church of small groups where our people model biblical community: a safe place where we accept one another and are accepted, love and are loved, shepherd and are shepherded, encourage and are encouraged, forgive and are forgiven, and serve and are served.

We envision helping all our people—youth as well as adults—to discover their divine designs so that they are equipped to serve Christ effectively in some ministry either within or outside our church. Our goal is that every member be a minister.

We envision welcoming numerous members into our body who are excited about Christ, experience healing in their family relationships and marriages, and grow together in love.

We envision our recruiting, training, and sending out many of our members as missionaries, church planters, and church workers all over the world. We also see a number of our people pursuing short-term missions service in various countries. We envision planting a church in America or abroad every two years.

We envision a larger facility that will accommodate our growth and be accessible to all the metroplex. This facility will provide ample room for Sunday school, small groups, Bible study, prayer, and other meetings.

While we do not believe that "bigger is better," numerical growth is a by-product of effective evangelism. Thus, we desire to grow as God prospers us and uses us to reach a lost and dying world.

This is our dream—our vision about what could be!

Aubrey Malphurs 1/97

Lakeview Community Church
Cedar Hill, Texas

Our comprehensive purpose is to honor our Lord and Savior, Jesus Christ, by carrying out his command to make disciples of all nations (Matthew 28:19–20). Specifically, we believe God has called us to focus on reaching those in Cedar Hill and the surrounding areas who do not regularly attend any church.

In order to accomplish this, Lakeview Community Church will be an equipping center where every Christian can be developed to his or her full potential for ministry. This development will come through: creative, inspiring worship; teaching that is biblical and relevant to life; vital, supportive fellowship; and opportunities for outreach into the community in service and evangelism.

As a result, the Cedar Hill area will be different in ten to fifteen years, with the Christian influence being increasingly felt in homes, businesses, education, and politics. We further intend to multiply our worldwide ministry by planting churches, by preparing our people for leadership roles in vocational ministries and parachurch groups, by sending out missionaries, and by becoming a resource center and model for Texas and the nation.

River City Community Church
Louisville, Kentucky

WE SEE . . .

. . . the light of truth cutting through the darkness!

At River City, we will seek to lead irreligious people from the darkness of separation from God to a relationship with Him by proclaiming clearly and often the truth of eternal life in Jesus Christ. Corporately, we will provide a Sunday morning service that is exciting, interesting, and friendly. We will also have outreach events such as concerts, block parties, sports, and festivals. Individually, the mature, trained followers of Christ will reach out to friends, family, and neighbors.

WE SENSE . . .

. . . the aroma of freedom from a selfish lifestyle!

At River City, believers are encouraged to shed the shackles of harmful and selfish behavior and enjoy the freedom of following Christ. They understand the characteristics of a fully-functioning follower and are challenged to become one. In formal teaching times and small groups, believers find the means for learning how to study the Word, pray to God, share their faith, and practice hospitality.

WE HEAR . . .

. . . the sound of laughter breaking down the walls of silence!

At River City, we will be a family that calls people from the loneliness of isolation to the joy of relationships. We will seek to know, serve, encourage, challenge, and love one another. We will welcome all people regardless of race, sex, or history into our family, just as God has welcomed believers into His family by His grace. We will not be afraid to laugh or have fun.

WE FEEL . . .

. . . the strength of a loving hand training us to serve!

At River City, men and women will receive further training in order to become leaders who make disciples. As a result of our worship, evangelism, assimilation, and leadership training, we will become a church of ministers that carries out the Great Commission, meets the needs of one another, builds safer communities, and glorifies the name of Jesus Christ in the city of Louisville, Kentucky.

Saddleback Valley Community Church
Mission Viejo, California

It is the dream of a place where the hurting, the depressed, the frustrated, and the confused can find love, acceptance, help, hope, forgiveness, guidance, and encouragement.

It is the dream of sharing the Good News of Jesus Christ with the hundreds of thousands of residents in south Orange County.

It is the dream of welcoming 20,000 members into the fellowship of our church family—loving, learning, laughing, and living in harmony together.

It is the dream of developing people to spiritual maturity through Bible studies, small groups, seminars, retreats, and a Bible school for our members.

It is the dream of equipping every believer for a significant ministry by helping them discover the gifts and talents God gave them.

It is the dream of sending out hundreds of career missionaries and church workers all around the world, and empowering every member for a personal life mission in the world. It is the dream of sending our members by the thousand on short-term mission projects to every continent. It is the dream of starting at least one new daughter church every year.

It is the dream of at least fifty acres of land, on which will be built a regional church for south Orange County—with beautiful, yet simple facilities including a worship center seating thousands, a counseling and prayer center, classrooms for Bible studies and training lay ministers, and a recreation area. All of this will be designed to minister to the total person—spiritually, emotionally, physically, and socially—and set in a peaceful inspiring garden landscape.

I stand before you this day and state in confident assurance that these dreams will become reality. Why? Because they are inspired by God!

Taken from *The Purpose-Driven Church* by Rick Warren. Copyright © 1995 by Rick Warren. Used by permission of Zondervan Publishing House.

Crossroads Community Church
Ontario, Ohio

The Vision

The writer of Proverbs wrote, "Where there is no vision, the people perish" (29:18). At Crossroads, it is our desire that you catch the vision

God has given us, that you begin to visualize the invisible. We have worked hard at defining our vision so that it is clear, challenging, and concise. It is our desire that you clearly see the future of the ministry— what it can be and what it must be. But most importantly, we want you to capture the concept of our vision so that it will capture you and provide a foundation for your personal ministry with us at Crossroads.

In part, the vision of Crossroads Community Church is to become a Biblically functioning community. This will become clear as you continue through the notebook. However, our complete vision statement more specifically defines our desires.

Crossroads Vision Statement

The vision of Crossroads Community Church is to creatively implement the Great Commission to build a growing community of churches around the perimeter of Mansfield by planting culturally relevant churches every three years that are committed to dynamic worship of God while extending his transforming grace to reach the unchurched community.

There are five key phrases that outline our vision. They represent the core of our vision and are essential for evaluating, redefining, and sharpening our focus. The five key phrases are:

Creatively Implement the Great Commission—

Jesus summarized his purpose for being on earth in Luke 19:10. He said, "For the Son of man is come to seek and to save that which was lost." In his final instructions he made the purposes of the church clear. "Go and make disciples of all nations, baptizing them in the name of the Father and of the Son and of the Holy Spirit, and teaching them to obey everything I have commanded you" (Matt. 28:19–20). Therefore, our vision includes pursuing the lost in the most culturally relevant format. This includes implementing Christ's commission in both an innovative and creative manner to the unchurched of our community.

Build a Growing Community of Churches—

Unchurched people are nine times more likely to come to a new church rather than an older, established church (*Christianity Today*). We feel that the best means of impacting our area with the transforming message of Christ is to plant culturally relevant churches, like Crossroads, around our community. For us, this means starting a new church every three years in strategic locations so as to build a perimeter of churches around the city.

Committed to Dynamic Worship—

Because our vision is to extend the transforming grace of Jesus Christ, we believe that the most fundamental relationship people can have is an active, living relationship with God through Jesus Christ his Son (John 10:10; Romans 6:23). Our worship services reflect this by promoting creative, inspiring, and authentic worship which demonstrates that God is living and active in this generation; therefore, the most contemporary medium is used to express our worship.

Extending His Transforming Grace—

By the grace of God, the city of Ontario will be a changed community in 10 to 15 years, due to the influence of the Spirit of God through the lives of our people who are devoted to extending the transforming grace of Jesus Christ. It is our vision that the members of Crossroads will take Christ into homes, marketplaces, political arenas, and educational settings. Our Sunday morning service reflects our vision by being a safe place for Crossroads members to bring their friends, relatives, and co-workers. In other words, Crossroads is a safe place to hear a dangerous message.

Reach the Unchurched—

Finally, our vision includes the intentional pursuit of reaching those who have stopped attending, or have never attended a church. In other words, those who have not experienced God's transforming grace.

Placing a vision in print is somewhat like attempting to hold water in your hand. It is nearly impossible! A vision is something that is caught rather than taught. It has been described as a mental picture of the future which finds its realization in the hands of the one who owns the vision. It is our desire that the Crossroads vision becomes your vision; something you "own" and take great pride in seeing fulfilled. In essence, our vision is not something that you can see, but something you must be.

Willow Creek Community Church
South Barrington, Illinois

Vision Night '96
Bill Hybels

Someone was introducing me at a conference not long ago and they introduced me as the senior pastor of the church that had just completed the most astonishing twenty-year ministry run in modern church history. And that person went on describing the various ways that Willow has made contributions to this community and the nation and the world, and I was all embarrassed wishing he would sort of bring it to a close. And then he said to the crowd, that he was introducing me to, he said sort of half jokingly, "We are all wondering tonight, what is Willow Creek going to do for an encore? What is ahead? Is it going to fizzle? Is it going to have another run?" And then he said these words, "And you can bet we will all be watching."

I had sensed that there are a lot of folks inside and outside this church who have been waiting and who are going to be watching what we do in this next season of ministry. For the last several years we have been meeting in leadership teams and we have been asking each other, "Where are we going?" "What is next?" And this has floated around the elders, the staff, the management team, board, pilot groups throughout the church, "Where from here?"

We decided not to try to look twenty years out, that was just a ridiculous prospect. Not even ten years out, but what in the reasonable, the foreseeable future, the next five-year run. And as we have been talking about this, we know five years from now, if the Lord does not return. We know that probably the land will still be like it is and the buildings will still be standing and the gates will still be here, but the question that we have been asking is, "What will the church be like?" "What will this church be like five years from now?" "It is going to be like something. What is it going to be like?"

But then we have refined the question and asked, I think the best question, "What would God love for Willow Creek to look like five years from now?" "What would God like us to look like five years from now?" "What values does God want us to pay special attention to?" "What goals should we set?" "What programs should be launched?" "What should we really focus on?" So after hundreds of hours of prayer and interaction and review, I am going to give you just three great big ideas that the whole vision for the next five years sort of falls out under. Three values that we have to lift up powerfully and live out passionately, and the first one is going to come up on the side screen.

Strategic Focus #1

We feel we need to reach an ever increasing percentage of the Chicagoland area with the gospel message. This one came quickly and it came unanimously. All of us in leadership feel absolutely certain that the next five years must be an all-out full court press to communicate the message of salvation to this community and the greater Chicagoland area. Simply put, friends, we believe God is saying to us as a church, you are not finished yet. We feel that God is saying there are thousands and thousands of lost people who matter to Him, who are not in His family yet, and we feel that God is saying that He is counting on the witness of this church to just burn brightly, brighter than ever in the next five years. To be a beacon of hope to people who are lost and facing a Christless eternity. We feel that God is saying, cast the gospel message out there, and be free with it and even be reckless with it, because there are lots of folks who need to hear who haven't heard it yet.

I fly into Chicago at night on a fairly regular basis and I look out the window and I see the shimmering lights of our city, and I am often reminded of the words of Jesus who looked over a metropolitan area one time and He started crying because He said there are just a lot of wandering sheep down there without a shepherd, without a savior. There are a lot of lost folks there. And I think that as God looks at our immediate community and the greater Chicagoland area, that God weeps as well. There is lots of, lots of work to be done. And again, we just feel that with great clarity that the next five years we need to enter into a time where fruit will be born and where hearts will be redeemed, where lives will be transformed, and where people will turn from sin toward repentance and Jesus Christ in record numbers.

And so as of tonight, the starting gun goes off and we charge into a future that is going to be marked with evangelistic intensity. And I for one just can't wait. It was evangelistic intensity that fueled the launching of this church. We used to pray in small groups in the basement of South Park Church when we were just a youth group before this church. We used to fast and pray for our friends who were outside the faith. And when we started this church, we felt so strongly about it, as you know, we sold tomatoes door to door to just raise enough money to launch the first service so we could pass the gospel out, so somebody who needed to hear it would hear it and come to faith. We're going to get back to that kind of intensity.

This evangelistic intensity will be expressed first and foremost in each one of our lives, all of us who are of the core of Willow Creek here at New Community, because we are all going to receive a new round of training and instruction. How to become contagious Christians ourselves. It doesn't start with me making some big statement about evangelistic intensity. The kingdom of God advances one life at a time. It happens when your heart is changed and you see lost people as Christ sees lost people. And you understand that there is a heaven and that there is a hell and real people go there forever, and you are called as I am called in our individual lives to love lost people and to build relationships with Him, and when the opportunity presents itself to share a bold witness for Christ to them and then invite them to our seekers services as God gives us power and unction to do them here on weekends. But friends, as we announce the new evangelistic intensity, it begins in your heart.

Now the ironic thing is that the last couple years this church and particularly through the association has developed the premier evangelistic training course in the western world. It is called "Becoming a Contagious Christian" and just out of the thousands and thousands of Christ followers in this church there are only one hundred eighty-five people or so who have been through this new training course. And so over the next five years we are going to set as an objective that every single person who considers himself a Christian here at Willow Creek is going to go through the Contagious Christianity course where we learn and relearn and get sharpened and resharpened how to look at a lost world. And how to live in vital union with Christ, such that we are salt with savor, and salt that has proximity to that which it is trying to affect. And where we have evangelistic impact in our individual lives. So we are going to start with us, all receiving additional training.

And then beyond that, we are going to turn up the thermostat at weekend services. I mean, we are just going to do a whole lot more presentations of the gospel, series for seekers. Series like reasons to believe. Lots of outreach kinds of things. We are probably going to have to offer a fourth weekend service. We don't know if it will be on Saturday or on Sunday; we are not sure yet. We are going to work the details out on that later. But you will sense that more and more the evangelistic thermostat of our weekend services will go up.

Because I kind of knew this was coming, just the last couple of weeks when I have been talking about monetary stuff, you notice that I have been ending the messages with a strong gospel approach. This last weekend at one of the services I said, look, we have talked a little bit about moving toward financial freedom. Some of you are still in spiritual bondage and every opportunity I get, and Lee who spells me most of the time at the weekend, we are just going to pledge to you that we are going to look for every way we can to make the gospel message come alive more and more at our weekend services so that you can just invite the friends that you are witnessing to, to come here, and we will help you lead them to Christ.

Another thing that we are going to do is stress throughout all of the small groups, ten thousand people are in small groups in this church, and we are going to pick up that empty chair, that open chair, and we are going to say for God's sake, fill it. For the sake of lost people, fill it. With ten thousand people in small groups if all of us would just invite over the course of the next twelve months or twenty-four months, one lost person to join our small group, just think ten thousand folks can spend eternity in heaven. If all of us in groups would just invite somebody in. Friends, this would be just an unbelievable thing, wouldn't it? We are going to say, start praying to fill that open chair. Make it a group goal. Commit yourself to it. Watch what God does.

We are going to launch Access as an outreach ministry. It has been building a core for the last year or so, but it is going to be an outreach ministry in just a little while. Another thing that we are going to do is go back to the days when we had evangelistic outreach concerts. And when we had pre-evangelistic outreach concerts. Another that I get to announce yet tonight, is just, in the short-term future coming up in here in a few weeks we are going to do the Choice again. It is just a unanimous decision. We are going to have multiple presentations of it. If you are new around here, it is one of the most powerful presentations of the last days of the ministry of Christ, Good Friday, and Easter. We have done it twice before in years past. It is powerful. Lost people respond to Christ when they are invited to it. We want to fill this place 8 or 10 times with people that you invite. And we will do our best to put it on in a way that will just honor Christ. But again we are going to do team evangelism. It is something that we can all do together. You do your part and the music/drama people will do their part. But we want to see thousands of folks be touched with the power of the gospel.

Then we will go to Easter, which will be an outreach-oriented Easter service. The post Easter series is one that I am working on right now that will be just ideal for you to invite friends to. So we are just going to hit the ground running on this. A verse that just keeps welling up in my heart these days, Romans 1:16: "For I am not ashamed of the gospel of Christ, it is the power of God unto salvation." It is what has to be cast out there. The gospel still changes hearts and lives. That is why you are in here tonight, because someone told you that Christ died for sinners and you believed it and it changed your heart. That message is going to go out with frequency and with power like never before.

There is another thing that we are going to do because we want to reach the Chicagoland area. We looked way down the road, and got within a hair's breadth of committing ourselves to starting a couple satellite churches. But, friends, at the eleventh hour and fifty-ninth minute and I am not kidding you, we came dangerously close, right at the end God used one particular individual on our leadership team to say hang on, back it up. Let's take one long look at this again. Who did God make us to be? Who are the leaders of this church? How are they best gifted to have impact around the country and around the world? What is the best usage of the team that God has put together? So we went all the way back to zero and we started again. In the meantime, Jimmy Miato, president of our Willow Creek Association, did some research and found out that there are somewhere between thirty and forty Willow Creek Association churches within a reasonable driving radius in the Chicagoland area. Thirty or forty association churches. And so we started brainstorming and we said, What if we at Willow put a special synergistic emphasis behind those thirty or forty churches and helped them become evangelistically intense, and said let's do that.

Instead of our assuming responsibility for one or two other churches, we could just lift the entire spiritual climate of the Chicagoland area through our existing organization of the association and put special emphasis into those thirty or forty pastors, and we just feel that it is the way God wants us to go. So we are going to work in tight synergy with those leaders.

To make sure that we are not just blowing smoke about this whole goal of evangelism, we have chosen a goal of having a weekend attendance of in excess of twenty thousand people in the next few years. I mean our goal is, we run about fifteen thousand right now, and we want to move that to twenty thousand in the next few years. And Lee Strobel has stepped up, and he has said that he is willing to be the point person, the champion of this stallion. And he will gather other leaders around it to make sure that the entire staff and all the leaders of the church are working together toward this goal.

But I will tell you friends a few weeks ago when we had a baptism up here, God did something in my heart. I barely made it through those two nights, because I think, I think it is because we have sort of been in neutral evangelistically the last couple of years because we have been doing infrastructure rebuilds. I was not meant to function in neutral evangelistically, I will tell you. It has been very difficult. I have been telling the staff, we have been in an unnatural mode through the last three years while we have been rebuilding stuff. I don't think I could have taken it another month or two. At that last baptism service was just person after person after person when I said, have you trusted Christ for the forgiveness of your sins? And they didn't just answer the way we told them to. We said to say yes or something like that. Folks, with tears streaming down their cheeks, they would say yes with all of my heart, yes, you don't know how glad I am that Christ has saved me. I just saw up close and personal again what happens to a human heart when Christ redeems it. And I just thought, that's it, no more neutral, no more neutral. Settle down. We are going, that's it. Okay? There are a hundred churches in neutral within a driving radius of this church. If you like neutral, go there. We are not going to be in neutral. Settle down, we are going that way, let it be clear.

It took days of prayer for me to stay that restrained. I am celebrating a little personal victory that I kept my spirit under control on that one. Let's move onto the second large focus that we are going to be moving toward.

Strategic Focus #2

We are going to move the congregation, of Christ followers, toward community, spiritual maturity, and full participation within the life of the church. If we have learned anything in the past few years, it's that, once a person trusts Christ, the challenge is not over, but just beginning. Our mission statement has always been we are trying to turn irreligious people, not just into Christians, but into what? Say it, fully devoted followers. You didn't say it convincingly. Let's say it once more. We are trying to turn irreligious people into fully devoted followers of Christ. That's right.

What we are saying in the second major value is that in the next five years we would like to see huge progress in this church, in moving Christ followers into community, into spiritual maturity, and into full participation in the church. And we have a long way to go. Here is a staggering statistic that we should not be proud of. Right now 74 percent of people who attend our weekend services say that they are not connected in any meaningful fellowship. Almost 45 percent of the new community, of you gathered here, are not in small groups yet. Listen, friends, God made your heart to yearn for community. You long to know and be known, to love and be loved, to serve and be served, to celebrate and be celebrated. You are not going to be fully whole in Christ until you experience community on a consistent basis.

When a few moments ago, Janice Yarrow, who has served faithfully as an elder for ten years, when she said she was going to transition off being an elder, but she is going to continue to be our small-group leader, when she said she was willing to continue I wanted to sing the Hallelujah Chorus because, when we meet together as elders first hour, we meet in her home and she fixes us a meal and she just shepherds us and she cares for us and she calls us during the week and says, how can I pray for you? Because I love you and I am committed to you, and I get notes from her and the other elders do too. And we enjoy community.

Our management team, we enjoy community. I have told you before, I am at a stage in my life where there are only two things that I want anymore really in life. I want to do God's bidding for my life with all of my heart, but I want to do it in the context of community. I want to do it with people, that I can know and be known with, love and be loved by, serve and serve with and they can celebrate me and I can celebrate them. Friends, the next five years are going to be wonderful years for all of you who are in community and they are not going to be as wonderful as they could be for those of you who are not yet in community. So we are just committed to saying, anybody in isolation that is just unacceptable. We want to encourage you and move you and pull you toward community. We want to move you toward community.

We want to move toward spiritual maturity. John Hartford has just been trying so hard to get us to understand that there are certain practices, there are certain relationships, there are certain experiences that we need to have in order to move toward maturity in Christ. Some of you who have been around this church a long time we like to say, I haven't been a Christian that long. We like to claim baby status. Friends, some of you are not babies anymore. Some of you were baby Christians 15 years ago. You ought to be shaving by now. You can't claim just the milk stuff anymore. You are far past in chronological years, you know, the baby status thing. If you are a year or two or three old in Christ, that is one thing, you can claim you need some diapers yet. The rest of you, it is time that you take responsibility to moving toward fullness of spiritual maturity. And we are going to do everything in our power, mostly here at new community through worship and through teaching and so and then in the small groups to mature you in the faith. There is a whole new spiritual formation emphasis that is coming out up the pike that you are going to be hearing more about. But it is time for the immature to move toward maturity in a very intentional way.

And it also says here that we are going to move the congregation toward full participation within the life of the church. Friends, we have said it over and over again, if this Willow Creek is just a wonderful place to hang around, if you just want to be around a place where there is spiritual vitality where you can be fed, where you can worship, where you can hear great teaching, where you can just have your heart touched consistently week after week after week, then this is the place to hang around.

But you don't want to stand before a Savior who shed His blood for you, you don't want to stand before Him someday and say I never committed myself to the body of Christ at Willow Creek, I never found my spiritual gift, I never put on a uniform and became a part of the serving core of the church. You don't want to have white unstained, uncalloused hands when you put your hand in the bloodstained hand with a hole in the middle of it. You don't want that to happen. And we are going to do everything in our power to move you out of nonparticipation toward participating in the body of Christ.

We are going to fire up the Network Ministry once again. In the next forty-five days you will have an opportunity to go into Network. And this is just like Contagious Christianity, but it is about spiritual gifts. Over the next few years we want every single person who considers himself a core member here at Willow Creek to go through the Network program to find out anew or to have a refresher course on what your spiritual gift is. Some of you thought you knew four or five years ago, but then you never took action on it, you never found a place where you really fit, and where you feel like you are making a difference.

Friends, we are going to be relentless in challenging you to identify your spiritual gift and to get off dead center and to get in the game. Because if you are in community and if you are growing in personal spiritual maturity and if you are a full participating, serving member in the body of Christ, then this next five-year run is going to be a ball. But if you are standing on the sidelines or if you are sitting in the stands, then when we hit the objectives that we are all aiming for and when we are a completely different church, a much more God-glorifying and Christ-honoring church five years from now, and we have some huge celebration where we honor God in that regard, you'll have to sit on the sidelines and say I wasn't a part of that. You don't want to do that. This is your best shot at doing something wonderful with the next five years of your life.

We are all going to make house payments, and we are all going to try to raise our kids, and we are all going to do the mundane stuff that life just includes. What are you going to do that is great for eternity? What are you going to do that is great for the Kingdom of God? What are you going to do that is going to make you feel proud when you stand before your Savior someday with some calouses on your hands saying I was a player? What are you going to do? Well again, we are going to move you relentlessly toward finding your spiritual gift and identifying it, developing it, taking responsibility on yourself to finding a place in the church where you can use that gift. And when you do, and you find a place of joyful service, you will just be so glad.

Now because we want to be very specific about these values, community, spiritual maturity, and full participation within the life of the church, we have set some specific target goals and they are aggressive and there are people taking responsibility in writing point on them. We want to see increased community. We want to move from ten thousand people in the small groups, over the next few years, this next five-year run, to twenty thousand people in small groups. The twenty thousand people who attend the weekend services, that was our first objective that Lee is going to champion, we say everyone who comes to weekend services, anyone who considers Willow Creek a part of their worshiping experience. We are going to try to move them toward participation in a small group. Russ Robinson, whom you saw on the stage here, is committing the next five years of his life to say I and my team will do everything we can do to pave the way, to train the leaders, to open the doors, to allow twenty thousand people to come into community. Friends, if we hit that goal that is going to be one of the most exciting God-honoring goals I can imagine toward increased maturity.

John Orthurg has said, "I will give the next five years of my life toward having eight thousand people become regular worshippers and learners at the new community." John said, "I will be the anchor teacher, I will direct the new community, have Joe and Deter and others lead us in worship" The goal is in the next five years, to fill this place to capacity on Wednesday and Thursday night so that we can just lift voices together and sing, shout to the Lord, and "Shine Jesus Shine," and "How Great Thou Art," and have eight thousand people regularly honoring God and learning together.

And also we have set a goal of having eight thousand participating members in this church. The highest that we have ever had, even under the old membership was two thousand. We were never pleased with that. But we have a membership system now that we just believe it honors God, it is right out of the pages of Scripture. It captures those five G's, grace, growth, group and gifts, and good stewardship. These are things that every Christ follower wants to have true in his or her life.

So here is the deal, we are serving notice. Some of you a little while ago we said, stand if you are already participating members, or if you fully intend on becoming one in 1996. Now there is a whole bunch of you that didn't stand. I am glad that you are here, but expect some heat. I am telling you friends, expect some heat. This is going to be hard for me to say. It is going to be harder for you to hear. Write all the letters you want to write, and don't expect a response, because I am standing on this one friends.

If you are unwilling, over time, to throw your hat in the ring and to say I am willing to get in the game and commit myself to the church that God has called me to, to be a responsible member of this place. If you are just resisting and you say I am not going to do it, I am just going to be a bystander, a fence sitter, someone on the sidelines, then here is what I want to say, sit in another church, because, listen friends, we need that seat opened up for someone who is going to come to Christ and someone who is going to get discipled and join a group and grow in full maturity and become a participating member here. Because listen, this is not about club membership, this is about redeeming the world.

There is a lost and dying world. And it is not going to be reached by folks who just sit on the sidelines. We have to turn a congregation into a mobilized army of people, who in the name of Christ will become players and servers and prayers and givers to achieve the objective that God has in mind for us. So once again, those are hard words and I know some of you are going to be very mad at me, and you are going to say, I like to sit in that church down the block, and I like to sit in this church on this block, and I like to do a little of this and I like to do a little of that. Friends, the heat is going to get so high that you are going to have to make a decision sooner or later. And we just want you, if you want to be a full participating member, a server, a player in the church down the street, get there, go there, be a full player there, but we need to have full players here and we are just going to knock back off that and we are going to head in that direction. As the strong sense of the leadership bodies of this church, so that is where we are going together.

Stretegic Focus #3

We are going to invest a greater percentage of our lives, and our knowledge and our resources with those in our city, our nation, and our world. John 3:16, the most often quoted verse in the Scripture, says, For God so loved, what? the world. God so loved the world. The Great Commission, Jesus said, you go out into the world. You see God always thinks globally, God acts globally, God loves globally, God redeems globally. His heart breaks for the hurting and the poor and the lost, globally. And God has made it abundantly clear to those of us in leadership over the last few years that these beautiful glass walls of this auditorium must never again be viewed as boundaries that hold back the explosive work of the Holy Spirit that is so obvious within these walls. We have the opportunity and even beyond that the responsibility in this new era, we have a responsibility to the world. And we are finally ready as leaders to stop playing down the extraordinary influence that God has given us as a church and we are ready to say, we will take on that responsibility, we will wear that mantle, humbly but seriously and intentionally. And by God's grace we will move out into the world and we will seek in the inner city, the Dominican Republic and various places all around the world. We will seek to expand the Kingdom of God regionally, nationally, and internationally.

This is just not about hype or rhetoric. We already have the infrastructures in place. We have been building them the last three or four years. We have community care ministries right here, a part of our own church here at Willow, that cares for the poor and the suffering among us. Ministries such as the food pantry, fellowship housing, the benevolence ministry, the car ministry and a dozen other ministries that already exist here. They are staffed up, there are volunteers in place. For some of the positions, we need more volunteers, but we are prepared to start to bring a lot of compassion and relief, and hope and help to the poor among us.

And then we have our international ministries department and it is staffed and it is funded and it is ready to go. And they are targeting the inner city and certain emerging churches. And then we have the Willow Creek Association that is staffed and it is working well. It has already linked up fourteen hundred churches around the world and to bring renewal and rejuvenation to them. So I mean we are spooled up, we are ready to release more of our lives, and our knowledge and our resources. And friends, I have to tell you, the world is waiting, the world is hoping, the world is depending on those of us in this church to bring some help and some hope.

In just the last few months, I have visited many of the projects that we are involved in, in the inner city and other places around the world and friends I just want to say this to you, when you go, when you make the visits, when you roll up your sleeves, when you volunteer, when you see God at work amongst the poor, when you see God at work in a foreign culture, you see God at work on the other side of the world that we have been able to influence and help a little bit, I will just tell you, you will never be the same. And so, what we are setting as a target goal, we are setting as a goal that by the year 2000 there will be eight thousand of us per year who are participating in the giving of our lives, in our knowledge, in our resources, to ministries outside Willow Creek. Be it through community care, through international ministries or the Willow Creek Association.

Maybe some of these numbers start making some sense. We are saying we want to see twenty thousand folks at our weekend services, many who are seekers, who are coming to know Christ. And then all of those folks we want to become members of small groups so they are at least moved into community. And then we want to see eight thousand people worshiping and learning at the new community, and eight thousand participating members and that represents the strong mobilized army, the core of Willow. And out of all of that eight thousand numbered group, we want to see every person in that group be involved on an annual basis at least once, going down into the inner city, and working side by side with someone who has only known hardship and tragedy. Or we want to get you onto an airplane to go to the Dominican Republic and help build a home for someone who has never had a home. Or we want to send you somewhere around the world where the association is putting on conferences, where you can help us put on conferences, be it in Germany, or Australia, or South Africa, or Brazil or wherever we are being invited these days to go to try and bring help, and hope, and renewal to the church.

But friends, this is a new day, and I for one am so grateful about this. Because for the last couple of years I have dealt with a lot of guilt, my heart and fundamental calling has always been to be the pastor here at Willow Creek, but every time I felt God leading me to speak to another group of churches, or to a conference at some other place or in another nation, I feel guilty flying away from this church. Sensing that I am shirking my responsibilities here, and lots of times, hundreds of times, before I would land to where I was going to go speak I would just say, that is it. I have just got to stop doing this because I really have to just pay all of my attention back at Willow, what is happening inside the walls. And then I would get up and I would give a talk, and while I would be giving the talk there would be this incredible surge of the Holy Spirit that I could just feel. And the Holy Spirit would say this is part of what I want you to do, and this is part of what I want other people, in and around Willow to do as well. I want you to think wider and more globally. This is the way God thinks. This is the way I want you to think more.

I have had such terrible inner tension in my spirit about all of this. And when the leaders of this church in just the past few years came together and said look we are going to make it intentional that part of what we are about as a church from here on out, this next five-year run is, we are about investing a greater percentage of our lives, that means my life too, and our knowledge, and our resources with those in our city, in our nation, and our world. And I think as eight thousand of us participate in this grand adventure—John Burke on our management team is the person who is writing point on this—I will give the next five years of my life through international ministries, the association, and others, I will give the next five years of my life to involve eight thousand people a year in an experience like that. When that happens to you, it is going to fill you up so full that you are going to wonder why we ever thought less than globally. That is where we are headed in these next few years and I am so glad we are.

The Willow Creek Association has as its goal to move to from fourteen hundred churches that we are helping, that are a member of the association, to four thousand churches. And Jim Miato says, you know he is the president of the association, he is saying I will give the next five years of my life to try to move our core from one thousand four hundred to four thousand churches. And that is an exciting venture. But anyway, those three big emphases, that sort of crystallizes where we are going together. We are going to reach a greater percentage of our community with the gospel. We are going to move our Christ followers here toward community, maturity, and participation in the body of Christ and we are going to invest more of ourselves, and our knowledge, and our resources, around our city and our nation and our world.

Now, friends, I have to say this in closing, we don't have a prayer of reaching these goals without you. I mean, we are not into grandiosity. This is not a few leaders in a room thinking these are great ideas, we think we can pull them off. We have a tremendous sense of humility and inadequacy surrounding each of these goals. But somehow, you know, we just feel that if every single person in this place said, that is it, I mean I will do the mundane stuff I have to do with my regular life, but I am going to be a part of this great adventure. Here is the way I am thinking about it, maybe this will help you. When we celebrated our 20th anniversary, so many folks, hundreds and hundreds wrote letters and said I would have given anything to be a founder. You all here tonight, I mean, you are here as the gun goes off for this five-year plan. You are founders in this five-year run. I mean you are here.

There is a famous verse in the Old Testament Book of Esther, where a man of God says to Esther, maybe in the scheme of God you were appointed to live for just such a time as this. Do you know what I want to say to you? I don't think it is an accident that you are in a room tonight. I think the whole course of your life led up to a point where you would be saved, and growing, and enough of a Christ follower to be sitting in a room tonight with an expectant heart, excited about where your church is going. And I just want to say I think God appointed you for such a time as this and we need you. And I don't want to end this talk by saying, you know, let's have a big applause if you are all with me. Let's have a big stomp your feet if you agree with the leaders that this is the way God is leading the church because that is easy. We could have a big hoopla and get all excited and blow up balloons and so. I don't want to do that, because I think what we are heading into is, I don't want to treat it in any way in a superficial, I don't want to trivialize it.

So I want to ask you to vote for this vision, but I don't want to ask you to vote now or with a vote with your voice or with your hand. I want to ask you to vote in the following ways over the next five years. First I want to ask you to vote with your mind. I want you to go home tonight and I want you to think. I mean really think. Who is going to turn this mess of a world around? Who has any answers to be unraveling in the disintegration that we see happening all around the world? The hope of the world, and I have said it a thousand times, the hope of the world is Jesus Christ and His gospel proclaimed through a local church. It is the hope of the world. And I want to ask you to be thoughtful about that. I want to ask you to say, you know what, I can be a part of the redemptive solution of God to a world that is facing problems that it cannot solve. So I want to ask you to think it through with your mind. And vote with your mind to be a part of this church's great adventure in the next five years and just be real calculated about it. And say, I want a significant part of my mind to be engaged in the adventure of world redemption through this five-year plan.

And then I want to ask you to vote with your heart. I want to ask you to get your heart connected to some loving hearts of other people around here in community, so that all of what flows out in the next five years will flow out of community. It is easy to get our minds fixed on a cause and to lose a sense of doing it together. I hope and pray that will not happen. I mean we are going to become a lot more focused and a lot more intentional but not at the loss of community. So I want to ask you to vote with your heart and to put your arms around some folks and say, with our hearts knit together let's walk in the direction of this great adventure.

And then I am going to ask you to vote with your feet. I talked about engaging in the discipline of assembling. I am going to vote every Wednesday or Thursday night and I am going to vote every weekend. I am going to vote by showing up, by just getting in the car and by coming and praying and supporting. Vote with your feet.

And then I am going to ask you to vote with your hands. Again, hands that are reached out to lost people. Friends, you have got to have your hand out, in the workplace, in the neighborhood, at the health club. You have got to put your hand out to lost people. And I am going to ask you to roll your sleeves up and work with your hands. To find your spiritual gift and to use it. Vote with your hands.

And vote with your lips. I am going to ask you to pray and to pray every day that we will achieve this plan for God's glory. Pray every day that we will push back the forces of evil and that with God's help we will achieve these objectives. And I want to ask you with your lips to worship. To come and just push back the forces of evil with the sheer volume of worship and praise that just turns the evil one to running. Just vote with your lips.

And then I want you to vote with your daytimers. I want you to rearrange your priorities and your schedules so that you seek first the kingdom of God. If you wind up five years from now and you say, you know what? I squandered the run, I just squandered it. I went out and I did that which was okay and I did a little of that and a little of that. I just didn't do the best part. I just never rearranged my life so that I was elbow deep in the best part. Vote with your daytimer.

And finally, vote with your checkbook. Resolve not to miss a single full tithe in this entire five-year run. I hope all of you are taking the teaching on the weekend seriously these days. You rearrange your finances and you say one thing I will not do is rob God or rob this church of the resources it will take to achieve these plans. Rearrange your finances so that you can at least get the full tithe to the work of God here so that we can unleash resources to achieve these objectives. And those of us who have a measure of affluence, now with clear objectives, if we have some extra earning power, let's earn a little extra and let's throw it into the pot and let's say that these are worthy objectives and that it is worth putting some extra resources into. But I will tell you this friends, if you vote that way, with your mind and your heart, and your feet and your hands, and your lips and your schedules and your checkbook. With that kind of investment someday we will achieve these objectives and Christ will be honored and you will be glad. And in heaven when we are all together forever all of us will say, you know that five-year run, that run from the twentieth anniversary to the twenty-fifth anniversary, what a ride, what an adventure, and we did it together.

Let's stand for closing prayer. And now as just a sign of unity, would you take the hand of someone next to you, and let's just connect all throughout the auditorium. Reach across the aisles, and let's commit what we believe are God's plans for the next five years. Just commit them to God. Oh God, I am so grateful that You lead, that You guide, that when leaders humble themselves and bow and pray and discuss that You lift us out of our petty preoccupations, You lift us out of our comfort levels. You show us a world. You show us Your power. You remind us of what our lives are to be about and You give us a dream, and You give us a vision and You call us to pursue it with all of our hearts. So Lord, here we are, hand in hand, heads bowed. May the gun go off. May You be honored and glorified and receive all of the praise when these goals are achieved. And may we just enjoy the adventure, and talk about it for eternity. And everybody agreed together and said, Amen. Thanks everybody.

Recorded by The Prestonwood Pulpit, Prestonwood Baptist Church, 15720 Hillcrest, Dallas, TX 75248

Martin Luther King Jr.

From "I Have a Dream"
August 28, 1963

I say to you today, my friends, that in spite of the difficulties and frustrations of the moment I still have a dream. It is a dream deeply rooted in the American dream.

I have a dream that one day this nation will rise up and live out the true meaning of its creed: "We hold these truths to be self-evident; that all men are created equal."

I have a dream that one day on the red hills of Georgia, sons of former slaves and sons of former slaveowners will be able to sit down together at the table of brotherhood.

I have a dream that one day, even the state of Mississippi, a desert state sweltering with the heat of injustice and oppression, will be transformed into an oasis of freedom and justice.

I have a dream that my four little children will one day live in a nation where they will not be judged by the color of their skin but by the content of their character.

I have a dream today.

I have a dream that one day the state of Alabama, whose governor's lips are presently dripping with the words of interposition and nullification, will be transformed into a situation where little black boys and black girls will be able to join hands with little white boys and white girls and walk together as sisters and brothers.

I have a dream today.

I have a dream that one day every valley shall be exalted, every hill and mountain shall be made low, the rough places will be made plains, and the crooked places will be made straight, and the glory of the Lord shall be revealed, and all flesh shall see it together.

This is our hope. This is the faith with which I return to the South. With this faith we will be able to transform the jangling discords of our nation into a beautiful symphony of brotherhood. With this faith we will be able to work together, to pray together, to struggle together, to go to jail together, to stand up for freedom together, knowing that we will be free one day.

This will be the day when all of God's children will be able to sing with new meaning, "My country 'tis of thee, sweet land of liberty, of thee I sing. Land where my fathers died, land of the pilgrim's pride, from every mountainside, let freedom ring."

And if America is to be a great nation this must become true. So let freedom ring from the prodigious hilltops of New Hampshire. Let freedom ring from the mighty mountains of New York. Let freedom ring from the heightening Alleghenies of Pennsylvania!

Let freedom ring from the snowcapped Rockies of Colorado!

Let freedom ring from the curvaceous peaks of California!

But not only that; let freedom ring from the Stone Mountain of Georgia!

Let freedom ring from Lookout Mountain of Tennessee.

Let freedom ring from every hill and molehill of Mississippi. From every mountainside, let freedom ring.

When we let freedom ring, when we let it ring from every village and every hamlet, from every state and every city, we will be able to speed up that day when all of God's children, black men and white men, Jews and Gentiles, Protestants and Catholics, will be able to join hands and sing in the words of that old Negro spiritual, "Free at last! Free at last! Thank God Almighty, we are free at last!"

Strategy Statement

Northwood Community Church

The following is a condensed, edited version of a working strategy for Northwood Community Church in Dallas, Texas.

Every strategy implements a mission. So this strategy begins with a restatement of our mission.

Mission

Our mission is to be used of God in helping people develop into fully functioning followers of Christ.

Fully functioning followers have three characteristics (the 3 Cs):

1. Conversion to Christ (they know Christ as Savior).
2. Commitment to Christ (they are committed to grow in Christ).
3. Contribution to Christ (they serve the body, share their finances, and seek the lost).

Goals

The strategic goals (to realize our mission):

#1 To see people converted to Christ (to interest in *becoming* a disciple).
#2 To bring people to a commitment to Christ (to become a *committed* disciple).
#3 To equip people to make a contribution to Christ (to become a *contributing* disciple)

Steps

The specific action steps to accomplish our goals:

The following three action steps are vital to our plan to move people from prebirth to maturity. The steps are represented by using the visual of a three-legged stool. Each leg represents a level of commitment. The range is from level 1 (the least commitment) up to level 3 (the maximum commitment).

1st Leg: Conversion to Christ

Goal: To lead people to faith in Christ and active involvement in the church (to interest in becoming a disciple). Luke 15:1–10; 19:1–10; Col. 4:2–6; 2 Tim. 4:4; 1 Cor. 14:22–25.

Strategy #1: A "people-friendly" large group meeting at 10:45 A.M. on Sunday to interest unchurched lost and saved adults and young people in becoming Christ's disciples. It will include the sermon, drama, celebrative worship, and a regular presentation of the gospel.

Strategy #2: Other events to minister to lost and saved people and assimilate them into the church such as Vacation Bible school, men's and women's ministries, aerobics, Pioneer Boys and Girls Clubs, Awana, Sports events, community events, and others.

2nd Leg: Commitment to Christ

Goal: To bring people to a commitment to Christ (to become a *committed* disciple). Col. 1:28; Eph. 4:12–13; 1 Tim. 4:7–8; Heb. 6:1–3.

(What does a committed disciple look like? The answer is found in Acts 2:41–47.)

Strategy #1: Discipleship Small Groups (fully functioning communities)

Lay leaders will oversee small group communities who help one another become more like Christ. Meeting twice a month, these communities could include the following: shepherding, studying the Bible, exercising spiritual gifts, biblical community, accountability, prayer, and evangelism.

Strategy #2: Christian Education

Christian education consists of a children and adult's Sunday school, a nursery, and children's church. The adult's Sunday school consists primarily of classes that will cover more in-depth than the sermon or groups topics that are vital to commitment and spiritual growth.

3rd Leg: Contribution to Christ

Goal: To equip people to make a contribution to Christ (to become a contributing disciple). This involves three things: serving the body, sharing your finances, and seeking the lost.

Strategy #1: Serving the body (Eph. 4:12).

A staff or lay Minister of Involvement will use our Sunday classes to assess our people and provide the necessary information for them to discover their divine designs (required of new members). The staff or lay minister will match the people with the church's ministries for which they are best suited according to their design.

Strategy #2: Sharing our finances (Acts 2, 5; 2 Cor. 8–9).

We will use the Sunday service, the Sunday school, and the small groups to teach our people the biblical principles that will help them to handle their finances in a Christ-honoring way.

Strategy #3: Seeking the lost (Luke 15, 19:1–10).

We will provide classes in evangelism so that our people will understand the importance of evangelism, discover their style of evangelism, and how to share their faith with the lost. We will involve our people in missions abroad as well as at home. We will plant churches as we grow.

Visual

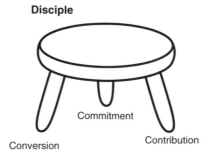

Disciple

Commitment

Conversion

Contribution

Appendix G

Ministry Description

Northwood Community Church

Job Title: Christian Education Director with a focus on Children's Ministries

Job Profile: The Christian Education Director ideally needs gifts or abilities in the following areas: Leadership, discernment, shepherding, administration, encouragement, and teaching.

The director needs a passion for adults as well as kids (works primarily with adults on behalf of the kids). A primary function will be the ability to work with and develop adults and teens as leaders.

This person's ideal temperament is a D/I on the *Personal Profile*.

The director needs to see life "through the eyes of a child." This person should be in touch with children—their world and culture.

Finally, the director should be a visionary who can take the children's ministry to the next level in its development.

Job Summary: The director is responsible for the children's Sunday school program (nursery through youth), children's church, the annual Vacation Bible school, and the Sunday school and worship nurseries. However, the director will focus primarily on children's ministries.

Duties:

A. Sunday School

1. Recruit teachers and floaters.
2. Train teachers and floaters.

3. Evaluate teachers and floaters.
4. Encourage teachers and floaters.
5. Assist teachers and monitor Sunday morning program.
6. Maintain supplies and facilities.
7. Select and approve all curriculum.
8. Plan and make preparation for class expansion.
9. Maintain a substitute teacher list.

B. Children's Church

1. Presentation of church program.
2. Recruit workers for leadership.
3. Train workers for leadership.
4. Select the curriculum.

C. Vacation Bible School

1. Recruit a director and other leaders.
2. Choose curriculum and coordinate other materials.
3. Recruit teachers and workers.

D. Sunday School & Worship Service Nurseries

1. Recruit directors.
2. Help recruit people as workers.

E. Miscellaneous

1. Develop the core values, mission, vision, and strategy for the Christian education program.
2. Attend board meetings.
3. Attend staff meetings.
4. Conduct personal background checks.
5. Conduct personal reference checks.
6. Preach as needed.

Reports to: Senior Pastor

Works with: Elder responsible for Christian Education

Appendix H

Strategy Implementation

Northwood Community Church

Strategy implementation involves the formulation of strategic priorities and specific actions. The following are ours.

Priority One: Christian education program

Develop a Sunday school program, nursery, and children's church that provide Christian education for all the people in our church.

Actions	Deadlines	Responsible Persons
1. Recruit Pastor of Christian Education.	November 1996	Elder over C.E.
2. Recruit teachers, helpers, and a director.	December 1996	Pastor of C.E.
3. Train teachers, helpers, and the director.	January 1997	Pastor of C.E.
4. Remodel rooms where necessary.	January 1997	Pastor of C.E.
5. Implement Christian education . program	February 1997	Pastor of C.E.

Priority Two: One to another groups

Develop small-group communities who minister to and help one another become more like Christ.

Actions	Deadlines	Responsible Persons
1. Evaluate current groups.	December 1996	Senior Pastor
2. Select and recruit leaders and apprentices.	December 1996	Senior Pastor
3. Establish a monthly small-groups training program.	January 1997	Senior Pastor
4. Launch small-groups program.	February 1997	Senior Pastor

Priority Three: Assimilation of newcomers

Develop an assimilation program so that we can assimilate our newcomers and keep track of our members.

Actions	Deadlines	Responsible Persons
1. Recruit a Minister of Assimilation.	December 1996	Senior Pastor
2. Assess assimilation trends.	January 1997	Assistant Pastor
3. Develop an assimilation plan.	January 1997	Assistant Pastor
4. Launch assimilation program.	February 1997	Assistant Pastor

Priority Four: Assessment of members

Develop an assessment program that assesses our members and places them in strategic positions of ministry (small group, Sunday school, etc.).

Actions	Deadlines	Responsible Persons
1. Recruit a Minister of Assessment.	December 1996	Senior Pastor
2. Train Minister of Assessment.	January 1997	Senior Pastor
3. Develop an assessment and placement program.	January 1997	Minister of Assessment
4. Launch the assessment and placement program.	February 1997	Minister of Assessment

Sample Evaluations

Northwood Community Church

Visitor Evaluation
Worship Service Evaluation
Ministry Description: Director of Christian Education
Ministry Appraisal: Director of Christian Education
General Appraisal: Director of Christian Education

Visitor Evaluation
Northwood Community Church

Please help us as a church by evaluating the following areas:

1. Were you warmly greeted as you entered our facility?

2. Were you able to find your way easily around our facility?

3. How would you rate the following:

	Poor	Fair	Good	Outstanding
Greeters	1	2	3	4
Ushers	1	2	3	4
Music	1	2	3	4
Worship	1	2	3	4
Sermon	1	2	3	4

Comments:

4. Any distractions?

5. Did you find our people to be friendly and accommodating?

6. How did you find out about Northwood?

7. Any comments or suggestions?

8. Will you come back? Why? Why not?

Signature (optional):_____

Date:_____

Evaluation
Sunday Worship Service

Evaluator (optional):_____

Date:_____

Directions: Please help us grow by constructively evaluating each area below. (Use back if necessary.)

	Poor	Fair	Good	Outstanding
1. **Announcements/Bulletin**	1	2	3	4

Comments:_____
_____
_____
_____

	Poor	Fair	Good	Outstanding
2. **Music/Band/Accompanists/ Slides**	1	2	3	4

Comments:_____
_____
_____
_____

	Poor	Fair	Good	Outstanding
3. **Special Events** (Communion, dedication, etc.)	1	2	3	4

Comments:_____
_____
_____
_____

	Poor	Fair	Good	Outstanding
4. **Sermon**	1	2	3	4

Delivery: (Mannerisms, speech, etc.)_____
_____

_____

_____

Application: (Relevant, how?)_____

_____

_____

_____

Content: (Biblical?)_____

_____

_____

_____

What was the main point of today's message?_____

_____

_____

_____

Ministry Description
Northwood Community Church

JOB TITLE: Director of Christian Education

JOB PROFILE: The Director of Christian Education needs abilities or gifts in leadership, discernment, shepherding, encouragement, teaching, and administration. While administering the present program, the director needs to be a visionary who can lead it to the next level. This person should have a passion for adults as well as children and youth because he or she will work primarily with the parents in behalf of children and youth.

JOB SUMMARY: The Director of Christian Education is responsible for the children's Sunday school program, children's church, the annual Vacation Bible School, and the Sunday school and worship nurseries.

DUTIES:

A. SUNDAY SCHOOL

1. Recruit teachers and floaters.
2. Train teachers and floaters.
3. Evaluate teachers and floaters.
4. Encourage teachers and floaters.
5. Assist teachers and monitor Sunday morning program.
6. Maintain supplies and facilities.
7. Select and approve all curriculum.
8. Plan and make preparation for class expansion.
9. Maintain a substitute teacher list.

B. CHILDREN'S CHURCH

1. Presentation of church program.
2. Recruit parents for leadership.
3. Train parents for leadership.
4. Select the curriculum.

C. VACATION BIBLE SCHOOL

1. Recruit a director and other leaders.
2. Choose curriculum and coordinate other materials.
3. Recruit teachers and workers.

D. SUNDAY SCHOOL & WORSHIP SERVICE NURSERIES

1. Recruit directors.
2. Help recruit people as workers.

E. MISCELLANEOUS

1. Develop the core values, mission, vision, and strategy for the Christian education program.
2. Attend board meetings.
3. Attend staff meetings.
4. Conduct personal background checks.
5. Conduct personal reference checks.
6. Preach as needed.

Reports to: Senior Pastor

Works with: Elder responsible for Christian education

Ministry Appraisal
Director of Christian Education

Circle the appropriate number:
SUNDAY SCHOOL

	Poor	Fair	Good	Excellent	N/O
1. Recruit teachers and floaters.	1	2	3	4	
2. Train teachers and floaters.	1	2	3	4	
3. Evaluate teachers and floaters.	1	2	3	4	
4. Encourage teachers and floaters.	1	2	3	4	
5. Assist teachers and monitor Sunday morning program.	1	2	3	4	
6. Maintain supplies and facilities.	1	2	3	4	
7. Select and approve all curriculum.	1	2	3	4	
8. Plan and make preparation for class expansion.	1	2	3	4	
9. Maintain substitute teacher list.	1	2	3	4	

Comments:

CHILDREN'S CHURCH

	Poor	Fair	Good	Excellent	N/O
1. Presentation of church program.	1	2	3	4	
2. Recruit parents for leadership.	1	2	3	4	
3. Train parents for leadership.	1	2	3	4	
4. Select the curriculum.	1	2	3	4	

Comments:

VBS AND SPECIAL EVENTS

	Poor	Fair	Good	Excellent	N/O
1. Recruit a director and other leaders.	1	2	3	4	
2. Choose curriculum and coordinate other materials.	1	2	3	4	
3. Recruit teachers and workers.	1	2	3	4	

Comments:

MISCELLANEOUS

	Poor	Fair	Good	Excellent	N/O
1. Develop values, mission, etc.	1	2	3	4	
2. Attend board meetings.	1	2	3	4	
3. Attend staff meetings.	1	2	3	4	
4. Conduct personal background checks.	1	2	3	4	
5. Conduct personal reference checks.	1	2	3	4	
6. Preach as needed.	1	2	3	4	

Comments:

General Appraisal
Director of Christian Education

1. **Job Knowledge**: The individual is familiar with the duties, requirements, practices, policies, and procedures of the position.

Poor	Fair	Good	Excellent	N/O
1	2	3	4	

Comments:

2. **Quality of Work**: The individual does thorough and accurate work.

Poor	Fair	Good	Excellent	N/O
1	2	3	4	

Comments:

3. **Productivity**: The individual produces a reasonable, acceptable amount of work in a timely manner.

Poor	Fair	Good	Excellent	N/O
1	2	3	4	

Comments:

4. **Organization**: The individual's files, records, etc. are in order and easily accessible.

Poor	Fair	Good	Excellent	N/O
1	2	3	4	

Comments:

5. **Initiative and Resourcefulness**:   Poor   Fair   Good   Excellent   N/O
The individual is a self-starter who   1   2   3   4
identifies opportunities, improves
procedures, and suggests new ideas.

Comments:

6. **Sociability**: The individual is   Poor   Fair   Good   Excellent   N/O
cooperative and supportive and gets   1   2   3   4
along well with people.

Comments:

7. **Communication**: The individual   Poor   Fair   Good   Excellent   N/O
is a good listener who communicates   1   2   3   4
clearly and accurately when writing
or speaking.

Comments:

8. **Character**: The individual is a   Poor   Fair   Good   Excellent   N/O
person of integrity (respectful, trust-   1   2   3   4
worthy, honest, not a gossip, hum-
ble, etc.).

Comments:

Notes

Introduction

1. Ken Blanchard and Terry Waghorn, *Mission Possible* (New York: McGraw-Hill, 1997), 82.

2. Aubrey Malphurs, *Planting Growing Churches in the 21st Century* (Grand Rapids: Baker, 1992), 13.

3. "Last Week? You're Sure?" *Dallas Morning News,* 21 September 1997, p. 1G.

4. In no way am I attempting to diminish the importance of preaching and teaching the Scriptures. The Bible communicates God's Word and will to mankind. Without it, we perish.

5. *Developing a Vision for Ministry in the Twenty-first Century* (Grand Rapids: Baker, 1992); *Values-Driven Leadership* (Grand Rapids: Baker, 1996); *Strategy 2000: Churches Making Disciples in the Next Millennium* (Grand Rapids: Kregel, 1996); *Developing a Dynamic Mission for Your Ministry* (Grand Rapids: Kregel, 1998).

6. Marc Spiegler, "Scouting for Souls," *American Demographics* 18, no. 3 (March 1996): 49.

7. Some examples are Karl Albrecht, *The Northbound Train* (New York: American Management Association, 1994); Nicholas Imparato and Oren Harari, *Jumping the Curve* (San Francisco: Jossey-Bass, 1994); and Gary Hamal and C. K. Prahalad, *Competing for the Future* (Boston: HBS Press, 1994). An extreme example is Randall P. White, Philip Hodgson, and Stuart Crainer, *The Future of Leadership* (Washington, D.C.: Pitman Publishing, 1996). They see no need for strategic planning.

8. Albrecht, *Northbound Train,* 57, italics mine.

9. Tom Peters, *Thriving on Chaos* (New York: Harper & Row, 1987), 615.

10. Pastors must think about and develop a hermeneutic for "doing" church, a theology of change, and a theology of culture. But these are topics that I will treat in a future book.

11. I have further developed this concept along with a theology of strategy in *Strategy 2000,* chap. 4.

Chapter 1: *Preparing to Think and Act*

1. The S temperament characterizes those who are patient, consistent, and loyal. They are good listeners who really care about people. They want to know how change will affect their relationships with people before they will accept it. The C temperament characterizes people who are very conscientious. They are detail-oriented and always look for the facts. They are natural skeptics and initially view any change with skepticism.

2. People who are more traditional in their thinking have the SJ temperament. They believe that the best is in the past and pride themselves on being the conservers of the past. They view change as a threat.

3. Some have found an outside consultant more harmful than helpful. I suggest that you consider the following when enlisting the help of a consultant: Ask for references from other churches and ministries (who else has used the consultant's services and were they pleased with the results?); ask for credentials (degrees, training, etc.); inquire about ministry experience (has he or she ever worked in your type of church?); what qualifies this person to consult in this area (what training or experience does he or she have?); does this consultant stay current in the field (is this person aware of the new ministry paradigms and is he or she well read?); does this person seem too eager to come and work with you (is this person truly qualified to consult in this area or is he or she in need of work?).

4. Leonard D. Goodstein, Timothy M. Nolan, and J. William Pfeiffer, *Applied Strategic Planning* (New York: McGraw-Hill, 1993), 102.

5. Mike Vance and Diane Deacon, *Think Out of the Box* (Franklin Lake, N.J.: Career Press, 1995).

Chapter 2: *Understanding Organizational Development*

1. Gary L. McIntosh, "How to Live to Be 100," *The McIntosh Church Growth Network* 9, no. 9 (September 1997): 1.

2. Ibid.

3. Peter Brierly, "Deserting the Churches," *Christianity Today* (10 January 1994): 52.

4. Jackson W. Carroll, Douglas W. Johnson, and Martin E. Marty, *Religion in America: 1950 to the Present* (San Francisco: Harper & Row, 1979), 13.

5. Win Arn, *The Pastor's Manual for Effective Ministry* (Monrovia, Calif.: Church Growth, 1988), 41, 43.

6. Randy Frazee with Lyle E. Schaller, *The Comeback Congregation* (Nashville: Abingdon Press, 1995), 11.

7. Charles Truehart, "The Next Church," *Atlantic Monthly* (August 1996): 38.

8. Constant H. Jacquet Jr., ed., *Yearbook of American and Canadian Churches, 1988* (Nashville: Abingdon Press, 1989), 261, compared with Kenneth B. Bedell, ed., *Yearbook of American and Canadian Churches, 1996,* 251–52, 255–56. I have rounded off these figures.

9. C. Peter Wagner, *Church Planting for a Greater Harvest* (Ventura, Calif.: Regal, 1990), 14, 16.

10. Carroll, Johnson, and Marty, *Religion in America,* 16.

11. *SBC Handbook* (Nashville: Convention Press, 1991).

12. Arnell Motz, ed., *Reclaiming a Nation* (Richmond, B.C.: Church Leadership Library, 1990), 16–17.

13. Bill Hull, *The Disciple-Making Pastor* (Grand Rapids: Revell, 1988), 20.

14. Bob Gilliam, "Are Most Churches Intentionally Making Disciples?" Findings from the *Spiritual Journey Evaluation* (29 March 1995): 1.

15. Charles Handy, *The Age of Paradox* (Boston: Harvard Business School Press, 1994), 51.

16. We learn from history and others' experiences that we do not learn from history and others' experiences.

17. Handy, *Age of Paradox,* 57.

18. See Aubrey Malphurs, *Maximizing Your Effectiveness* (Grand Rapids: Baker, 1995).

19. I have written *Pouring New Wine into Old Wineskins* (Grand Rapids: Baker, 1993) to help those who find themselves in this situation.

20. I have not commented so far on the church's purpose. That does not mean that it is not important and does not pose questions for the church to answer. I cover purpose under the mission step.

Chapter 4: *Discovering Core Values*

1. I am using congregational or corporate soul in this context as a leadership not a theological concept.

2. I have included the Jerusalem church's values as a credo in appendix C.

3. Ken Blanchard and Michael O'Connor, *Managing by Values* (San Francisco: Berrett-Koehler Publishers, 1996), 3.

4. Lyle E. Schaller, *Getting Things Done* (Nashville: Abingdon Press, 1986), 152.

5. If you desire a more complete, in-depth presentation of core values, see my book *Values-Driven Leadership.* However, this chapter contains information that I have learned since writing that book.

6. James C. Collins and William C. Lazier, *Beyond Entrepreneurship: Turning Your Business into an Enduring Great Company* (Englewood Cliffs, N.J.: Prentice Hall, 1992), 66.

7. Thomas J. Peters and Robert H. Waterman Jr., *In Search of Excellence* (New York: Warner, 1982), 281.

8. Blanchard and O'Connor, *Managing by Values,* 31, 108, 121.

9. It is common for people to mistake what they value with their values. We value all kinds of things, such as a particular method of evangelism, a preaching style, the way we serve communion, small groups, the way we study the Bible, and so on. But these are not values.

10. James C. Collins and Jerry I. Porras, *Built to Last* (New York: Harper Business, 1994), 74, 219.

11. Ibid., 74.

Chapter 5: *Developing a Mission*

1. Stephen Covey, *The Seven Habits of Highly Effective People* (New York: Simon & Schuster, 1989), 139.

2. Warren Bennis, *On Becoming a Leader* (New York: Addison-Wesley, 1989), 183.

3. Peter F. Drucker, *Managing the Non-Profit Organization* (New York: Harper Business, 1990), 3.

4. Peter F. Drucker, *Management: Tasks, Responsibilities, Practices* (New York: Harper & Row, 1973), 75.

5. Ibid., 78.

6. Allan Cox, *Redefining Corporate Soul* (Chicago: Irwin Professional Publishing, 1996), 25.

7. Ibid., 26.

8. Patricia Jones and Larry Kahaner, *Say It and Live It* (New York: Doubleday, 1995), 264.

9. I covered this important hermeneutical principle at the end of chapter 2.

10. Frazee, *The Comeback Congregation*, 6.

11. Fred Smith, *Learning to Lead* (Waco: Word, 1986), 34.

12. If you desire a more thorough, in-depth coverage of how to communicate the mission or the development of a mission statement, see my book *Developing a Dynamic Mission for Your Ministry.*

Chapter 6: *Scanning the Environment*

1. In my section on a theology of culture at the end of chapter 2, I noted that culture can be used for good or bad. John's use of the "world" in 1 John 2 is that world under the dominion of Satan and the antichrists.

2. Bennis, *On Becoming a Leader*, 2.

3. Ibid., 199.

4. Edward Cornish, "The 1997 Conference," *World Future Society* (November 1997), 3.

5. James A. Belasco and Ralph C. Stayer, *Flight of the Buffalo* (New York: Warner, 1993), 129.

6. Ibid.

7. I use the term *claims* carefully here. I have no reason to doubt his research, but he does not present it in the book.

8. Christian A. Schwarz, *Natural Church Development: A Guide to Eight Essential Qualities of Healthy Churches* (Carol Stream, Ill.: Church Smart Resources, 1996).

9. Russell Chandler, *Racing toward 2001: The Forces Shaping America's Religious Future* (Grand Rapids: Zondervan, 1992).

10. I got the idea for this from Rick Warren who pastors Saddleback Valley Community Church in Mission Viejo, California.

Chapter 7: *Developing a Vision*

1. If after reading this chapter, you desire a more in-depth treatment of the vision concept, see my book *Developing a Vision for Ministry in the Twenty-first Century.*

2. "The Man Who Brought Marketing to the Church," *Leadership* XVI, no. 3 (summer 1995): 124–25.

3. David Goetz, "Forced Out," *Leadership* XVII, no. 1 (winter 1996): 42.

4. Lewis Carroll, *Alice in Wonderland* (New York: Book-of-the-Month Club, 1994), 85.

5. You may take the MBTI through a private counseling agency or one located at a college or university. You may order the Kiersey Temperament Sorter from Prometheus Nemesis Book Company, Box 2748, Del Mar, CA 92014; 619-632-1575; fax: 619-481-0535. The Sorter costs twenty-five cents per copy plus shipping.

6. Smith, *Learning to Lead,* 38.

Chapter 8: *Developing a Strategy*

1. Belasco and Stayer, *Flight of the Buffalo,* 138.

2. Ibid.

3. Ibid.

4. I do not have the time or space here to develop a theology of strategy. For more on this, see my book *Strategy 2000,* chap. 4.

5. For a more in-depth treatment of these questions and others, see my book *Strategy 2000,* chap. 7.

6. In the job descriptions at Northwood, we carefully spell out all the ministry responsibilities. Consequently, we cannot randomly dump new responsibilities on staff without first discussing it and their current load. We also discuss increased compensation for increased responsibilities.

7. I got the idea for these three terms from Jim Dethmer, a former teaching pastor at Willow Creek Community Church.

8. Blanchard and Waghorn, *Mission Possible,* 46.

9. Gary L. McIntosh, *How to Develop a Pastoral Compensation Plan* (Lynchburg, Va.: Church Growth Institute, 1991), 32–33.

10. Ibid., 36.

11. Ibid., 43–48.

12. The early churches met initially in the temple courts and in homes (Acts 2:46; 5:42). Later they met primarily in homes because of persecution (Rom. 16:5; 1 Cor. 16:19; Col. 4:15).

13. Jan Jarobe Russell, "Coming to a Mall Near You," *Good Housekeeping* (December 1997): 116–19.

Chapter 9: *Implementing the Strategy*

1. Ken Blanchard, "Turning Vision into Reality," in *Renewing Your Church through Vision and Planning,* ed. Marshall Shelley (Minneapolis: Bethany, 1997), 84.

2. I have written *Pouring New Wine into Old Wineskins* to help churches deal with change and go through the revitalization process.

3. Aubrey Malphurs, *Maximizing Your Effectiveness: How to Discover and Develop Your Divine Design* (Grand Rapids: Baker, 1995).

4. A number of good ones are on the market. There is one in appendix A of *Maximizing Your Effectiveness.*

Chapter 10: *Preparing for Contingencies*

1. Steven Fink, *Crisis Management: Planning for the Inevitable* (New York: The American Management Association, 1986), 67.

2. Ibid., 20–27.

Chapter 11: *Evaluating the Ministry*

1. Actually the New Testament does not tell us a lot about what the early church practiced. I believe that God did this because he knew that we would try to mimic it and become needlessly bound up in the first-century culture.

2. I have gleaned most of these from Rod MacIlvaine who is the pastor of Grace Community Church of Bartlesville, Oklahoma.

Appendix B: *Scenario Planning*

1. Peter Schwartz, *The Art of the Long View* (New York: Doubleday, 1991).

2. Ibid., 62.

3. Ibid., 64.

4. Ibid., 66.

5. Ibid., 68.

6. Ibid., 73–74.

7. Ibid., 79.

8. Ibid., 81.

9. Ibid., 86.

10. Ibid., 136.

11. Ibid., 141–50.

12. Ibid., 151-57.

Index